OCTOVIAN

EARLY ENGLISH TEXT SOCIETY

No. 289

1986

the schypp come by an yle syde
and schyp men bade þm goo abyde
[...]for watur haue we none
so goo when wall a foote hye
a wolf faym wolld þere they [...]e
come rynnyng onys a foote
two men in the londe they saw
by þe streme they [...]
[...] wolld [...] fonde anone
Alysande lay in hur dame
And was full fayne of þe two men
Anone she hyd them slon
So sone on duke can they ryde
And two men for so a byst
[...]enone was on the day
þy men know can they dyght
wyth halues and helues the schyppe
to londe when wente they
they fonde þe hende done
A man chylde honyr þer ynne
wyth the hende to play
Some tyme he [...] the hende [...]
And some tyme they can kysse þe schyppe
[...] fete they fleed a way
they goos did[...] whyle þay fye
they fonde on þis þothe on hye
a hende in hur dame
A man chylde þer in lay
wyth the hende to play
And þere was lowde they men
than sente the lady mylde
mercy lordyngys þat þe my chylde
on londe he let me come
þe boto they smen on þe flode
to londe alone the lady yede
Sore wepyd the schyppman than
whon she came on þe þothe on hye
Sche gan[...] whyll she myght
wyth full sore mode
þe hende therow goddys grace

whon she[...] þe þe lady oc faro
[...] þat þe rode
þorow the mynde of mercy mylde
sche saued hur to take vp þe chylde
did wyth the lady to goo þe rode
whon þe schypmen þe hende sye
the londe þyste þay not come nye
for feer they were nye wode
Some hente an ores þa some a spryte
þe hende for to mete
Out of þer schyppe to wey[...]
the lady vn to the shyp wente
þer fore the hende dym[...]nce
[...] durste no man hur [...]eye
there men myght yeme see
[...]men lepe vn to the see
So sayde of the hende they weys
[...] the lady þe hende downe lay
And [...] the chylde can she play
And no man swore stye deye
they drewe þe stole of ryche hewe
the wynde out of þe haven þem blewe
Onyr the wanne streme
þe fyste londe that they see
was a cite wyth toweyr hye
that hyste Jerusalem
As glad they weyr of that syght
As fowlys be of day lyght
And of the sune leme
whon hyt was ebbe þnot flode
the schypmen þe lady to londe yode
In to that ryche paleme
Onyr all þe cyre wyde and londe

Cambridge, University Library, MS Ff. 2. 38, f. 93[r]

OCTOVIAN

Edited from Lincoln, Dean and Chapter Library, MS 91
and Cambridge, University Library, MS Ff.2. 38

BY

FRANCES McSPARRAN

Published for
THE EARLY ENGLISH TEXT SOCIETY
by the
OXFORD UNIVERSITY PRESS
LONDON NEW YORK TORONTO
1986

Oxford University Press, Walton Street, Oxford OX2 6DP

Oxford Glasgow New York Toronto
Delhi Bombay Calcutta Madras Karachi
Kuala Lumpur Singapore Hong Kong Tokyo
Nairobi Dar es Salaam Cape Town
Melbourne Auckland

and associates in
Beirut Berlin Ibadan Nicosia

OXFORD is a trade mark of Oxford University Press

British Library Cataloguing in Publication Data
[Octovian, the Emperor (Romance). Middle English].
Octovian.—(Original series/Early English
Text Society; 289)
I. McSparran, Frances   II. Octovian   III. Series
821'.1   PR2065.03
ISBN 0-19-722291-9

Typeset by Joshua Associates, Oxford
Printed in Great Britain
at the University Press, Oxford
by David Stanford
Printer to the University

FOREWORD

In this edition of the northern *Octovian* the two surviving manuscript copies (Lincoln, Dean & Chapter Library, MS 91, and Cambridge, University Library, MS Ff. 2. 38) are printed as parallel texts. Rather less than half of the romance is also preserved in an early print (San Marino, Huntington Library 14615); this print is valuable for the light it throws on the relative reliability of the two manuscript copies, and it is presented here in an appendix.

I wish to thank those who have given me help and information as I prepared this edition: Mr M. B. Parkes and Miss P. R. Robinson for information on palaeographical matters; Professor W. H. Ingram of the University of Michigan, who helped me to make computer concordances for both Middle English texts; the Department of English of the University of Michigan for financial assistance with typing costs; Dr. Pamela Gradon for her help in seeing this edition through the press. The facsimiles are reproduced by courtesy of Cambridge University Library and the Dean and Chapter of Lincoln.

ABBREVIATIONS

EETS, os, es	Early English Text Society, Original Series, Extra Series
EGS	*English and Germanic Studies*
ES	*Englische Studien*
MÆ	*Medium Ævum*
Med. Stud.	*Medieval Studies*
NM	*Neuphilologische Mitteilungen*
PMLA	*Publications of the Modern Language Association of America*
PQ	*Philological Quarterly*
TPS	*Transactions of the Philological Society*

CONTENTS

INTRODUCTION

I THE MANUSCRIPTS AND EARLY PRINT   1
II THE TRANSMISSION AND AFFILIATION
   OF THE TEXTS   10
III LANGUAGE AND PROVENANCE   21
IV VERSIONS AND LITERARY RELATIONSHIPS   38
V ORIGINS OF THE OCTAVIAN STORY   53
VI TREATMENT   60

SELECT BIBLIOGRAPHY   69

THE TEXTS   73

NOTES   181

GLOSSARY   201

NAMES OF PERSONS AND PLACES   221

APPENDIX   223

PLATES
   Cambridge, University Library, MS Ff. 2. 38, f. 93^r Frontispiece
   Lincoln, Dean and Chapter Library, MS 91, f. 98^v Facing p. 73

INTRODUCTION

I. THE MANUSCRIPTS AND EARLY PRINT

L Lincoln, Dean and Chapter Library, MS 91 (The Lincoln
    Thornton MS)

This is a paper manuscript, imperfect, consisting now of 314
leaves, foliated 1-314, followed by seven fragments and stubs,
foliated 315-21. In 1974 the manuscript was disassembled for
restoration and rebinding, and at that time it was examined
and collated by A. E. B. Owen.[1] Prior to this the manuscript
(which Sir Frederic Madden had had rebound in or after
1832) was too tightly bound for a full collation, though a
substantial amount of information about its make-up could
be derived from catchwords, an incomplete set of quire signatures, and a note on f. 163[v] by the scribe, Robert Thornton:
'Here is ix qwayers'. Owen's emended collation of 1977 is
necessarily tentative in estimating the total number of missing
folios, but he believes that the manuscript when complete
probably contained seventeen quires, and not less than 340
leaves. The quires vary considerably in the number of leaves
they contain. The evidence of stubs, cancellations, catchwords, and the texts themselves suggest that much of the
present irregularity of structure dates back to the original
assembly of the manuscript for binding. Furthermore, Owen
points out that the 'decayed' binding which Madden replaced
and described as: 'thick oaken boards, covered with white
leather, and fastened by a clasp', was almost certainly a
fifteenth-century binding.[2] It seems likely, then, that both

---

[1] For a detailed description of the manuscript and its contents, see *The Thornton Manuscript*, Introductions by D. S. Brewer and A. E. B. Owen (rev. edn., London, 1977), pp. vii-xx. The revised edition modifies and supplements the description
in the 1975 edition in several important respects. For further discussion see A. E. B.
Owen, 'The Collation and Descent of the Thornton Manuscript', *Transactions of
the Cambridge Bibliographical Society*, vi (1975), 218-25 and J. Thompson,
'Textual *Lacunae* and the Importance of Manuscript Evidence', ibid., viii (1982),
270-75.

[2] On Madden's account of the existing binding, which he replaced when he

the present organization of the quires and the earlier binding were those provided by the fifteenth-century scribe and owner, Robert Thornton.

Madden found not only the binding in sad shape, but the leaves in 'loose disorder'; at least 20 folios are now missing, and a number of the extant folios are damaged. The lower corners of ff. 144–51 are torn, large portions of ff. 108, 152, 153, and 159 are missing and only fragments or stubs remain of ff. 122, 133A (a stub following f. 133), 315–21. As a result of loss and damage to the manuscript there are two major gaps in the text of *Octovian*: one folio of text has been lost after f. 102, and much of the text copied on the damaged f. 108 is missing.[1]

The leaves have rounded corners, and their average size is 290 × 200 mm. The size of the written space varies (e.g. 210 × 135 mm., 225 × 165 mm.) as does the number of lines to a column (ranging in *Octovian* from 37 to 44 lines). The layout of texts varies also: items in prose and alliterative verse are written in one column, other verse items in two columns, but other styles of presentation are also used, and there is sometimes variation within the copying of a single text, as in the treatment of the four-line 'wheel' in *The Awntyrs off Arthure*, or the occasional use of braces to mark rhyme schemes in the romances. Frame ruling in black or red ink is used and the top line of text is written either below or through the ruling. The initials beginning a line of verse, or sentence of prose, are often touched with red. Larger initials, most in red, or red touched with purple, are used at the beginning of texts or new narrative sections; they are sometimes flourished, sometimes inhabited by grotesque faces or animals, or filled with vegetal motifs. Four such initials occur in *Octovian* marking major sections of narrative.

The hand is Anglicana of the mid-fifteenth century, and watermarks which occur in the manuscript have been found

borrowed the manuscript from the Dean and Chapter of Lincoln Cathedral in 1832, see further *The Awntyrs off Arthure at the Terne Wathelyn*, ed. R. Hanna (Manchester, 1974), p. 1 and fn. 2, and Owen (1975), 225, Brewer and Owen (1977), p. xvi.

[1] See further below, p. 11.

in documents dated from 1413-61.[1] Internal evidence suggests that the manuscript was probably copied in the second quarter of the fifteenth century. Folios 250^v-258^r contain an account by a woman of visions of purgatory. The title describes the piece as: 'A Reuelacyon Schewed to ane holy woman now one late tyme', and the opening claims that the visions began 'appone saynt lowrence day at nyghte, þe ȝere of oure lorde a thowsande fowre hundrethe twenty and two'.[2] Folio 49^v bears, besides pentrials and several religious invocations, a note on the birth of 'Robertus Thornton in Ridayll anno domini m° cccc liij'. These dates show that parts of the manuscript, at least, were produced after 1422 and before 1453. The possibility, discussed below, that the manuscript is a compilation of booklets, copied separately and subsequently bound together, prevents us from being quite certain that these dates provide a *terminus post quem* and a *terminus ante quem* for the copying of the entire manuscript.

The Robert Thornton whose birth in 1453 was recorded is believed to have been the grandson of the compiler of the manuscript, who is identified as Robert Thornton by a colophon on f. 98^v, by the tag: 'R. Thornton dictus qui scripsit sit benedictus' on ff. 98^v and 213^r, and by the recurrence of the name in other places in the manuscript (ff. 53^r, 211^v, 278^v, etc.). The marginalia include the names of later members of the Thornton family, together with sketches, scribbles, brief religious invocations, and Latin epigrams. Over forty years ago Mrs M. S. Ogden investigated the Thornton family history, and identified as the likeliest compiler Robert Thornton, who in 1418 became lord of the manor of East Newton, near Helmsley in the North Riding of Yorkshire, and who, according to a family pedigree, was dead by 1465, since his widow remarried in that year.[3] Oswaldskirk, whose rector is

---

[1] I am indebted to Mr M. B. Parkes of Keble College, Oxford, for this opinion on the date of the hand. On the watermark evidence for date, see *Facsimiles of Ancient Manuscripts*, ed. E. M. Thompson, *et al.* (The New Palaeographical Society, Second Series, vol. 1), London, 1913-30, plate 45 and facing notes, and K. Stern, 'The London "Thornton" Miscellany', *Scriptorium*, xxx (1976), 211.

[2] See the facsimile, Brewer and Owen (1977), f. 250^v.

[3] See *The Liber de Diversis Medicinis*, ed. M. S. Ogden. EETS, 207 (1938, repr. 1969), pp. viii-xv. For a valuable recent investigation of Robert Thornton, the Thornton family, and the history of the manuscript, see G. R. Keiser, 'A Note on the Descent of the Thornton Manuscript', *Transactions of the Cambridge*

cited twenty times as an authority in the collection of medical recipes in the manuscript, is nearby, and Ryedale, mentioned as the birthplace of the later Robert Thornton, is a wapentake in the south-eastern part of the North Riding.

Other contents of the manuscript also connect it with this area. It contains many works ascribed to, or associated with, Rolle. Rolle was born in Thornton Dale, near Pickering, in the wapentake of Pickering Lythe, adjacent to Ryedale, and about fourteen miles east of Oswaldskirk and East Newton. Much of his adult life seems to have been spent in this area, and he was lodged for some time with John Dalton of Pickering.[1] This local connection may well explain Thornton's interest in Rolle, and his access to so many of his works. A more general association with Yorkshire is suggested by the presence in the manuscript of a copy, belonging to the northern tradition, of *Gaytryge's Sermon*, an English version of Archbishop Thoresby's 1357 instruction to the clergy of the York diocese on the teaching of basic doctrine. Gaytryge belonged to St. Mary's Abbey in York, and his translation was made at Thoresby's request. A further Yorkshire connection is afforded by a reference to St. Everild in a litany contained in the abridged Psalter and Office (ff. 258^v-269^v).[2] St. Everild belonged to a Wessex family, but founded a community in Yorkshire, with the help of St. Wilfrid, and is commemorated only in litanies according to the use of York.[3]

The manuscript is a personal compilation, and the contents therefore represent the taste and interests of Robert Thornton, as well as the sources available to him. The rather frequent occurrence in its pages of the names of Thornton himself, and of other members of the Thornton family, suggest that it

Bibliographical Society, vi (1976), 346-8, and G. R. Keiser, 'Lincoln Cathedral Library MS 91: Life and Milieu of the Scribe', *Studies in Bibliography* 32 (1979), 158-79. Keiser's discussion throws some doubt on the 1465 remarriage date.

[1] See *English Writings of Richard Rolle*, ed. H. E. Allen (Oxford, 1931), pp. xi, l.

[2] For this, and for other information on the Lincoln Thornton, I am indebted to Miss P. R. Robinson, of Queen's University, Belfast.

[3] See *Horae Eboracenses*, ed. C. Wordsworth (Surtees Society, CXXXII), London, 1920, p. 94 and n. 9; *York Breviary*, ed. S. W. Lawley (Surtees Society, LXXV), London, 1882, col. 388; *The Prymer or Lay Folks Prayer Book*, ed. H. Littlehales. EETS, OS 105 (1895), pp. i, lxiii.

was used in a Thornton household over several generations. Like various other Middle English miscellanies, it contains an assortment of contents: in this case, devotional and didactic material, works of entertainment and a substantial collection of medical recipes. A survey of the list of contents gives the somewhat misleading impression that they occur in a random or casual order. Analysis of the structure of the quires, their watermarks, the presentation and nature of the texts and their linguistic features suggests that Thornton organized his material, roughly according to kind and subject matter, into a series of groups of gatherings or 'booklets', which may have existed separately for some time before being bound up together.[1] Five major groups of gatherings emerge: each group consists of a major text or a cluster of texts of a similar kind; short unrelated items occur typically as 'fillers', copied into space left at the end of one or other group of gatherings.

The composition and principal contents of these groups or 'booklets' are as follows:

1. ff. 1–52 The prose *Alexander*.
2. ff. 53–178 A collection of Arthurian and other romances (*Morte Arthure, Octovian, Sir Isumbras, Earl of Toulous, Sir Degrevant, Sir Eglamour, Awntyrs of Arthure, Sir Perceval of Galles*), a life of St. Christopher, and other short unrelated items (all verse, except for 'fillers' in prose on ff. 176ᵛ–178ᵛ).
3. ff. 179–222 Prayers and devotional works in English and Latin, most of which are either attributed to, or associated with Rolle (verse and prose).
4. ff. 223–79 Devotional treatises, some ascribed to Rolle, an

---

[1] On the identification of booklets in manuscripts, see P. R. Robinson, 'The "Booklet": a Self-contained Unit in Composite Manuscripts', *Codicologica*, 3 (1980), 46–69. Among her criteria for establishing 'booklets' relevant here are the following: (i) The coincidence of the end of a text and the last leaf of a gathering. (ii) Variation in the customary size of gatherings between one booklet and the next. (iii) The addition of extra leaves in a booklet to complete a text, or the cutting away of unwanted leaves. (iv) Blank leaves at the end of a gathering, or the filling up of such leaves with additional items, often unrelated to the primary contents, and often edited to fit available space. (v) Signs of wear on the outside leaves of a booklet, suggesting use or circulation unbound. (vi) Change in the layout of texts between one booklet and the next, reflecting the layouts of different exemplars.

abbreviated Psalter, religious poems, hymns, and prayers, in English and Latin (verse and prose).

5. ff. 280–321 *Liber de diversis medicinis*, in English (prose).

It is difficult to know for certain if these groups were conceived of and used as independent units of reading material before being bound up together, or if they merely result from a sorting and classifying process, carried out by Thornton as he gathered items for a projected book. A sorting process might encourage him to begin each substantial item on a new gathering, thus allowing him eventually to separate and assign to different parts of the manuscript secular and religious texts derived from the same written source, as he did in the case of the *Morte Arthure* and the *Previte off the Passioune*.[1] Various features, however, do suggest that the groups did for a time have some independent status and use. Thus, for example, many of the outer leaves (where extant) of the 'booklets' show marked signs of wear and tear. The most conspicuous example of this is f. 53^r (where *Morte Arthure* begins) which is soiled and worn, and which bears Robert Thornton's name, perhaps to identify the owner of the 'booklet', while this was its outer leaf.

C Cambridge, University Library, MS Ff. 2. 38

This is a paper manuscript, imperfect, consisting now of 247 leaves, foliated 3–261.[2] Until recently the first two gatherings were misbound.[3] Two nineteenth-century systems of foliation are visible. The earlier, cancelled, foliation numbers the surviving leaves 1–247, in the order in which they were still wrongly bound; the second, by Henry Bradshaw, numbers

[1] Thornton may even have used this method to divide texts between different manuscripts, since he copied at least one other, London, British Library, MS 31042. On the relationship between *Morte Arthure* and *The Preuite off the Passioune*, see A. McIntosh, 'The Textual Transmission of the Alliterative *Morte Arthure*', in *English and Medieval Studies presented to J. R. R. Tolkien on the occasion of his seventieth birthday*, ed. N. Davis and C. L. Wrenn (London, 1962), pp. 231–40.

[2] For a detailed description by P. R. Robinson of the manuscript and its contents, see *Cambridge University Library MS Ff. 2. 38*, Introduction by F. McSparran and P. R. Robinson (London, 1979), pp. xii–xvii, xxi–xxv.

[3] The sequence of the sixteenth-century quire and leaf signatures shows that at the time of signing ff. 1 and 2 were already missing, the first two quires were placed in the wrong order, and that a bifolium (ff. 21 and 40) and ff. 19 and 20 (the conjoint leaves of ff. 1 and 2) were assigned to the wrong quire.

them in the order in which they should occur. This foliation, which is in general use, allows for missing folios, and thus runs 3-261. Notes in pencil at the appropriate places show where folios are missing, and how many. Rebinding in 1972 has restored the correct sequence of leaves in the first two gatherings, and Bradshaw's foliation agrees with the present sequence.

Texts are written in Anglicana, with some Secretary letter forms; colophons, titles (and often opening lines) are in a Bastard display script. The hand belongs to the late fifteenth, or early sixteenth, century; the watermark evidence supports this dating, while the contents provide no useful internal evidence as to date. There is a marked change in the size of the writing and the density of the ink from f. 93rb, sixth line (C466 of *Octovian*) to f. 156^v.[1] In this portion the script is larger and looser, and several letter forms, notably *h*, are modified. Some editors believe a different scribe copied this part of the manuscript, but Miss Robinson ascribes the differences to an opening out of the scribe's hand as he continued a long stint, and points out characteristic letter forms occurring in both parts.[2] My own examination of the language of *Octovian* shows no significant differences in spelling habits between the first 465 lines of *Octovian* and the remainder, and it may be that the abrupt change in scale and ink density here was caused by the resumption of copying by the same scribe after some interval.

The manuscript is written in two columns, except for item 33 (in long lines), and the end of item 40, *Guy of Warwick*. The average size of folios is 297 × 210 mm. Frame ruling in hard point is used. The written space varies in *Octovian* from about 200 × 135 mm. (where the hand is smaller, up to f. 93rb) to 200 × 160 mm. (f. 93rb onward). The number of lines in the column varies in the same way from 39-42 (usually 42) in the first part of *Octovian*, and from 32-35 (usually 33) thereafter. Large initials in a metallic red, or red and white, mark the beginning of new texts, or of new sections of narrative within a text, and there are four such in *Octovian*.[3] In many places the ink has faded and is difficult to read, but this is not a problem in *Octovian*.

[1] Throughout this edition, line references to Ff. 2. 38 are preceded by C.
[2] See McSparran and Robinson, p. xiv. [3] See further, pp. 18-19.

The manuscript has suffered loss and damage; ff. 1 and 2 were lost early (see above) and eight more folios were lost subsequently;[1] half of f. 135 is missing, a strip (without text) is torn from the bottom of f. 99, and trimming has removed some letters on ff. 134[r] and 150[r]; f. 140 is damaged and was earlier patched with a fragment from a printed Primer.[2] Five items, including the first and last, are defective because of missing folios.

There are various scribbles, words, and lines on margins; none gives any information about owners or the history of the manuscript. The marginalia include an alphabet (f. 10[v]), four lines of a prayer in Latin (f. 152[v]), eight lines of English verse, begins: *Adewe my prettye pussey* (f. 147[r]), seven lines of the same verse recurring on f. 179[v], and a line in Latin, *liber iste constat mihi*, on f. 170[v]. Item 22, a life of St. Thomas, has been cancelled, presumably in obedience to Henry VIII's proclamation of 1539 removing him from the calendar of English saints.

C, like L, contains devotional and didactic material and works of entertainment, though unlike L it contains no medical material, and its contents are all in English. It is a more professional-looking compilation than L, systematic in the organization of contents, and rather consistent in its manner of presenting them. Items, identifiable by title or incipit in display script, follow each other neatly, laid out in similar fashion, with little space between them.[3] There is no sign of 'filler' texts being added. The first quarter of the manuscript contains religious and didactic material, and proceeds, though not with absolute consistency,[4] from meditative and penitential material, through a collection of pieces dealing with basic

---

[1] In addition to these ten folios, the last four leaves of the eighth quire are missing, following the conclusion of *The Seven Sages of Rome* on f. 156[v]. They were probably blank, and cancelled before binding this section of the manuscript together with the remaining quires.

[2] Now detached and bound in at the end of the manuscript.

[3] The first 156 folios seem to have been conceived of as a unit, and no sizeable blank spaces occur until that point, perhaps originally intended as the end of the collection. The second part (ff. 161–261) is also efficiently organized, though some miscalculation or reorganization is evident at f. 231, an added leaf, containing the conclusion of the story of Guy of Warwick and, on the verso, the beginning of the account of his son Reinbrun.

[4] On the nature and arrangement of the contents, see my discussion in McSparran and Robinson, pp. vii–xii.

doctrine, ending with saints' legends and exemplary tales offering guidance on the conduct of a decent Christian life. The remainder of the manuscript consists of eight romances, *The Seven Sages of Rome*, and the exemplary *Robert of Sicily*, but the nature of this substantial entertainment section harmonizes well with the kind of material which precedes it.

The Ff. 2. 38 romances are unsophisticated adventure stories, generally pious and moral in tone and homogeneous in style and content.[1] Heroic exploits against Saracens, dragons, or giants occur in almost all of them, within plots hinging on the persecution of virtuous women, especially faithful wives wrongfully accused of adultery, the separation of children from parents, noble children brought up in humble circumstances, vindication of the innocent, and family reunions. The association in this manuscript of popular devotional texts, simple verse summaries of basic doctrine, exemplary stories about the conduct of daily life, and stories about families and virtuous women, suggest that Ff. 2. 38 was compiled for devotional and recreational reading in a pious household.

H Huntington Library 14615 (STC 18779) (printed as appendix)

This book is a quarto, in black-letter.[2] It is incomplete, containing only twelve leaves (signatures A[8], B[4]). There are 727 lines of text, which break off at a point corresponding to C742 (L is defective here). The text is preceded by a title page bearing a woodcut of a knight on horseback, and, on a ribbon, the title: 'Here begynneth Octauyan the Emperoure of Rome'. Most earlier references to this book assigned it to Copland's press, but in 1824 Sir Frederic Madden attributed it to Wynkyn De Worde, and Mr Mead's examination has confirmed this.[3] The woodcut used here appears also in De

[1] This homogeneity is apparent despite the fact that five of the romances (*The Erle of Tolous, Sir Eglamour, Sir Triamour, Octovian*, and *Le Bone Florence of Rome*) are in tail-rhyme stanza, and three (*Guy of Warwick, Bevis of Hampton*, and *Sir Degaré*) are in couplet. The influence of early couplet romances, especially *Guy* and *Bevis*, on the style and content of the tail-rhyme romances is demonstrable.

[2] For a description, see H. R. Mead, 'A New Title from De Worde's Press', *The Library* (5th series), ix (1954), 45–49, E. Hodnett, *English Woodcuts 1480–1535* (London, 1935), p. 292.

[3] Mead, op. cit., 45 quotes Madden's footnote to this effect in an 1824 revised edition of Warton's *History of English Poetry*.

Worde's print of *Oliver of Castile* (1518), where the crack visible in the *Octavian* print has widened further. Mr Mead dates the book about 1504–6 on the evidence of the type used. This printed version, title, and woodcut match well the description of a printed edition of *Octavyan* given by Bagford in London, British Library, MS Harley 5905, f. 17, quoted by J. O. Halliwell in the introduction to his edition of C.[1]

> Octavyan, the emperour of Rome, a romanse in rime; a man and horse in complete armour, with a dogge running; imprented at London, in Flet Strete, at the signe of the Sonne, in q., no date; a well printed booke.

Halliwell knew of no surviving copy of this book.

Large capitals mark the opening word of the romance and textual divisions at H319, H516, H588.[2]

II. THE TRANSMISSION AND AFFILIATION OF THE TEXTS

A comparison of the three texts, L, C, and H, shows that they are derived from an archetype *LCH. It is not clear how close this archetype was to the original English version (*O) of the Northern *Octovian* (NO). That the archetype *LCH was not itself the original English redaction of the French source seems certain. Shared textual problems in L and C show that the archetype itself contained textual corruption (see, for example, the notes on 45, 342, 643–5, 1305). Furthermore, there are inconsistencies and confusions of detail common to L, C (and H, where it exists), which seem much more likely to have developed in the course of transmission of the original English version *O (and hence either in *LCH or an antecedent) than to have been introduced in the initial redaction of the OF source to produce the original English version *O. For example, in FO (and the Southern *Octovian* (SO)), the emperor identifies his son Florent at the end of the poem, in a classic family reunion, and Clement, the foster-father, provides the

---

[1] See *The Romance of the Emperor Octavian*, ed. J. O. Halliwell (Percy Society, xiv), London, 1844, p. xi.

[2] See further pp. 18–19. Throughout this edition line references to Huntington are preceded by H.

necessary corroboration. In both L and C, however, this identification has been shifted to an earlier point in the poem
(1125 ff.), and the resulting inconsistencies in later references
to the possible kinship of the emperor and Florent have not
been resolved.[1] This looks like incompetent reworking of the
original English version. So does the more local disturbance
apparent in the L, C, and H accounts of the killing of the *knaue*
early in the poem, though here addition of new material,
rather than displacement of material derived from the OF
source is involved.[2]

(a) *Omissions and Additions to the Texts*

L and C offer different and conflicting claims to authority,
some of which will be discussed below. H, which is generally
close to C, is late, fragmentary, and corrupt, and offers few,
if any, best readings, but it is valuable for other reasons.

As the oldest text, L has the presumed sanctity and authority of age, and on examination and comparison with C, this
is largely confirmed. In its favour are its earlier date, its apparent closeness to the language of the original poem as evidenced
by rhymes, its preservation of northern and North Midland
words and phrases, the fuller text it contained, and various
points of agreement with H against C.

Neither L nor C preserves the full text of the poem, but
for rather different reasons. In L a folio is missing after f. 102
(which ends at line 664, corresponding to C661).[3] Because of
this L wants 142 lines, corresponding to C662–804 (almost
twelve stanzas), and also wants the first five lines of the stanza
with which it resumes at 665, a total of 147 lines. It is likely
that yet another stanza of L is lost here. The number of lines
contained in a folio of L (recto and verso) varies between 151
and 171, averaging 160 lines. 147 lines have been accounted
for; if the folio contained another stanza detailing the giant's
love for the sultan's daughter, and the opening of his negotia-
tions with the sultan for her hand, the total would be 159
lines. This number would correspond better to the customary

---

[1] See the note on 1125–60. [2] See the note on 175–83.
[3] This is the first half of a missing bifolium. Its conjoint leaf occurred in the
Life of St. Christopher.

amount of text on a folio. This probability, however, cannot be confirmed, since the interview with the sultan, partly preserved when L resumes at 665, does not occur in FO or in C.

L has also suffered damage at f. 108, where more than half the page has been torn away, eliminating almost completely two columns of text, and damaging two more.[1]

L otherwise preserves a fuller version of the poem than does C, and in almost all cases its additional material seems to be derived from the OF source.[2] It lacks lines present in C in two places, following 872 (three lines wanting) and 1571 (three lines wanting). On the first occasion the lines in C are original, and their omission produces the only 9-line stanza in L; on the second, they may be original, but cannot be confirmed from FO, and their omission reduces a 15-line stanza in C to the normal 12 lines in L.

The text of C is continuous and undamaged, but it lacks some lines and stanzas present in L. It agrees with H in omitting three lines corresponding to 133-5 in L, which are paralleled in FO, but whose faulty rhyme-sequence is suspicious. If archetypal, these lines may have been omitted deliberately from C to avoid the partial repetitions of 134 and 136, and to regularize the length of the 15-line stanza.[3] L concludes with a 6-line stanza lacking in C; I think that this was added to *L rather than omitted from *C.

There are quite extensive lacunae elsewhere in C and in almost all cases these are the result of revision and condensation in *C (or perhaps *CH).[4] This process has been accompanied by some rewriting to remove the inconsistencies that were generated, but the repair work is not always adequate. The major discrepancies between the two texts are:[5]

(i) C omits the interview between the sultan and the giant, partly preserved in L in the incomplete stanza (665-71) discussed above. The rhyme words and content of C811-16

---

[1] The damage begins at 1479, and ends at 1559.

[2] For discussion of the evidence leading to the conclusions summarized here, see the notes to the various passages referred to.

[3] C's one 15-line stanza, C1669 ff. (L1569 ff.), discussed above, may not be authentic.

[4] On *CH see further below. Since H ends before the first of this group of omissions, we cannot know if the omissions took place in *CH or in an antecedent copy of C (*C), or perhaps even in C itself.

[5] For detailed discussion of the authenticity of these sections, see the notes.

suggest that C's version is closer to the archetype than L is, and that material was probably added to *L here.

(ii) Two stanzas in L, 720–43, are wanting in C. These deal with the giant's attack on Paris, and his challenge to Dagobert. Much of this material is paralleled in FO, and must be original, though it has been removed by editing in *C.

(iii) Two stanzas in L, 768–91, are wanting in C. This is another clear instance of editorial revision of *C, resulting in the elimination of original material, preserved in L.

(iv) C lacks 60 lines corresponding to 1032–91. These lines in L are certainly original; the events described are closely paralleled in FO, and a faulty tail-line sequence in C1117–28 betrays the omission.

(v) A faulty tail-rhyme sequence confirms that C has either lost or removed material following C1590, but L, for other reasons, is also defective here.[1]

Much of the condensation took place in the giant-killing episode (ii, iii), where the archetype itself incorporated new material, but it is difficult to see any editorial principle at work in C other than a no-frills approach to trimming the text. Material essential to the action is not removed, but the giant–Saracen princess–Florent triangle carefully developed in L is weakened, and some colourful material is lost. Clement's role in the arming of Florent is reduced in (iii), and the boisterous comedy of Clement's behaviour at the feast is eliminated by (iv).

(b) *The Affiliation and Reliability of the Texts*

C and H are closer to one another than either of them is to L, and they are close in date. They agree in error in the rhyme-word of line 3 (though not at H596, where H, but not C, repeats the same error), and agree in falsely identifying Clement's own son with Florent, while L preserves the FO account of the two boys being set to different trades, 643 ff. (H626 ff.).[2] They agree against L in omitting 133–5, and in replacing 142 with a less forceful line (H127). They have the

---

[1] This is probably a case of accidental loss; see the note on these lines.
[2] Since C is printed facing L in this edition, a reference to L will also serve for C; line references for H are given to facilitate reference to the Appendix.

same content as L in the stanza beginning at 244 (H229), but the units occur in a different sequence from L.[1] They agree in the first element of the name *Octavian* against *Octo-* in L. Other agreements against L are pervasive, and include identical or near-identical lines (C49, H43; C51, H45; C82, H73; C93, H81, etc.), shared rhymes (C316-17, H304-5; C322-3, H310-11; C651 ff., H637 ff., etc.) and shared original readings (C501, H488; C613-14, H600-1, etc.).[2] C and H must be derived from a common source which differed from L in various respects.

Agreements between H and L against C, and cases where H is independent of both C and L, show that H is not a descendant of C, but derived independently from their common source *CH. Thus H565-6 shares the second person pronoun with L, where C578-9 wrongly uses the first person, and, thanks to a misunderstanding of the word, H241-2 preserves a rhyme on *grette* which has been removed in C254 (and elsewhere in H). Where C408 makes poor sense, L and H395 agree in a much better reading. Where C704 wrongly refers to Clement's other sons, H690 has the singular form which is correct. Many of the numerous agreements in wording between H and L against C must be derived from *LCH, from which C has deviated, although some may be the result of revision or recasting in H.[3] Cases where H differs from both L and C are discussed in the notes to 45, 175-83, 643-5.

The affiliation of the texts suggested here may be represented very simply:

```
            *LCH
           /    \
          /      \
        *CH       \
        /  \       L
       /    \
      C      H
```

---

[1] The source of this contrast between C/H and L may, however, be displacement in L.

[2] Other examples could be added; the most important of these are discussed in the notes.

[3] Thus, for example, when L and H agree on *bukes of Rome* (10, H10), where C has *bokys of ryme*, H may have preserved the archetypal reading, corrupted in *C, or the corruption, introduced in *CH, may have been emended by a moderately intelligent scribe of *H, familiar with the phrase from other romances.

That an *LCH and a *CH existed is, I think, beyond doubt, but the number of intervening stages in the transmission of the texts cannot be established. The corrupt state of H suggests several stages of progressive deterioration from *CH. There are, on the other hand, signs of a close connection between C and L, and between them and *LCH, which would preclude many intervening stages in their transmission.

The kinship of C and H means that we cannot assume that their shared readings are necessarily archetypal, since they may have been introduced in *CH. On the other hand, agreements between L and C, and between L and H, are probably archetypal; in view of the late date and the corruption of H, the numerous L/H agreements seem particularly significant, even if some have to be discounted as possible revisions in *H.[1]

A close comparison of L and C with the extant portion of H reveals some characteristic patterns of alteration of *LCH in the three texts. These must be taken into account in evaluating different readings.

L shows a disposition to create over-long lines by adding explanatory material, such as words introducing direct speech (55, 867, 1105, 1131, 1269, 1572, etc.), and redundant conjunctions and adverbs, such as *full, bothe . . . and, bot, so, and* (43, 141, 327-8, 479, 513, etc.). C's austerity in this respect, however, may not always be archetypal; L and H agree in a longer tail-line at 186 (H171) against C; L has an excessively long tail-line at 333; H318, though shorter, is still closer to L than it is to C. Furthermore, C repeats lines very frequently, and, on at least one occasion, uses exactly the same line as a four-stress couplet line and as a three-stress tail-line (C205, C1560), which is a clear sign of disorder. L does not always preserve rhymes which are probably, or certainly, original in C (C313-14, C501-4, C613-14, etc.), and its revisions of rhyme, like its expansions of text, often yield lines which are metrically and syntactically crude. C sometimes preserves original readings lost in L, or corrupted readings which seem closer to the original than do those in L (C45, C339, C995, etc.). Lines are misplaced in L at 411 and 627;

[1] The most important of these agreements are discussed in the notes on the texts. See, for example, the notes on 214-19, 333, 411, 646-57.

one cannot know if this happened in L or *L. The differing arrangements of three-line units in L and C at 244 ff., 1227 ff., 1557 ff., and the inversion at 1422-3, may be further instances of such displacement in L.

L's deviations from the archetype seem the outcome of two different tendencies: on the one hand, casual carelessness and garrulity, on the other a zeal to clarify things by identifying speakers. C shows signs of similar carelessness, and also of rather more extensive and systematic modification; much of this is shared with H, and must be derived from *CH. It should probably be associated with the substantive editorial revision apparent in C, described under (a) above. What is involved here is the replacement in C and H of northerly dialect features of inflexion and vocabulary preserved in L.[1] The evidence has to be viewed with caution, since not all northerly forms in L need be original. Some, however, are confirmed as such by rhymes, and by their occasional occurrence in C or H. H is more radical and careless than C in its changes, which may reflect a somewhat later date, as well as a corrupt copytext.[2] A comparison of both these texts with L shows that sometimes one shares the original reading with L while the other replaces it (48, H42; 257, H242), sometimes they share a new reading (28, H28; 267, H252), and sometimes they both have new, but different, readings (94, H82; 307, H292; 428, H412; 604, H588). A good example of this kind of tinkering occurs at 288.[3]

Besides replacing items of vocabulary and inflexional forms, C and H avoid syntactic features apparently found unacceptable; thus, impersonal constructions, the historical present, and unmarked possessives are often replaced (258, H243; 229, H214; 909, etc.). These signs of revision, whether they took place in *CH, *C, or C, coupled with occasional inferior

---

[1] The discussion in III of the language of L, C, and the archetype, provides more evidence; further examples are discussed in the notes. The language of H is closer to C than L (pr. 3 sg. in -eth, pr. p. in -yng, neuter pronoun hit (and it), predominance of -ond spellings, &c.); H does, however, use the auxiliary gan form of L, rather than the can of C, which is rare in H.

[2] Thus, for example, C preserves the pr. p. in -and only twice, when required by rhyme (C164, C267). On the first occasion H151-2 shows revision of the rhymes of the couplet; on the second, which involved the whole tail-line sequence, H255 ff. has broken the sequence: wepynge : stonde : hande : londe.

[3] See the note on this line.

readings, repetitions of lines, and other signs of carelessness, seriously weaken the authority C otherwise deserves in view of its generally careful copying and good preservation of original forms.[1] The restylings and prunings apparent in C produce a text which is neat and rather neutral in style, and which suggests competent but rather perfunctory professional handling. The text of L is stylistically idiosyncratic and sometimes clumsy, but in its preservation (and augmentation) of source detail it offers a text which is livelier and more colourful than C.

The weaknesses of H are obvious: there are numerous typographical errors; corruption is shown by the frequent breakdown of the twelve-line stanza into units of six lines (H55 ff., H97 ff., H325 ff., H707 ff.), or of seven or five lines (H265., H331 ff.) and by the omission of text. H has omitted lines corresponding to NO 30-36, 69-70, C721-3 following H30, H62, and H706 respectively. These omissions gave rise to inept attempts to patch up deficient stanzas by padding, or by stealing from the next stanza, which caused more difficulty. H has many readings inferior to L and C (321, H306; 345, H330; 592 ff., H576 ff.) and some that are nonsense (67, H61;[2] 231, H216; 399, H383; C685, H671). It is of particular interest for its intermeshing of correspondences with both L and C, and for its occasional readings which differ from both, though at 120-1 (H109-10), 157-9, 175-7 (H142-4, H160-5) it may have rationalized confusing sequences of events in *LCH.

(c) *The Process of Transmission*

I have discussed above omissions and variations in the texts, and some patterns of corruption of the archetype *LCH typical of the different texts. Beyond these, however, is ample evidence of that apparently random variation in vocabulary and phrasing which can be seen in most manuscript copies of a single romance. A comparison word by word, and line by line, of almost any stanza in the three texts will show a series

---

[1] See, for example, the notes on C45, C307-8, C501, C613-14.
[2] This may represent or perpetuate a printer's error (the *l* and *d* of *lond* being taken respectively as 'long' *s* and *e*).

of partial but not total correspondences between one text
and the other. This kind of variation is typical of the copies
of ME popular romances, but it is puzzling because so many
of the variations seem quite insignificant. They are of a kind,
in fact, which is often associated with oral composition and
transmission. Professor Baugh has discussed exactly this kind
of variation; he rejects the idea of minstrel composition for
most romances in favour of composition in writing by semi-
learned, often clerical authors; he rejects also the notion that
all variants in the manuscripts of the popular romances are
due to the scribes, and suggests instead that:

for those popular romances in which the manuscripts show extensive
variation of a kind that cannot be explained as scribal errors we have in
each case the story as told by some minstrel.[1]

The minstrel, he believes, has written down, or dictated, his
own modified version of the original composition, incorporat-
ing the variants which developed in oral recitation. This view
therefore posits written composition, oral transmission, and,
for the surviving copies, the eventual commitment to writing
of an orally transmitted text.

Whatever the merits of this argument in relation to other
romances preserved in a number of manuscripts, it is, I think,
untenable here. L and C are related in a way that can be plausibly accounted for only by a continuous line of transmission
through pen and paper. The evidence for this is the transmission of textual divisions from the archetype, and the presence
in both texts of residual features of the spelling system of the
archetype.

The archetype *LCH must have been divided into narrative
sections, which are well preserved in L and C, though, as one
might expect, much less faithfully in H.[2] L and C agree in the
beginning of a second section, marked by a large initial N at
532 (C529). C marks the transition to a third section by a
large initial A at C757; the corresponding passage in L is missing, since a folio is lost there after f. 102. Both texts agree in

---

[1] A. C. Baugh, 'The Middle English Romance: Some Questions of Creation,
Presentation, and Preservation', *Speculum*, xlii (1967), 30.

[2] H, which ends at line H728, has large initials at H319, H516, H588; of these
only H516 corresponds with a division in L and C (at 532).

the large initial T marking a further section at 1029; L marks one more section, not recorded in C, at 1485, and I think it likely that this division is authentic, and was overlooked in C.

The probability that these divisions in L and C are derived from the archetype, rather than arrived at coincidentally, is reinforced by a survey of the presentation and layout of other romances in the two manuscripts. Practices concerning the use and style of titles, the use of braces to mark rhyme-schemes, the break-up of individual romances into sections marked by initials, vary within each manuscript, and the lack of uniformity suggests that in each manuscript the scribe is preserving features present in his various exemplars. The substantial agreement in the positioning of these initials in L and C suggests further that the narrative sections were inherited, by way of the exemplars, from the archetype *LCH.

L and C show some curious agreements in spelling practice which I think can most reasonably be explained as vestiges of the spelling practice of the archetype which have persisted into the surviving copies. Most occur in rhyme position, where, in any case, we expect scribes to be more conservative than elsewhere. (i) Both manuscripts occasionally double the vowel of certain monosyllabic words ending in a long vowel when they fall at the end of a line; within the line, and generally at the end of the line also, these words occur with a single vowel. What is significant is how frequently these untypical forms with double vowel turn up in both L and C at exactly the same point.[1] This must surely reflect the same feature in a shared written source. C has more such forms than L, and was apparently more reliable in preserving them. (ii) Apart from its regular form ȝyt 'yet',[2] C uses initial ȝ on only three occasions, all in rhyme: ȝelde 'yield' C252 (also in L), ȝelle 'cry' C330 (also in L), ȝyng 'young' C1567 (L defective, but cf. line 1). Elsewhere the initial palatal fricative is represented

---

[1] A couple of examples may serve to illustrate this: soo occurs three times in each text at the end of the line, beside final so (10 examples in L, 4 in C). L and C agree in soo at 88, 109; at 82 L has soo while C has thoo (a different reading, but with double vowel); at 27 C has soo beside so in L. Goo occurs 6 times in each text at the end of the line, beside final go (11 examples in L, 9 in C). L and C agree in goo at 267, 277, 284, 1354; at 118 C has a different rhyme; the remaining three forms do not agree. There are other examples of this shared spelling feature.

[2] L's form of 'yet' is ȝitt. On the vowel, see p. 28 below.

by *y*, and *3* forms are clearly unusual in C. I believe these spelling forms, all paralleled in L and all in rhyme, must have been preserved from the archetype. (iii) C habitually uses the form *tyll* (15 examples) while L uses *till* (18 examples); the only exception to this is the form *tylle* which occurs in rhyme in both L and C at 1016, and again in rhyme at C1571, where L is defective. This agreement in a form untypical for either text is striking.[1]

The rather free variation of wording described at the beginning of this section seems inconsistent with this preservation of phonologically non-significant details of spelling from the archetype. The first would be compatible with oral transmission, the second could not survive it, and must depend on a written tradition. Both can, I think, be attributed to the scribe if we consider the cultural context in which popular romances were produced and circulated, and how the copyist of such a romance is likely to have approached his task. We are not dealing with Chaucer's circle, where Adam can be rebuked, but with the production of copies of adventure stories, almost certainly without authorial supervision, for what was clearly an undemanding audience.[2] We have seen above how the texts of NO have been changed in the process of transmission, not just by error, but by abridgement and expansion. We must think of the scribes who copied these and similar romances as scribe-editors, revising content and recasting form as they write, partly deliberately and partly automatically.

Major structural modifications, expurgations of the text if and when they occur, the elimination of archaic or extreme dialectal features of the language are likely to be deliberate. The recasting of lines and the substitution of one idiom or cliché for another are, I think, like many of the modifications of the language, mechanical changes, introduced by scribes who simplified their task by reproducing content and sense rather than exact details of wording and language. Exact copying is difficult, and a needless labour if neither author or

---

[1] On C's use of *tyll(e)* as a preposition only in rhyme, see p. 32 below.

[2] On the likely clientèle for the Ff. 2. 38 romances, see F. McSparran and P. R. Robinson, Introduction to the facsimile of *Cambridge University Library MS Ff. 2. 38* (London, 1979), pp. vii-xviii.

audience demands it. I think these scribes read their copy, perhaps in couplets or three-line units, and then rendered it from the mind rather than the page before them. This method of procedure would encourage 'translation' into the scribe's own dialect, and minor variations in wording. It would also explain the differences in spelling and wording which occur when scribes copy the same material twice. Robert Thornton, for example, introduced a host of trivial variations when he inadvertently copied the same twenty lines of *Richard Coer de Lion* twice over in London, British Library Add. MS 31042, ff. 131ª, 142ª.[1]

On the other hand, tinkering with the rhymes introduces serious problems for the copyist, and, in the interests of saving labour, scribes copying in this fashion would be wise to cling to the formal control and security afforded by the stanza-form and rhyme-scheme of the exemplar.[2] I think C and L have been transmitted through scribes who, through their attentiveness to this, have sometimes preserved by an accident of the visual memory even phonologically non-significant spelling features of the all-important rhyme-words of their archetype.

III. LANGUAGE AND PROVENANCE

The account which follows confines itself to those features of spelling, rhymes, inflexion, and vocabulary which are most significant for localization and date.

The Language of L

1. The reflex of OE *a* before *l* + consonant is usually written *a*: *alle* 193, *falle* 795, but it appears as *au* in *haulle* 605, etc. (9 examples), *haulsynge* 1363 (beside one occurrence each of

---

[1] On these lines see Brunner's edition (Wiener Beiträge zur englischen Philologie, xlii), Vienna, 1913, pp. 5–7; also K. Stern, 'The London "Thornton" Miscellany', *Scriptorium*, xxx (1976), 34–36.

[2] It is worth noting that in the duplicated lines from *Richard*, despite the variations within the line, Thornton is very consistent in his representations of rhyme-words; he alters one rhyme-word (*me* becomes *be*), varies in his use of –*e* in the rhyme-word *kyng*, and otherwise has the same forms for rhyme-words throughout.

halle 1068, *halsynge* 1582). Dobson, §60, dates this diph-thongization about or shortly before 1400.

2. The reflex of OE *a* before *ld* is usually written *o*: *byholde* 1095, *bolde* 794, but occasionally as *a*: *halde* 581, 670.

3. The reflex of OE *ā* is usually represented by *o*: *brode* 579, *go* 296; forms with *oo* occur occasionally in open syllables at the end of a line: *goo* 118, *twoo* 693. It is written *a* quite often in rhyme-position: *sare* 174, *hare* 354, and on a number of occasions within the line: *sary* 206, *wafull* 303.

4. The reflex of OE *ā*, ON *á* before the voiced guttural spirant and *w* is usually written *ow*: *knowe* 1579, *owen* 926, but sometimes as *aw*: *awen* 230, *knawe* 1224, *lawe* 1319. These latter forms occur typically, though not exclusively, in northern texts (cf. Jordan, §105, Anm., Dobson, §241).

5. The reflex of OE *ā* before *ht* is written both as *a* and *au*: *bytaghte* 283, *bytaughte* 646, *laghte* 888, *raughte* 889. Forms without a glide are northern, though *au* forms also appear in the north (see Jordan, §121).

6. The reflex of OE *e* is usually represented by the spelling *e*: *bedde* 71, and occasionally by *ee*: *beedd* 143. It is represented by *i* in *riste* 1164. The raising of *ĕ* to *ĭ*, especially before dentals, occurs from the thirteenth century and became very common in the north (cf. Jordan, §34, Dobson, §76, n. 4).

7. The reflexes of OE *ē* before the voiceless guttural spirant (spelt *g*, *h*) (including *ē* by smoothing) are represented by various spellings (*ey*, *ye*, *y*), but the most common spelling for both is *–egh*: *seghe* (pa.t.) 409, *eghe* 572, *heghe* 336, *neghe* 470. Such spellings are generally northern or North Midland.

8. The reflex of OE *i* is usually spelled as *i* or *y* in L, but there are a number of forms spelled with *e*. Many of these are shared with C and are probably archetypal (*reden* 1443, *hedir* 1188, *peté* 232, *mekyll* 54, etc.). L has additional forms with *e*: *smetyn* 902, *petous* 745, *fethils* 200, *sekirly* 1123, etc. One cannot tell if these are further archetypal forms, or forms representing Thornton's own practice.

In most cases it is impossible to be sure if the forms show ME lengthening of *ĭ* > *ę̄* in open syllables of disyllabic words, which is chiefly northern, or ME lowering of *ĭ* > *ĕ* which occurs more widely. In the fifteenth century the latter is par-ticularly common in the York and Towneley plays, but is also well attested in eastern texts (see Jordan, §271, Dobson §80, and n. 3). The problem is complicated by the fact that ME *e* spellings for *i* in closed syllables, the only sure evidence for *ĕ* < *ĭ*, occur chiefly in those same texts which also afford evidence of open syllable lengthening of *ĭ* > *ę̄*. Since this is the case, *e* spellings in open syllables are ambiguous. However, *ĕ* < *ĭ* in closed syllables is not a feature of L or C, so it seems probable that these forms show lengthening of *ĭ* > *ę̄*, and are northern.

9. The reflex of OE *ī* is usually represented by *i* or *y*: *dryve* 721, *chide* 779, but occasional spellings with *ie, ye* also occur: *wyefe* 679, *wiefe* 1566, beside the usual *wyfe*.

10. The reflex of OE and ON *y* is usually written *y* or *i*: *giltles* 158, *kysse* 728, but appears as *e* in *brene* 849, *euyll* 241. Forms of *brene, brenie* with *e* occur in other northern or North Midland texts, including *Awntyrs of Arthure*, the alliterative *Morte Arthure* (both Thornton texts), *Wars of Alexander*, and *Sir Gowther*, and probably have *ę̄* by lengthening in open syllables of disyllabic words (cf. 8 above).

11. The reflex of OE *o* before lengthening groups is usually spelled *o*, but *burdes* 910, 1089, beside *borde* 1228, shows northern raising of *ō*.

12. The reflex of OE *o* before *ht* is written *oght*: *boghte* 1134, *wroghte* 312. One form: *doughetir* 990 shows a glide before *h*.

13. The reflex of OE *ō*, ON *ó* is usually represented by *o*: *bote* 418, but is sometimes written *u*: *buke* 353, *gude* 883, *luke* 770, etc. On the northern raising and fronting of *ō*, see Jordan, §54. The *oy* spelling in *soyty* 800 is a hypercorrection, reflecting northern monophthongization of *oi* in the second half of the fourteenth century (on which see Jordan, §238).

14. The reflex of OE *ō* before the voiceless guttural spirant (spelt *g, h*) is usually written *ogh*: *sloghe* (pa.t.) 158, *woghe* 564, etc.; sporadic forms with a glide occur: *ynowghe* 1618, *loughe* 844.

15. The reflex of OE *u* + voiced guttural spirant is spelled *ow* in *fowle* 660, *fowlles* 333, but the northern form *fewle* occurs three times (352, etc.).

16. The reflex of OE *ū* is represented regularly by the spelling

ou, ow: *broune* 936, *down* 316. The *uy* spelling in *ruysty* 796 is a hypercorrection, depending on the northern monophthongization of *ui* in the second half of the fourteenth century (cf. 13 above, and see Jordan, § 132).

17. For unstressed inflexional syllables L favours *-es, -ede, -en* forms over more typically northern forms with *-i-*. Elsewhere, however, *-ir, -ill* are used regularly in *fadir, modir, wondir, mekill, littill*.

The main points of interest in the treatment of consonants are the following:

18. Beside the regular form *if, gyff* appears once in 1412 and *ʒif* in 336. Forms of 'give' and 'gift' always appear as: *gyff* 5, *gyffe* 75, *gyftes* 95. 'Again', 'against' appear always as *agayne* (52, 539, 721, etc.).

19. OE *cw*, OF *qu* are written *qw*: *qwykke* 718, *qwene* 261, *qwne* 523.

20. Words spelt with *hw* in OE are written with *wh* in L; the form *whilde* 299, 366, beside *wilde* 520, must be a hypercorrect spelling, reflecting the reduction of [hw] to [w]. Thornton also wrote, but corrected, *whyd* 'wide' at 842. Kristensson's survey of the six northern counties and Lincolnshire shows that, though [hw] was apparently the normal pronunciation throughout the area he investigated, spellings with *w* are frequent throughout.[1]

21. Words beginning with *sc* in OE are usually written with *sch*: *schame* 560, *schelde* 692; forms of 'shall' and 'should', however, are written consistently with *s*: *sall* 66, *salle* 728 (*schall* occurs only at 76 and 135), *solde* 284, *sold* 425, *sulde* 985. In final position *s* is also used in *Grekkes* 407, 569. These forms show the northern development of [š] to [s] in unstressed forms and syllables (see Jordan, §183). OE *sc* is written *ch* in *chippe* 'ship' 474, 475, beside forms with *sch* (cf. Kristensson, p. 202, who refers to *ch* spellings as exceptional).[2] Such forms reflect the French *ch* spelling for [š], developed from earlier [č] in CF in the thirteenth century.

22. OF *s* is written as *sch* in *Paresche* 600, etc. (12 examples),

[1] G. Kristensson, *A Survey of Middle English Dialects 1290–1350: the six northern counties and Lincolnshire* (Lund Studies in English, 35, Lund, 1967), 211–15, 246.

[2] Thornton uses the form *chippe* again in *Sir Eglamour*, line 865.

Parische 1255, and as *ch* in *Pareche* 574. These may be hyper-correct spellings reflecting the change of [š] to [s] described above, or instances of the dialectal and vulgar development of final [s] to [š] chiefly in the East Midlands and the north (see Dobson, § 373).

23. The form *þofe* 346, 357 (beside *þoghe* 258) shows the late ME change of [χ] to [f].

24. Thornton's regular use of *f(f)* in the verbs *gyff(e)* 5, 75, *hafe* 134, 165, *lyf(f)e* 68, 105, *lufe* 374, 1350, beside occasional forms with *u* or *v*, may reflect northern unvoicing of final *v*, following the early loss there of final *e*.

25. A recurrent feature of Thornton's spelling practice is the doubling of consonants, particularly *t* and *n*: *twentty* 587, *wonndir* 346, *knyghttes* 270, *wellde* 249, *lyghttede* 958, *thykke* 307. These forms, and others, occur beside forms without doubling (*twenty* 693, *wondir* 448, *knyghtes* 283, etc.). They occur after short vowels, after long vowels, and vowels that were presumably lengthened, and are apparently of no phonological significance.

26. Nouns, whatever their historical form or declension, usually end in *-e* in uninflected forms. Where forms with and without *-e* occur, forms with *-e* are always more numerous: *knyght* (3 examples), *knyghte* (27 examples), etc. The plural, like most gen. sg. forms, ends in *-es, -is* or *-s*; *-es* and the much less common *-is* occur chiefly, though not exclusively, with monosyllabic nouns; *-ez* occurs once only in *kyssyngez* 1582. *-s* occurs with monosyllabic stems ending in a vowel: *knes* 256, *trees* 313, and more commonly with nouns whose stems have two or more syllables: *auenturs* 1334, *maydyns* 512, *eldyrs* 11. Syncope of the vowel of the final syllable in trisyllabic or polysyllabic forms is fairly common by the late fourteenth century. The plural of *childe* is always *childir* 44, 115, and the pl. *brethir* occurs once (1585).

The most significant features of verbal inflexion are the following:

27. Almost all infinitives end in *-e*. Exceptions include some twelve verbs which occur at least once without ending: *haf* 104, *com* 470, *sadill* 1170, etc. Infinitives in *-ne* occur only in rhyme; two are shared with C: *vndone* 841, *bene* 971, and the third, *gone* 892, may also be archetypal.

28. The pr. 1 sg. almost always ends in *-e*; *hase* 392 occurs, once only, beside regular *hafe*. The pr. 2 sg. has no ending in *sall* 688, ends in *-t* in *willt* 774, *art* 1461, ends in *-se* in *hase* 871, and in *-s* in *werreys* 1190. The pr. 3 sg. usually ends in *-es*, beside occasional *-is*: *endis* 1629, *gretis* 916; *-se* occurs in *dose* 106, *hase* 116, *sayse* 109, and *-s* in *has* 1389, *sais* 55, and *answers* 1017. When preceded or followed by a personal pronoun, the pr. pl. ends in *-e*: *hafe* 64, *rede* 282, *saye* 109. Plural forms in *-se*, *-es* occur in *hase* 65, *gamnes* 1145. Forms with *-n* occur in *sayne* 27, *duellyn* 196, *bene* 1203 (which may be subjunctive).

29. The present participle ends in *-and(e)*: *byrnand(e)* 167, 169, *sayland* 424, *sowkand* 443, etc. No other ending occurs.

30. The imperative pl. has *-es* in *helpes* 758, *tukes* 768, *lukes* 1269, and *-s* in *herkyns* 2. As with the pr. pl., forms with *-e* occur when the imp. is used with a personal pronoun: *ʒe late* 456, *ʒe do* 250, *gyffe ʒow* 75, etc.

31. In the past tense of strong verbs, sg. and pl. have fallen together. Levelling in both directions takes place in the pa.t., but more often the vowel of the sg. is extended into the pl., as was generally the case in the north (see Brunner, p. 206). Some verbs have alternate pa.t. forms containing the reflex of both OE vowels, which are used both for sg. and pl.: *fonde* 309, *found* 311 (sg.): *fonde* 442, *found* 432 (pl.), etc.

32. The past participle of strong verbs usually ends in *-en*: *broken* 1245, *comen* 31, *spoken* 184, etc., less often in *-yn*: *comyn* 565, *smetyn* 902, etc. Forms with *-ne* occur also: *borne* 265, *lorne* 1031, *done* 230, *tane* 1382, *slayne* 435.

33. Among the personal pronouns, regularly used forms which are of interest include 3 sg. *scho*; acc., dat. and poss. *hir*; 3 pl. *þay* (beside occasional *thay*, almost always at the beginning of a line, and two instances of *they* 298, 484, in the same position); acc. and dat. *þam* (except for *þem* 1373, *thaym* 1520); poss. *þair(e)* (*thaire* once at 45).

34. The plural of *þat* is *þose* 354, *those* 551. The plural of *þis/this* is *thies* (twice), *theis* (once). *ʒone* 'that, yon' current in the north from the beginning of the fourteenth century, occurs twice (1117, 1580). The acc./dat. form of *who* is *whaym* (3, 8).

35. L contains a few words which are predominantly northern

or North Midland in distribution, and a number of forms or uses of other ME words which occur chiefly in the same areas.[1]

The most distinctive words in L are *jwhil(l)s* (conj. and adv.), otherwise only in the *Alphabet of Tales, Lay Folk's Mass Book*, and Rolle, *vnfrely*† 'ugly',[2] otherwise only in *Morte Arthure* and *Cursor Mundi*, *blyschede vp* 'looked up', *belle* 'cauldron', otherwise only in the *Awntyrs of Arthur* and *Life of St. Robert of Knaresborough*, *syte* 'grief' (see the note on 1305), *haghten* 'eighth' (*aght-* forms are northern or North Midland, though *eʒt-, eght-* forms occur elsewhere). *Bydene*† (adv.) is northern or North Midland.

Other words which are chiefly, if not exclusively, northern or North Midland in distribution include: *abowne* (adv.), *barne, bere*† 'cry out', *bodworde* 'message:, *brymli* 'loudly', *garte, gerte* as a causative verb, *ʒone* 'that', *nerhande*†, *samen* (adv.), *sprente*†, *till*† (conj. and prep.), *intill* (prep.), *þer(e)till* (adv.), *whills* (conj.), *vnto* as a conj. 'until', *will of wone*†.

Northern or North Midland forms of other ME words are: *hare* 'hair', *ware* (pa.t.), *are* (adv.), *bynke, dede*† 'death', *kirke, gyff, ilke*† (adj.), *swylk(e), whilke, fra, sall(e), mekill*†, *sen* (conj.), *wate* 'wet'. The plural forms *childir*† and *brethir* occur usually in northerly texts. Some of these words and forms are of native origin, others are Scandinavian.[3]

The evidence presented above demonstrates the distinctively northern character of L, and fits well with the identification of Robert Thornton, scribe, with Robert Thornton of East Newton in the North Riding of Yorkshire.[4] The diphthongization seen in *haulle* (see 1) and the *þofe* forms (see 23) suggest copying in the fifteenth century, which accords with the evidence for date provided by the manuscript itself.[5]

---

[1] Kaiser's list of northern forms (see R. Kaiser, *Zur Geographie des mittelenglischen Wortschatzes* (Palaestra 205, Leipzig, 1937)) must be modified somewhat in view of additional evidence on the distribution of forms in material published subsequently in fascicles of the *MED*, and in its files. As might be expected, the words which he records widely in northern texts often drift into other areas, and in practice only rare words remain distinctive for one area.

[2] Forms which occur also in C are marked with † and are probably archetypal. They are included here because Thornton, presumably familiar with them, preserves them in his copy, often within the line as well as in rhyme position.

[3] Other words occurring in L which Kaiser takes as northern but which seem to me of doubtful value as evidence are: *grett(e)* (pa. t.), *haylsed* (pa. t.), *myrk*.

[4] See pp. 3–4.   [5] See pp. 2–3.

The Language of C

1. The reflex of OE *a* before *ld* is regularly written *o*: *bolde* C24, *beholde* C691.

2. The reflex of OE *a* before the lengthening group *nd* is usually written *o*: *brondys* C231, *stonde* C239. Forms with *a* occur mostly in rhyme position, either in self-rhymes, or in rhyme with the present participle in *-and*, though even here the scribe sometimes reverts to his preferred form with *o*: C163 *stronde* : *brennand*, C267 *wepande* : *stande* : *hande* : *londe*. Before *ng* both *a* and *o* spellings are used, with *o* the more frequent: *amonge* C196, *longe* C130, *sprange* C962.

3. The reflex of OE *ā* is usually written *o*: *bote* C454, *brode* C760, sometimes *oo*: *moost* C1098, *goon* C31; as in L, *oo* forms are favoured in open syllables at the end of a line: *soo* C27, *moo* C30, *goo* C274. Spellings with *a* occur only in rhyme position: C51 *sare* : *care* : *fare* : *mare*, etc., and seem to represent a concession by the scribe of C to the rhymes of his source.

4. The reflex of OE *ā* before *ht* is spelled with *a* or *aw*: *lawght* C976, *raght* C977, beside *o* in *oght* (pa.t.) C1643, a form which Jordan, § 129, characterizes as northern.

5. The reflex of OE *e* before *ld* is represented by *e*: ʒ*elde* C252, but beside one occurrence of *felde* C1534 there are six examples of *fylde*, C243, C804, etc., and *schylde* always has *y*. OED records forms of *schyld* with *i/y* in *Cursor Mundi*, Wyclif, and *Avowing of Arthur*; like *fylde* these forms probably show shortening of ME *ę̄* to *ĭ*.

6. ME *er*, from various sources, is occasionally spelled *ar*: *farre* C185, *harkenyd* C858, *harte* C975, etc. These forms show the lowering of *ĕ* before *r* which began in the north in the fourteenth century, and gradually spread southwards. *Pertynge* C203 is a hypercorrect spelling illustrating the same development.

7. The reflex of OE *ē* is represented by *y* in ʒ*yt* C544 (six examples), with shortening and raising either directly from *ę̄* > *ĭ*, or by way of *ĕ*.[1]

8. The reflex of OE *ē* before *h* appears in *hygh* C1155. The form *hyght* occurs at C457; Jordan, §96, Anm., takes this

---

[1] On ʒ*yt*, see also p. 19.

as the typical northern form, contrasted with southern *height*.
The forms *ye* : *hye* C284, *nye* C467 derive from OE *ēʒ* (cf.
Luick, §407, 1).

9. As in L, the reflex of OE *i* is sometimes represented by *e*:
mekyll C54, *hedur* C1216, *redyn* C1471.[1] It is worth observ-
ing (i) that *e* forms are more numerous in L; (ii) that *e* forms
in C correspond to *e* forms in L, almost always at the same
point in the text; (iii) that the reverse is not true, since L has
e forms for some words which occur only with *y* in C. These
facts suggest that at least the shared *e* forms are derived from
the common source of L and C; the scribe of C has preserved
a number of these forms, but seems to have been less familiar
with them than Thornton was.

ON *i* is spelled *ey* in C's rendering of the northern phrase
weyle . . . of won C318. This must be an error, perhaps reflecting his unfamiliarity with the phrase, which must also
have baffled the transmitters of H, since it was eliminated
there (cf. H306).

10. The reflex of OE and ON *y* is usually written *y*: *hylle*
C307, *kysse* C443, *kyn* C200; beside these, however, *u* and *o*
spellings are regular in *moche* C303 (25 examples), beside
four occurrences of *mekyll* (and one each of *mykyll*, *mykull*),
dud C50 (11 examples), *furste* C484, C1633, *churche* C182,
192, and *soche* C212 (15 examples). Although *u* forms occur
sporadically in texts from various ME dialectal areas, they are
in general West Midland or south western.

11. The reflex of OE *eo* is usually spelled *e*: *erthe* C893,
herte C36, but it is represented by *y* regularly in *swyrde*
C537 (8 examples) beside *swerde* 545 (once only).[2]

12. C favours *-ys*, *-yd*, *-yn* spellings for unstressed inflec-
tional endings, though some past participles in *-on* occur (see
24). The unstressed vowel is regularly spelled *u* before *r*:
aftur C34, *brodur* C1636, *fadur* C188, *wondur* C51, etc., but
before *l* both *y* and *u* forms occur: *lytyll* C554 (3 examples),
lytull C374 (3 examples).

The main points of interest in the treatment of consonants
are the following:

13. Forms of 'give' have initial *y* in the infinitive and present:

---

[1] On the significance of these spellings, see further p. 22.
[2] On *harte*, *farre*, see 6 above.

yeue C400, *yeuyth* C1151, though *geue* occurs twice, C78, C1509. The initial consonant is lost in *yf* 'give' (imp. sg.) C75. Past tense forms have *g*: *gaf(e)* C96, C274; *gyftys* (n. pl.) occurs once at C95. Within the line *ageyn(e)* occurs as prep. and adv. C175, C1218, and *agenste* C780, etc., as prep.; in rhyme position the form is always *agayn(e)* C52, C665.

14. OE *cw*, OF *qu* are spelled *qu*: *quyte* C1494, *quene* C508; *qw* is used only in some occurrences of *qwene* C258, etc.

15. Initial glide consonants are shown in the forms *yerly* 'early' C100, *wodur* C341.

16. *Smyght* 'smite' C1526 is a hypercorrect spelling reflecting the loss of [ç] in the sequence *iht*, a development which Dobson, §140, says was completed by about 1400, and which he considers predominantly eastern in the fifteenth century. There is otherwise no evidence for this development in C, and it is noteworthy that the form occurs in C1526 in rhyme with *fyʒt*, itself an error for, or scribal emendation of, the northern word *syte* (see the note on 1305).

17. Words beginning with *sc* in OE are usually written with *sch*: *schall* C66, *schame* C557, *schewe* C56, but occasional *sh* forms occur: *shall* C1228, *shewe* C1583, *shylde* C941.

18. The plural of most nouns ends in *-ys*: *armys* C1267, *gyftys* C95; *-es* occurs occasionally: *armes* C61, *seges* C1084. Nouns ending in a vowel have a plural in *-es*: *partyes* C1319, or *-s*: *ladys* C266. As in L, nouns whose stems have two or more syllables usually form plurals with *-s*: *auenturs* C1362, *prysoners* C1621, though occasional *-ys* forms occur. The pl. *brethurn* occurs once (C1688), and the pl. of *chylde* is *chyldren*, except for *chyldyr* C344 (once only).

The most significant features of verbal inflexion are the following:

19. Almost all infinitives end in *-e*; there are less than a dozen exceptions to this, which include *dyght* C436, *fyght* C546, *couyr* C522, *crysten* C627. L and C share two infinitives in *-ne*: *ondone* C926, *bene* C1059. C has in addition *gone* C315, C721, *han* C44, *bene* C808, *sene* C809, *ouyrgone* C862, *comyn* C1514, all in rhyme. Some of these may be archetypal, but *ouyrgone* has been introduced into C in the process of revision (see the note on 744-55).

20. The pr. 1 sg. almost always ends in *-e*; exceptions are

few: *wyll* C3, *pray* C1144. The pr. 2 sg. ends in *-t* in *wylt* C617, *art* C954, *schalt* C731, in *-est* in *trowest* C148, and in *-ste* in *mayste* C149, *haste* C674. The pr. 3 sg. ends in *-yth*: *deryth* C106, *gretyth* C1004, occasionally written *-yþ*: *comyþ* C529, *stondyþ* C791; *-th* occurs in *hath* C116, and *dothe* occurs in C1385. Pr. pl. forms usually end in *-e*: *lye* C693, *rede* C1695; *-n* occurs in *seyn* C27, *ben* C1297 (if the latter is not subj.); *be* occurs at C395 and C488.

21. The present participle ends in *-yng*: *brennyng* C166, *rennyng* C338. Two forms in *-and(e)* occur in rhyme: *brennand* C164, *wepande* C267.

22. C has a distinctive imperative plural form in *lystenyth* C2, C207; otherwise there is no distinction between sg. and pl. which usually end in *-e*: *crepe* C136, *drede* C1107, *loke* C1297.

23. The past tense of weak verbs usually ends in *-yd* for all persons sg. and pl.: *armyd* C1199, *gamyd* C1173, *openyd* C1131, though syncopated forms in *-de*, *-te* (sometimes *-d*, *-t*) are common. Strong verbs usually end in *-e* for all persons sg. and pl.; C has one pl. in *-yn*: *stodyn* C1468.

24. The past participle of strong verbs usually ends in *-yn*: *redyn* C1471, *comyn* C1127, etc.; it occurs five times with *-on*: *beton* C682, *bowndon* C1629, *eton* C1129, *forgeton* C1130, *schapon* C1421. Other endings which occur are: *-en*: *taken* C662, *folden* C654, *-e*: *bede* C189, *woxe* C326; as in L, *-ne* occurs with stems ending in a vowel or *r*: *borne* C262, *done* C227, etc. The prefix *y-* occurs infrequently both for strong and weak pps.: *ybrokyn* C1273, *ydrawe* C1357, *ydyght* C1648.

25. C uses *can* frequently as an auxiliary of the past tense (C8, 49, 53, etc.). This form is generally associated with western or North-West Midland texts.

26. Forms of interest among the personal pronouns include the regular 3 sg. *sche* beside *she* (11 examples); acc., dat. and poss. *hur*; 3 sg. *hit* (the invariable form); 3 pl. *they*, occasionally *þey*; acc. and dat. *them* or *þem*; poss. *ther*, occasionally *þer* (*hur* once only, C1559).

27. The demonstrative pl. *þo* occurs twice, and the pl. of *þys* is *þes(e)* or *thes(e)*.

28. C has very few interesting words or forms of words which

it does not share with L. On the pr. p. *stryking* 'flowing, running' see the note on C426. Beside its regular form *as*, C uses *os* twice (C41, C339). Northern and North Midland words and forms of words are much less common in C than in L, and it is clear that the text of C has passed through the hands of a scribe (or scribes) who rejected various archetypal forms either because they were regional or were felt to be archaic. Those which occur are noted above (pp. 27, 36); to them may be added the rare verb *wele* 'choose' C1577 (otherwise only in *Ywain and Gawain* and Robert of Brunne). L is defective at this point, but the form is probably archetypal. Of the northerly forms C shares with L, *bedeene* C882, and *sprente* C473 occur only in rhyme. *Tyll(e)* as a preposition occurs only in rhyme (C56, C251, C1104, C1571); two of the three examples of *nerehonde* are in rhyme (C501, C788), and *dedd* 'death' occurs once in rhyme C236.[1] Incomprehension must underlie the garbling of the northern word *syte* 'grief' (cf. 16 above), of an archetypal northern, North (West) Midland *bremli* at C1449, and may explain the spelling *weyle* (. . . *of won*) C318, beside *will* (. . . *of wone*) in L321. C cannot in fact be shown to have any northern or North Midland vocabulary items peculiar to itself, since, except where L is defective, all its northerly forms are matched in L.

C shows more diverse dialect features than L. It contains northern, East Midland, western, and even South Midland forms. Since a comparison with L shows that northern features from the archetype are often either eliminated or confined to rhyme position (3, 21), and are sometimes misunderstood (28), its language must be placed south of Thornton's. Failing the north, the East Midlands are suggested by *y* for OE *y* (10). A western colouring is contributed by *o* and *u* spellings for the reflex of OE *y* (*soche, moche, dud,* etc.) (10), *-ur, -ull* in unstressed syllables (12), *hit* (26), and *can* as an aux. (25). The present ind. endings are Midland, as is the pr. p. in *-yng* (21); the imp. pl. *lystenyth* (22) points further south, but occurs only twice, in one of the conventional formulas of romance, the call for attention. The pp. forms are varied (24), with North East Midland *-yn*, western *-on*, and South Midland

---

[1] *Dede* C1037, within the line, may be another instance of this noun; if so, it may, as the form suggests, have been understood as *dede* 'deed'.

or southern *-e*, with occasional *y-* prefix. *Sche, she* and the
3 pl. forms are Midland (26). The language then is mixed,
apparently late (cf. the identification of *er* and *ar* (6), of *ir*
and *er* (11), the loss of the fricative in *-iht* (16) and is probably best placed in the western fringes of the Central Midland
area: that is to say, characterized as West Central Midland.

The Language of the Archetype

This section outlines the most significant features of the language of the archetype as evidenced by rhymes, inflexions, and
vocabulary. The evidence gained from the rhymes is limited
by the repetitiveness of the rhyme schemes, and by the preva-
lence of self-rhymes. It is clear, moreover, that convenient sets
of rhymes for the tail-lines were part of the stock in trade of
authors of these romances, so that, for examples, the 'northern'
sequences in NO showing OE *ȳ* in rhyme with OE *ī* as in 1619
tyde : *pryde* : *syde* : *ryde* can be matched in many other tail-
rhyme romances (cf. *Launfal* 207 *ryde* : *-tyde* : *pryde* : *wyde*,
Emaré 747 *pryde* : *syde* : *ryde* : *wyde* (cf. 987), *Athelston*
533 *abyde* : *hyde* : *ryde* : *wyde*, etc.). The value of such
evidence for localization is, therefore, questionable.

Only rhymes common to L and C are discussed here, and
only selected examples are given for the forms under discussion. Rhymes of interest which occur in one text only are
discussed in the notes on the texts.

1. Anglian *a* + *ld* rhymes with the pa.t. of *will*: 220 *tolde*
(pp.) : *wolde*, 580 *wolde* : *halde* (v.) cf. 804). These cannot
safely be taken as showing the rounding of *ā*, as they may be
rhymes on Anglian *walde* (see Campbell, §156). Strandberg,
§131,[1] discusses the same rhymes in *Cursor Mundi*, and
assumes that the vowel is *ă*. A short vowel occurs in 631
tolde (pp.) : *callde*.

2. OE *ā* occurs frequently in rhymes with OE *ă* lengthened
in open syllables: 51 *sore* : *care* : *fare* : *mare*, 354 *hare* (adj.)
: *ware* (pa.t. sg.) : *bare* : *kare* (cf. 123, 414, 522, etc.). In
self-rhymes and in rhymes with ON *á*, the quality of the
vowel cannot be confirmed. A rounded vowel is confirmed in
only one rhyme: 1416 *oste* : *alþirmoost*.

[1] O. Strandberg, *The Rime-Vowels of Cursor Mundi* (Uppsala, 1919).

3. OE *æ* rhymes on *a*: 190 *allas* : *was*, 1607 *was* : *br̆asse* : *rase* : *anelase*, 226 *faste* : *caste*. The unstressed form *wes* is confirmed by rhymes: 370 *lyones* : *was*, 292 *wyldirnes* : *was*. Rhymes such as 414 *fare* : *were* : *bare* (pa.t. sg.) : *sare* (cf. 354, 1163) must, if exact, depend on levelling of the pa.t. sg. vowel into the pl., followed by open syllable lengthening, and levelling of the lengthened vowel throughout the preterite.

4. OE $\bar{æ}^1$ (non-WS $\bar{e}$) and $\bar{æ}^2$ rhyme (i) together: 1387 *dede* : *lede*; (ii) with OE $\bar{e}$ and $\bar{e}o$: 282 *rede* (pr. pl.) : *lede* : *thede* : *blede*, 1511 *wede* : *stede* : *ʒode* : *lede*, 298 *strete* : *mete*; (iii) with OE *e* lengthened in open syllables: 474 *werre* : *bere* : *were* : *dere* (v.), 1175 *bere* : *dere* : *here* (n.) : *were*. ME $\bar{ę}$ (< OE $\bar{æ}^2$ and *e* lengthened in open syllables) has been raised to $\bar{ę}$. On northern and eastern raising of $\bar{ę}$, recorded chiefly before dentals, *r* and in final position, see Dobson, §121.

5. Anglian *e* (WS *ie* by palatal diphthongization or *i*-mutation) rhymes on *e* (probably lengthened) in 1283 *welde* : *schelde* : *felde* : *byhelde*, 246 *vphelde* : *wellde* : *ʒelde* : *felde*. On 330 *welle* : *ʒelle* : *hyll* : *felle* see 8.

6. Anglian $\bar{e}$ (WS $\bar{ie}$) by *i*-mutation rhymes on OE $\bar{e}$: 1413 *fere* : *were* : *bere* 'cry out' : *here* (v.) (cf. 1026), 210 *here* : *chere* : *ʒere* : *were*.

7. OE *i* + *ld*, $\breve{e}$ + *ld* rhyme together in 625 *child* : *helde* 'age', 366 *whilde* (adj.) : *childe* : *felide* : *mylde*. These must be inexact rhymes, probably on $\bar{i}$: $\breve{i}$, since *helde* and *felde* (OE $f\bar{e}lde$) may have $\breve{i}$ by raising of $\bar{ę}$ (see Dobson, §11, and compare *fylde* (n.) 'field', the usual form in C). A similar sequence occurs in *Eglamour* (L)711 *felde* (n.) : *mylde* : *childe* : *wylde*, and Strandberg, §337, discusses similar rhymes in *Cursor Mundi*.

8. OE *y* rhymes on *i*: 400 *jn* : *syn*, 1371 *wyn* : *kyn* (cf. 1395). It appears also in rhyme with *e*: 330 *welle* (n.) : *ʒelle* : *hyll* : *fell*. This rhyme, if exact, must depend on ME variation between $\breve{e}$ and $\breve{i}$. Raising of $\breve{e}$ to $\breve{i}$, and lowering of $\breve{i}$ to $\breve{e}$, seem to have been particularly common in the north in ME (see Dobson, §§76, 80). It is often impossible when dealing with rhymes to tell which has occurred; here, however, the rhyme must be on $\breve{i}$, as $\breve{e}$ forms for OE *hyll* are rare, even in the south east.[1] Strandberg, §62, records rhymes on $\breve{e}$: $\breve{i}$ in *Cur-*

[1] On this see M. L. Samuels, 'The Role of Functional Selection in the History

sor Mundi; all his examples show the vowels before *n* or dentals. Another *e* : *i* rhyme involving *hylle* occurs at C307-8, and is probably archetypal (see note on C307-8).

9. OE $\bar{y}$ occurs in rhyme with OE $\bar{\imath}$: 562 *besyde* : *pride* (cf. 1451, 1617), 1271 *ryde* : *byde* : *hide* : *syde*, 3 *kythe* : *blythe* : *lythe* : *sythe* (cf. 606, 1547).

10. OE *ea* rhymes on lengthened *a*: 1269 *ȝare* : *fare*, 568 *ȝare* : *bare* (pa.t. pl.) (see 3), and presumably underwent open syllable lengthening. OE *ea* + *rd* rhymes with OE $\bar{e}$ in 981 *herde* : *berde*; if the vowel is long, the $\bar{ę}$ must have undergone raising to $\bar{ę}$ (cf. 4). Strandberg, §260, confirms a short vowel for the pa.t. *herd*, and in the NO sequence both words may have $\breve{e}$ by shortening.

11. OE $\bar{eo}$ rhymes (i) with OE $\bar{e}$: 87 *free* : *see* : *hee* : *three* (cf. 151, 262, 265), 472 *sprete* : *mete*; (ii) with $\bar{æ}^1$ (non-WS $\bar{e}$): 139 *crepe* : *slepe*; (iii) OF *é*: 959 *knee* : *thre* : *solempnyte* : *he* (cf. 983); (iv) with OE $\breve{e}$ lengthened to $\bar{ę}$ before *ld*: 246 *vphelde* : *wellde* : *ȝelde* : *felde*, and with OE $\breve{e}$ lengthened in open syllables and raised before the dental in 186 *lede* : *stede* 'place' : *bede* : *ȝede*. OE *geēode* rhymes on $\bar{e}$, and $\bar{o}$, with change of stress: 1182 *stede* : *ȝede* (cf. 186), 150 *stode* : *ȝode* : *wode* : *blode* (cf. 710, 1314). Shortened, it rhymes with *e* in 208 *telle* : *byfell*.

12. The archetype probably contained forms showing northern lengthening of *i* > $\bar{ę}$ in open syllables of disyllabic words. The evidence for this is the agreement between L and C on some -*e*- forms within the line (see *The Language of L*, 8).

13. An infinitive without final nasal is confirmed by frequent rhymes: 34 *welde* : *elde*, 67 *fare* : *kare*, 76 *make* : *sake*, etc. Beside these, infinitives in -*n* are confirmed by rhyme twice: 840 *sone* : *vndone*, 971 *bene* : *kene* : *bydene* : *tene*. For other infinitives in -*n* in rhyme, but occurring in one text only, see *The Language of C*, 19.

14. A pr. pl. without final nasal is confirmed by rhyme: 15 *rede* (pr. pl.) : *dede* : *wede* : *stede* (cf. 282, 1583). These examples all, however, occur in a stereotyped phrase which is a commonplace in romance. See the note on 15. L and C

of English', *TPS* (1965), 15-40, Figure 1, and *Linguistic Evolution* (London, 1972), p. 123.

agree on several untypical forms with *-n* within the line (*sayne* 27, *bene* 1203); L has in addition *duellyn* 196. These forms are probably archetypal.

15. A pr. p. in *-and* is confirmed by rhyme: 166 *strande* : *birnand*, 270 *wepande* : *stande* : *hande* : *lande*.

16. Strong pps. in *-n* are confirmed by rhyme. They occur most often with vocalic stems: 28 *bene* : *bytwene* (cf. 391), 1259 *bene* : *bytwene* : *sene* : *kene*, 31 *gone* : *none*, 1446 *sone* : *done*, 304 *byforne* : *forlorne* (cf. 1031), 717 *slayne* : *agayne* (cf. 1223). In the sequence 426 *nane* : *stone* : *anone* : *slayne*, the rhyme requires the analogical pp. *slān* (cf. *gān*). This form occurs also in *Cursor Mundi* (see Strandberg, §113), and *OED* records *slan, slon* forms only from Scottish and northern texts.

17. The pa.t. pl. and pa. subj. of 'to be' occur in rhyme with both *ā* and *ē*, but more frequently with *ā* (< ON *váru*). The frequency of rhymes on *ă* lengthened in open syllables: 123 *kare* : *mare* : *there* : *ware* (cf. 354, 414, 522, etc.) suggests an unrounded vowel for the *ā* forms.

18. The Scandinavian form of the third person pl. pronoun occurs once in rhyme: 438 *daye* : *þay* : *playe* : *awaye*.

19. The northern or North Midland items of vocabulary in L and C are discussed under *The Language of L*, 35, and *The Language of C*, 28, to which reference should be made. Northerly forms common to both texts in rhyme are: *sprente* (pa.t.) 476, *till* (prep.) 56, 251, etc., *bydene* (adv.) 797, *dede* (n.) 'death' 239, *bere* 'cry out' 1421. The adverb *nerehonde* occurs twice in rhymes confirming a form with *e* at C501 (H488) and C788; I have not found a form with *-e-* recorded elsewhere, but like *hend(e)* forms, it must be northern or North Midland. L has a different reading for the first, and is defective at the second, but in view of C's tendency to purge northernisms it seems very probable that these forms are also archetypal. The phrase *will of wone* 321 and *vnfrely* 1415 occur at the same points within the line in both texts, and are almost certainly derived from the archetype, and I believe the same is true of *syte* (n.), in rhyme at 1305 (not in C), *brymly* 1421, and *wele* (v.), in rhyme at C1577 (L is defective) (see the notes on these lines).[1] Within the line C's occasional

---

[1] On the 'northern' form *ȝynge*, see note on line 1.

mekyll forms beside regular *moche, childir* (once) beside regular *chyldren*, both matching the same forms in L, are also probably archetypal.

It is clear that this romance was composed in the North East Midlands or the north; the evidence for deciding between the two is inconclusive, and points, I think, to a border area, perhaps near the Lincolnshire/Yorkshire boundary.

Forms without any trace of palatal diphthongization, or of *ĭe* as the product of *i*-mutation are consistent with an origin in the East Midlands or the north (5, 6); the East Midlands or the north are suggested by *ĭ* as the reflex of OE *ў̆* (8), by the raising of *ę̄* to *ē̜* (4), and by the third person plural pronoun in *þ-* (18), and by infinitive forms without an ending (13).

A northern origin is suggested by the frequent occurrence of OE, ON *ā* in rhyme with *ă* lengthened in open syllables (2),[1] by present participles in *-and* (15), and by strong past participles in *-n* (especially by the pp. *slan*) (16), and, to some degree, by the vocabulary (19).

The occasional occurrence of infinitives in *-n* (13) need not argue against an origin in the area suggested. It is significant that they are confirmed only for vocalic stems, that they occur in other tail-rhyme romances, and that they are identical in form with their own past participles, constituting with them a group of monosyllabic verb forms convenient for use in rhyme. Strandberg confirms for *Cursor Mundi* occasional infinitives in *-n* for vocalic stems, such as *slan* (Strandberg, §113) and *don* (Strandberg, §360) including for the latter the rhyme on *sone* (adv.) which occurs in NO 840.

I believe it probable that the language of the original poem was not very different from that of L. Many of the northern forms in L cannot be confirmed (nor for that matter excluded) by the rhymes. Those that can include *a* for OE *ā*, present participles in *-and* and strong past participles in *-n*. Northern features of the vocabulary are matched in L, and it is also significant that L either preserves, adds, or restores within the line some forms which C tolerates only in rhyme, and which must there be archetypal: the pa.t. *ware* (4 examples

---

[1] Kristensson (Map 17, p. 283) shows the border between *ā* and *ǭ* forms running approximately from the Ribble to the Humber, then south, then east, to include the northern half of Lincolnshire in the *ā*-area.

within the line), *till* as a preposition (10 examples other than in rhyme), the adverb *þore* (14 examples within the line), the preposition and adverb *nere* (9 examples within the line), the noun *may(e)* (3 examples within the line) and the noun *dede* 'death' (6 examples within the line).

The rhymes afford no significant evidence for date; composition about or shortly after the middle of the fourteenth century seems likely.

IV. VERSIONS AND LITERARY RELATIONSHIPS

French and English Versions

The earliest surviving French version of the story is the romance *Octavian* (FO), 5371 lines in octosyllabic couplets, preserved in a single manuscript, Oxford, Bodleian Library, MS Hatton 100, copied by an Anglo-Norman scribe about the beginning of the fourteenth century. Vollmöller, in his edition of the text, suggested that it was composed by a Picard poet between 1229–44; his evidence for this dating (Christian occupation and rule of Jerusalem during this period) is tenuous, and was rejected by G. Paris in favour of a date of composition close to that of the manuscript.[1]

Recently, K. V. Sinclair has drawn attention to what was almost certainly another Anglo-Norman copy of FO.[2] In 1389, John Whytefeld listed the *Gesta octouiani imperatoris in gallicis* as the seventh item in a volume (no longer known) in the library of the Benedictine Priory of the Blessed Virgin and St. Martin in Dover. According to Whytefeld's table of contents the manuscript contained fourteen items, both secular and religious (including three on St. Thomas of Canterbury); the *Gesta octouiani* followed *La Romonse de Ferumbras*, and the eleventh item was the *Gesta karoli magni* 'in gallicis'.[3]

---

[1] See *Octavian*, ed. K. Vollmöller (Altfranzösische Bibliothek, 3), Heilbronn, 1883, p. iv. G. Paris, review of Vollmöller, *Romania*, xi (1882), 609–14.

[2] K. V. Sinclair, 'Evidence for a lost Anglo-Norman copy of *Octavian*', *NM*, lxxix (1978), 216–18.

[3] See M. R. James, *The Ancient Libraries of Canterbury and Dover* (Cambridge, 1903), pp. 460–1.

This cannot have been the Bodleian manuscript, since Hatton 100 contains only FO, on 108 folios, while according to the Whytefeld catalogue, the *Gesta octouiani* occupied folios 123ᵃ–164ᵇ. The *incipit* given by Whytefeld does not correspond with that in Hatton 100, but does in fact occur in the Hatton text at line 1185, the seventh line of f. 24ᵇ. It seems that these must be different copies, and that the Dover text was either imperfect, misbound, or wrongly catalogued. The recurrence of the same line of text confirms what the immediate context suggests: that this was indeed an Octavian romance; the form of the title associates it with FO, rather than the second version, F&O, described below.

Another much longer fourteenth-century French version, *Florent et Octavian de Rome* (F&O),[1] monorhymed alexandrines, in *laisses* of unequal length, is preserved in three unpublished manuscripts in the Bibliothèque Nationale in Paris. The dates of two of these are known; a note on the last leaf of Paris, Bibl. Nat., MS fr. 24384, in the same hand as the text, dates the copy 1455–6, and MS fr. 12564 is known to have been copied by Druet Vignon in 1461. The third and best copy, MS fr. 1452 belongs to the first half of the fifteenth century, and is probably close in date to the other two. MSS 24384 and 12564 are in the Picard dialect, MS 1452 is in Francien with some Picard features.[2]

These copies of F&O range in length from 16,000–18,576 lines, and are thus over three times as long as FO. Scholars have offered different explanations of the relationship between the two versions. Gautier's view that FO is a condensation of an earlier version of F&O is unconvincing, though it

[1] The title refers to the twin sons of the emperor Octavian, after whom the first version is named, and reflects a further shift in interest, already apparent in FO, from the parents to the exploits of the children.

[2] For a summary of F&O, with excerpts, and a brief account of the manuscripts, see P. Paris, 'Florent et Octavian de Rome', in *Histoire Littéraire de la France*, XXVI (Paris, 1873), 303–35. See also Vollmöller, p. iv, and R. Bossuat, '*Florent et Octavian*, chanson de geste du xivᵉ siècle', *Romania*, lxxiii (1952), 289–331. An inventory of the library of Charles V and VI in 1411 refers to what seems to be another and earlier copy of F&O: 'Florens et Octovian de Romme, rymé, en ung petit livret couvert de rouge . . . Fait à Paris'. G. Paris, *Romania*, 610, believes, for not very clearly defined reasons, that this was yet another redaction, making a third version of the story. On the dialect of the French texts, see Bossuat, 327.

has been repeated by many.[1] F&O bears all the signs of being
an expanded version, full of diffuse, confusing, and repetitive
secondary accretions. Others, following Vollmöller (p. xviii),
have argued that both are independent redactions of a lost
twelfth-century chanson de geste.[2]

Bossuat's comparison of the best manuscript of F&O with
FO leads him to yet another explanation. There is no need to
posit a lost earlier version; the first third of F&O is an adapta-
tion, 'pur et simple', of most of FO. In the second third, the
same fourteenth-century redactor developed extensively the
summary account of the deeds of young Octavian presented
in FO, by drawing on various sources, especially the *chanson
de geste Floovent*. The third section he views as a later con-
tinuation, close in date to the three extant manuscripts, and
inferior in every way to the two parts which precede it. It
repeats tediously many of the incidents and motifs of the
earlier sections, and concludes with an account of Othon, son
of Florent, grandson of the Emperor Octavian and father of
Florence, heroine of the romance *Florence de Rome*. A bridge
passage in all three manuscripts makes it clear that (though in
fact this occurs only in MS fr. 24384) *Florence de Rome* was
supposed to follow F&O, as it does in the three surviving
copies of a French prose version of 1454.[3]

The Octavian story was clearly a popular one; prose versions of FO and of F&O were made in the fifteenth century,
and were the sources of early printed versions.[4] Italian derivatives of the story are preserved in chapters 17–81 of the

---

[1] L. Gautier, *Bibliographie des Chansons de Geste* (Paris, 1897), p. 104. Compare D. Mehl, *The Middle English Romances of the Thirteenth and Fourteenth
Centuries* (London, 1968), p. 111.

[2] See Vollmöller, p. xviii, P. Streve, *Die Octaviansage* (Halle, 1884), R. Eule,
Untersuchungen über die nordenglische Version des 'Octavian' (Halle, 1889),
A. H. Krappe, 'Florent et Octavian', *Romania*, lxv (1939), 359–73.

[3] See Bossuat, 297 and fn. 1; R. M. Walker, 'From French Verse to Spanish
Prose: *La Chanson de Florence de Rome* and *El Cuento del Enperador Otas de
Roma*', *MÆ*, xlix (1980), 230–1. The only known copy of a ME version of this
romance, *Le Bone Florence of Rome*, occurs in the same manuscript as C (MS
Ff. 2. 38), but not in the same section of the manuscript. There is thus some
evidence for the development of an Octavian cycle in France, but not in England.

[4] Vollmöller, pp. xvi–xviii, and P. Paris, F&O, p. 335, cite catalogue references
to other manuscript and early printed versions in verse and prose. The French
prose versions are fully described by G. Doutrepont, *Les Mises en prose des
Épopées et des Romans chevaleresques du XIVᵉ au XVIᵉ siècle* (Brussels, 1939),
pp. 176–84.

fourteenth-century *Libro delle Storie di Fioravante*, and in book ii, chapters 42-52 of *I Reali di Francia*.[1] A French prose version was translated into German (1535) and became a popular German Volksbuch, printed a number of times, and itself the source of popular Danish, Dutch, Icelandic, and Polish versions.[2] The story was obviously popular in England also; the prime evidence for this is the provenance of FO itself, and the existence of the ME versions of the romance. But there is other evidence too: there are three references to Octavian among the heroes of romance, and he is named in the Lincoln Thornton copy of *Sir Eglamour* (lines 769-70); he is probably referred to also by Chaucer in the *Book of the Duchess* (line 368).[3] Henry V had tapestries illustrating both religious subjects and romances, and an inventory lists among his possessions a tapestry depicting 'Le Octavion roy de Rome'; this is probably the romance hero rather than the historical figure.[4]

There are two English versions of *Octovian*: the northern version (NO) preserved in L, C, and H, and edited here, and the southern version preserved in London, British Library, MS Cotton Caligula A. II (SO), which was probably composed in the London-Essex area.[5] In the Caligula manuscript *Octovian* precedes *Sir Launfal* and *Lybeaus Desconus*, and it is generally held that Thomas Chestre, the self-proclaimed author of *Launfal*, composed all three works.[6] Both English

[1] *Libro delle Storie di Fiorovante*, ed. P. Rajna (Bologna, 1872), *I Reali di Francia*, ed. G. Vandelli (Bologna, 1872).

[2] See L. A. Hibbard, *Mediaeval Romance in England* (1924, repr. New York, 1960), p. 267; M. Schlauch, 'A Polish Analogue of the Man of Law's Tale', in *Chaucer and Middle English Studies in Honour of Rossell Hope Robbins*, ed. B. Rowland (London, 1974), pp. 372-80.

[3] For details of these references, see *Octovian Imperator*, ed. F. McSparran (Middle English Texts 11), Heidelberg, 1979, p. 26.

[4] Quoted by Halliwell from an inventory of 2 Henry VI. See *The Romance of the Emperor Octavian*, ed. J. O. Halliwell (Percy Society, XIV), London, 1844, p. x. See also J. Evans, *English Art, 1307-1461* (Oxford, 1949), p. 93.

[5] For all subsequent references to SO, see my edition; on the language of the original and of the manuscript, see SO pp. 14-25. Both NO and SO were edited by G. Sarrazin (Altenglische Bibliothek, 3), Heilbronn, 1885. The C text of NO has been edited by M. Mills, in *Six Middle English Romances*, London, 1973.

[6] For bibliography and discussion of this, see M. Mills, 'The Composition and Style of the "Southern" *Octavian*, *Sir Launfal* and *Libeaus Desconus*', *MÆ*, xxxi (1962), 88-109, and his edition of *Lybeaus Desconus* EETS, 261 (1961), *passim*. See also *Sir Launfal*, ed. A. J. Bliss (London, 1960), pp. 12-14.

versions were composed about the same period, which was probably the second half of the fourteenth century; there is no conclusive evidence for priority of composition for either version, though there are interesting and suggestive agreements in wording and details between the two, which point to some connection between them. The following discussion will consider the question of the OF source of the English versions, and the relationship of NO and SO to one another, and to their source.

Relation of the English to the French Versions

The English versions are obviously related to FO rather than to F&O. They present an abbreviated version of the story common to FO and the first third of F&O, but where these two differ, the English versions almost invariably agree with FO. They lack the supplementary episodes and motifs of F&O,[1] and they share with FO one very distinctive and important feature absent from F&O, the double theft of the second child by a lioness and a griffin and their airborne trip to an island in the sea. It is generally assumed that the English versions are derived from FO;[2] in my view the close agreement in plot and details, and the verbal correspondences between the English texts and FO confirm that they are derived either from FO itself or from a text closely related to it.

In an early study, concerned primarily with NO, Eule reaches a different conclusion, and argues that both NO and SO were derived independently from a lost French source, collateral with FO and F&O, but independent of both, and like them derived from the lost twelfth-century *chanson de geste* posited by Vollmöller.[3] He argues that in general NO is not as close to FO as its editor, Sarrazin, suggests, and that

[1] Thus, for example, F&O has added the motif of the red cross on the shoulder of the twin babies as a sign of their royal birth, and exploits this later in the recognition of the children. Neither FO nor the English versions employs this motif, which, of course, renders the charge of their mother's adultery implausible, as her attendants point out in F&O (P. Paris, F&O, p. 304).

[2] See Sarrazin, pp. xviii–xxiii, M. Schlauch, *Chaucer's Constance and Accused Queens* (1927, repr. New York, 1969), p. 87.

[3] R. Eule, *Untersuchungen über die nordenglische Version des Octavian* (Halle, 1889). See especially his stemma (p. 16). For a brief discussion of Eule's views, see my edition of SO, p. 30 and fn. 44, p. 31.

many details in L and C are not paralleled there. There is some truth in this, but Eule has not allowed for the possibility that the changes developed as the English version evolved, beginning with the initial reworking of the source by an English author working within a different literary context (that of the existing ME romance tradition), and continuing with modifications in the course of transmission, brought about by the incorporation of material from other romances, and probably by the influence of one English version on the other.

The most significant differences he cites between the English versions and FO fall under two heads:

1. Agreements between NO and SO against FO

(i) In both English versions the emperor throws the head of the supposed lover at his wife, 176, SO 209 ff. The reference to the youth as a *kokes knaue*, 116, SO 122, is peculiar to the English versions. In FO 230, he is merely a *garcons*, and in F&O he is a *valet* (P. Paris (F&O), p. 304). (ii) The empress's father is named only in the English versions; in NO he is the *kyng of Calabire* 221, and in SO 43 *Dagabers*. (iii) Both English versions refer to the *Grekkes se*, 407, SO 1837. (iv) Both English versions say that the sailors go ashore for water, and thus find the lioness and the child, 426 ff., SO 549. (v) The king of France is taken prisoner by the sultan in NO, C1553 (L defective), and SO 1520, but not in FO. (vi) There are some close verbal parallels between the English versions.[1]

2. French place and personal names

(i) NO introduces the place names *Cleremont* 955, etc., and *Borow Lerayne* 1216, etc. Neither occurs in FO. (ii) In NO the sultan's daughter has a confidante named *Olyue, Olyuayne* in L1011, 1008, etc., and *Olyvan* in C1099, etc. This is not paralleled in FO, yet the forms in *-n* preserve an OF inflexional ending.

A survey of Eule's evidence shows that it requires reanalysis,

---

[1] I omit here Eule's supposed parallels between NO, SO, and F&O against FO. They involve numerals, which are unreliable as evidence, and which were, in one case in the English versions, clearly chosen for convenience in rhyme (SO 265 ff., NO 283–4, the latter rhyme used twice already between 264 and 278). His comments on the age of the children when the narrative returns to them are also of no weight.

because it is of different kinds. To begin with, we can exclude from discussion the naming of the empress's father in the English versions (see 1(ii)), since they do not agree on who he is, and he plays a different role in each. In NO his title has been introduced from some other source (a Duke of Calabria, for instance, is the heroine's father in *Ipomedon*); in SO the identification with Dagobert occurs in a different context and is a typical instance of the modification of source material in that romance. FO opens with an account of Dagobert himself taking a wife and then being crowned at Rheims. SO replaces the 'barren marriage' motif proper to the Octavian story with the 'exhortation to marry' motif, probably influenced by its use in other persecuted wife stories (compare *Lai le Freine* and Chaucer's *Clerk's Tale*). Thus, Octavian is urged to marry, and the bride proposed for him is Dagobert's daughter.[1] The barrenness of the marriage for a period of years, common to the other versions, is transformed in SO into Octavian's five year period of rule as a single man. None of this has anything to do with the King of Calabire's unwitting condemnation of his own daughter in NO.

The real agreements between NO and SO against FO consist of the remaining details of plot and verbal parallels cited by Eule, to which I can add others. What must be decided is the reason for these agreements. Do they suggest, as Eule supposed, a common OF source different from, though obviously similar to, FO? Are the agreements all attributable to the same cause, or are different factors involved in different cases? The verbal parallels (including the *kokes knaue* and the *Grekkes see* mentioned above under 1) are much more easily and convincingly explained as borrowings from one English version into the other. The shared details of plot are more problematic, since they might be transmitted from the putative OF source, or might also be borrowings.

The only significant evidence so far for an OF source other than FO is the names cited under 2 above, but I think this is important, though unfortunately scanty and ultimately inconclusive evidence. It must be pointed out, first, that these names do not occur in SO, and secondly, that this need not be significant, nor can it be used to argue that NO and SO

[1] See further on this SO, lines 31–60 and note.

are derived from different OF sources. NO and SO treat their material very differently. SO lacks the focus and detail of NO, and has generally the character of an outline or synopsis. Thus, in SO, the sultan's daughter plays a very small part, and we do not learn her thoughts. In FO she has twenty beautiful maidens as attendants, and unburdens herself to them (3777 ff.); they reply *communaument* (3796). In NO she has a modest version of that kind of helpful confidante found in various French romances, most fully realized in the Lunete of *Yvain*. The reduction to a single attendant could, of course, take place as easily in an English redaction of FO as in an alternate French version of the story, but if the name were then appropriated from some other romance, either French or English, it seems unlikely that the OF case distinction would have been preserved as it has been in the *Olyue, Olyuayne* forms of L.[1]

The place name evidence is also suggestive, though once again the NO forms are not paralleled in SO. The two episodes in which *Cleremont* is mentioned (955, 1180) do not appear there. *Borow Lerayne* occurs in three episodes in NO (C790 (L defective), 1216, 1332); the first two are omitted in SO, the third appears in a very abbreviated form, and no place name occurs in the corresponding passage. In using these place names, NO offers apparently circumstantial details about the Paris region. The sultan camps at Cleremont, his daughter moves to Montmartre:

> To þe kynge of Fraunce þe maydyn sende
> To lye at Mountmertrons þere nerehonde,
> From Parys mylys thre,
> At Mountmertrons besyde Borogh Larayn,
> That stondyþ ouyr the banke of Sayne,
> For auentours wolde sche see.
>
> (C787-92)

This arrangement agrees in general with FO, but not in the details of *Borogh Lerayne* and *Cleremont*, which do not occur

---

[1] In SO, p. 31, n. 46 I suggested the posited ME Charlemagne romance *Olive and Landres* as a conceivable, but undocumented source for the name. On this romance see *A Manual of the Writings in Middle English*, ed. J. Burke Severs, Fascicule 1 (New Haven, 1967), p. 81.

there. In FO the sultan camps, rather surprisingly, near *Dan Martin*, modern Dammartin-en-Goële, some thirty kilometers north-east of present-day Paris, while his daughter, for a good view of proceedings, moves to Montmartre (FO 1761 ff., 1825 ff.), a celebrated vantage point. The names are not derived either from F&O, since it places both the Saracen army and the princess at Montmartre.[1] *Cleremont* is an unlikely site for the sultan's camp because of distance (see the note on 955), and the account of the location of *Borogh Lerayne* is inaccurate (see the note on C787-92); both are, however, genuine place names, and suggest some familiarity with the Paris region, but no concern for topographical exactness. NO has thus derived them from some source other than FO or F&O; the occurrence of *Borogh Lerayne* twice in rhyme with *Sayne*, like the use of the inflected form of *Olyue*, strengthens the probability that this source was French.

There are, moreover, various respects in which NO, SO, or both, parallel F&O rather than FO, and two of these may be outlined here.

(i) In NO 115-16 the use of *þou* shows that the emperor's mother attributes the couple's childless state to his sterility:

> 'For þou myghte no childir haue,
> Scho hase takyn thy kokes knaue.'

In F&O the same reason is implied, though rather more discreetly, by the emperor's mother to her son during his wife's pregnancy (P. Paris (F&O), p. 303):

> Il a six ans passés que vos cors l'espousa,
> Et onques en sa vie nuls enfans ne porta.
> Cuidiés-vous donc avoir engendré celuy-la?
> Ce a fait un garson qui o luy soy coucha.

There is no suggestion of this in FO or SO, where the mother adduces the mere existence of twins as evidence of infidelity; twins are proof that two men have made love to the mother (FO 119-22, SO 127-32).

(ii) In their respective accounts of the exiled empress's life

---

[1] Bossuat, 306 ff., points out several improvements in topographical accuracy and plausibility in F&O, and associates them with other evidence which convinces him that the redactor of F&O was writing for a Parisian public.

in Jerusalem, NO and SO show parallels with F&O rather than FO. In FO 942 ff. the lady takes lodgings and disappears from the story until the concluding action of the romance. In NO 496 ff., SO 631 ff. she is summoned by the king of Jerusalem, and made part of his household, though in NO she is recognized and becomes an honoured guest, while in SO she is a seamstress. F&O provides a model for features in both accounts; there the impoverished lady plans to earn her living by embroidery and sewing, but is recognized as of noble rank by King Amauri, who becomes her patron, and supplies her lavishly with food and drink every day (see P. Paris, F&O, p. 306). She does not literally join his household.[1]

I do not believe that F&O can be the source of the English versions, but these and other minor parallels between them, and the French names discussed above, lead me to think there is a case for supposing that the source of NO was not FO, but an OF text very closely related to it (*A). If *A existed, it may also have been the source of SO, though it need not necessarily have been, since the evidence on which we may tentatively posit the existence of *A is derived primarily from NO.

In view of the otherwise close correspondence between the English versions and FO, I think it most improbable that *A could have been derived independently from a lost twelfth-century source, as Eule suggested; there is no evidence for such an early source, and Bossuat's account of the relation between FO and F&O renders one unnecessary. If *A existed, it must have been another representative of the FO tradition, otherwise represented only by the surviving Hatton copy. The relationship between a French *A and the Hatton copy would have to be a close one, comparable to that between L and C rather than between NO and SO. In the present state of knowledge and evidence, however, the numerous agreements between the Hatton copy of NO and the English versions remain as significant and useful as ever. It is tempting,

---

[1] This discussion revises somewhat my account of this detail in the English versions (see SO, p. 37 and references). SO may have derived the occupation as a serving-woman from a source resembling F&O in this respect, or may have introduced it independently; the verbal parallels with *Emaré* remain, and suggest its influence. For another parallel between F&O and the English versions see the note on NO 610–21.

but must remain pure speculation, to wonder if the lost Dover Priory manuscript described above may have contained *A.

Other agreements between the English versions against FO may be considered in the light of a possible *A, but we move here into an area of speculation and uncertainty, where an all-explaining lost source is a convenient but dangerous hypothesis. It is, for example, possible, but not provable, that the detail of the sailors going ashore for water and finding the lioness and the child in both English versions (see 1(iv) above) is derived from *A. In F&O the baby is stolen by the lioness, seen by pilgrims, and reclaimed by its mother before she boards a ship for the Holy Land; in FO the second theft of the child (and lioness) by the griffin occurs, and they are transported to an island in the sea (FO 599). Yet in FO the child is found by the sailors and recovered by its mother without any mention of a sea voyage (669 ff.). The manuscript of FO is not defective here, but the account does not quite hold together, and something seems to have been lost; *A, however, might have been more explicit, or contained material omitted in FO. On the other hand, an English redactor might have made good a discrepancy in his source by introducing this detail, and this might explain its appearance in both English versions.

The relationship between the English versions

A comparison of the extant English versions with each other and with FO shows that they must have been derived independently from their OF source. The authors have made substantial and different modifications to the story, omitting much, changing the sequence of events, conflating episodes, and rarely agreeing in such changes, yet both preserve a broad general agreement with the action of FO. Neither of the extant ME versions can be derived from the other, since each contains details present in FO, and close verbal parallels to it, not shared by the other. It would be impractical and unnecessary to list all the evidence for this, but a few representative examples from both SO and NO will show their close and independent agreements with FO; other parallels are discussed in the notes.

1. *Agreements between NO and FO*

(i) In FO 88 the empress is childless for fifteen years, in NO 64 for seven years, while in SO 97 ff. she conceives and bears children in the first year of marriage.

(ii) In FO 506 and in NO 580 the outlaws ask Clement for forty pounds, in SO 396, 409 the sum is not specified. He hires a wet nurse in FO 530 ff. and in NO 595, but not in SO.

(iii) In FO 561, as in NO 345, the baby is kidnapped by the lioness who is hunting for food for her whelps; in SO 470 the whelps are born later on the island.

(iv) In FO 1156 ff. Clement entrusts Florent with forty pounds, the merchant asks for thirty pounds, and Florent insists on paying forty pounds for the horse. L is defective, C710 ff. corresponds exactly with this, SO 812 ff. changes the character of the scene.

(v) In FO 2046 ff. the giant promises Marsabile to bring her the king of France if she will reward him with a kiss. In NO 678 ff. he promises the king of France's head for the same reward; all of this is omitted in SO.

(vi) In the description of the arming of Florent, C and L parallel the ironic comments of the bystanders in FO; an exact parallel to *le hardi bachelier* (FO 2276) occurs in the reference to *an hardy bachelere* C932 (L reads *doghety*).

(vii) In FO 3701, etc., the sultan's daughter is called Marsabile, and Clement's son is called Gladouains (FO 967, etc.). NO preserves these names, though Gladwyn occurs only once, and has been transferred to Clement's wife, NO 805. In SO the Saracen princess and Clement's wife are nameless, while his son is called Bonefey, SO 679.

(viii) In FO 3261 ff., Florent visits the Saracen camp as a messenger, bearing an olive branch, as in NO 1172. This episode is omitted in SO.

2. *Agreements between SO and FO against NO*

(i) In FO 118 ff. the emperor's mother charges the empress herself with adultery, citing the mere existence of twins as proof positive. SO parallels this both in detail and in wording (see SO 115-32 and note).

(ii) In FO 251 ff. and in SO 196 ff. the empress dreams that her children are carried off by an eagle; in NO 167 ff. a dragon carries them away.

(iii) In FO 275 ff., as in SO 217 ff., the empress is put into prison, in NO 184 ff. there is a curious hiatus in the action, and apparently nothing happens until the churching ceremony.

(iv) SO 309 ff., preserves the narrative sequence of FO in its accounts of the theft of both children; it therefore deals with the theft of the first child by the ape, and its subsequent history up to the arrival in Paris, then returns to the second child. NO mentions the theft of the first child, then deals with the second child up to the arrival of mother and child in Jerusalem, then reverts to the first child and its history.

(v) In FO 669 ff., as in SO 547 ff., one party of sailors goes ashore and discovers the lioness and the baby; the incident is expanded in NO.

(vi) In FO 1231 ff., Clement's wife rebukes him for his rough treatment of Florent, and says the boy's extravagance is a sign of his good breeding. SO preserves this in 843 ff., but it is much weakened in NO.

(vii) In FO 3501 ff., the sultan beats Mahon in anger; this is paralleled in SO 1303 ff., but not in NO.

In view of this independence of each other, how are we to explain the agreements of NO and SO against FO? These include: the throwing of the head of the supposed lover (the kokes knaue of NO 116, SO 122), at the hapless empress, the circumstances and details of the empress's recovery of young Octovian (NO 424 ff., SO 547 ff.), the explanation of the conduct of the lioness apprivoisée in NO 349 ff. (L only), SO 475 ff., and the inclusion of King Dagaberde among the distinguished prisoners carried off by the Saracens (NO C1553, SO 1517 ff.).[1]

Various possible explanations can be considered for each of these agreements: descent of the feature in question from a French *A or from a common English source of the two English versions; independent rationalizations in each version of a discrepancy in the source; independent borrowings of related motifs from other romances; the interpolation of

[1] These agreements are discussed both in the notes to NO and, in some detail, in SO, pp. 32-38, to which reference should be made.

material from NO into SO, or the reverse, or both, over a period of time; occasional borrowing from a lost third contemporary English version of the story.

Fortunately, in some instances, the texts themselves help us to evaluate these possibilities. In addition to these agreements against FO, there are numerous agreements in wording and rhyme between NO and SO, scattered throughout, but clustered most densely in two early and distinctive episodes: the entrapment of the empress by the wicked mother-in-law, and the recovery of young Octovian by his mother. These are the very episodes in which most of the agreements against FO occur. This convinces me that either borrowing took place between NO and SO, or that they are linked by way of another ME version, either earlier or contemporary. I find it impossible to establish definitively which of these is the correct explanation, because the evidence is ambiguous.

A number of the parallels suggest that SO borrowed from NO, while a few suggest the reverse;[1] the apparent reduplication of three lines of authentic source material in L133-5 (see the note on these lines) seems to suggest the incorporation of material from a third English version of the story, but might have been arrived at independently in an effort to identify the speaker of the lines which follow. I have found no clear evidence that NO and SO are independent redactions of an earlier ME version, nor that they may both have derived details from another contemporary version of the romance.[2] My own view, as I have already stated in my edition of SO, is that SO probably drew on an earlier text of NO, closer to L

---

[1] The parallels, and, where it can be determined, their significance, are discussed in the notes. See the notes, especially the notes on 334, 344-5, 484-5, 496-529, 610-21, 939, 1110-12, 1389.

[2] The earliest ME references to Octovian as a romance hero are in *Richard Coer de Lion* (composed probably in the early fourteenth century), and in the *Speculum Vitae*, which probably belongs to the mid-fourteenth century. The *Richard Coer de Lion* reference might be to either a French or English romance, the *Speculum Vitae* denunciation of the *veyn spekyng* of minstrels and gestours at feasts seems directed at English romances. The *Speculum Vitae* allusion is of some interest, since it mentions *Octouian and Isanbrace* side by side (see J. Ullmann, *ES*, vii (1844), 468-72, line 40), and they occur again side by side a century later in the Lincoln Thornton manuscript. One wonders if Thornton is preserving a traditional northern grouping of the two romances, so that they circulated in tandem.

than to C, as one might expect, since L is generally more faithful to the archetype. It seems to me inherently unlikely that the author of NO, who tried to produce a coherent and lively version of the story, would have found the choppy and inaccurate summary version of SO of much use, even if we assume an earlier copy of SO free from some of the wilder flights of the extant copy. This subjective judgement of the relationship is supported by the analysis of some of the parallels between NO and SO (on these, see SO, pp. 32-8). One further case (not discussed in my edition of SO) where FO helps to establish that SO has incorporated material from NO may be outlined here. In FO 2783 ff. the sultan's daughter is brought to her father:

> A tant la pucele descent . . .
> Et ele sant plus d(e)'arester
> S'agenoilla deuant son pere
> La face auoit et tendre et clere.
> Li soudans l'a par la main prise.
> Si l'a deiouste lui asise.
> (FO 2783-80)

NO's version of this preserves many of the details, the lady dismounts, kneels, is welcomed by her father, and he seats her.

> And jn hir fadir paveleone
> Thore lyghttede þe mayden down,
> And knelede appon hir knee.
> Than was þe sowdane wondir blythe
> And to his doghetir went he swythe,
> And kyssed hir sythes thre.
> He sett hir downe appon þe dese . . .
> (957-63)

SO omits this episode, but transfers some of the content and rhymes which occur in NO to the preceding episode, when Florent visits the lady and kisses her:

> þat hed he heng on hys arsoun
> And rod to þe maydyns pauyloun:
> He fond þat mayde of greet renoun
> Er he hyt wyst,

> And of hys stede he ly3t adoun,
> And swete her kyste.
>
> (SO 1171-6)

The father's tent becomes the daughter's, and the *paveleone* : *down* rhyme is preserved; the lady's dismounting (*lyghttede . . . down*) becomes Florent's (*ly3t adoun*), and the father's kiss becomes the lover's. As a result of this transfer, SO's account of this first meeting of the young lovers differs from that of FO 2654 ff., and NO 929-31, where Florent wisely remains on horseback, snatches the lady up beside him, and tries to carry her away.

In the light of this, and of some of the other passages discussed in the notes and in SO pp. 32-38, I think that the author of SO probably drew on an earlier copy of NO, closer to L than to C or H, as he reworked his French source. His version is an odd and scrappy one, with little of the enlivening detail which makes NO attractive, and his incorporation (and occasional reallocation) of rhymes and details from NO seems in keeping with his apparent indifference to the work at hand, his borrowing of material from various other romances, the confusions of details of the action, and the general carelessness of his version.

V. ORIGINS OF THE OCTAVIAN STORY

The action of the extant versions of the Octavian story (**Octavian**) deals with the break-up of a family through the machinations of a wicked mother-in-law, the patient endurance of the wronged wife, the quest for recognition and achievement by her twin sons, and the eventual happy reunion of the family. The plot combines familiar romance elements of love and adventure with a complex of motifs derived from various story cycles dealing with trials and suffering, but from three in particular; the typical features of each of these cycles is outlined below, and their relationship to **Octavian** is described.[1]

---

[1] This account of the origins of the Octavian story duplicates, with some modifications, the account in my edition of SO, pp. 39-44.

The Constance Story (Constance)[1]

1. A king wishes to marry his daughter.
2. She cuts off her hands, or mutilates herself in some other way to make herself repellent to him.
3. She is forced into flight or exile, either by sea or into a forest.
4. She marries the king who gives her shelter.
5. A child is born while her husband is absent.
6. Her wicked mother-in-law substitutes for the news of the birth of the child a report that she has given birth to a monster.
7. By another substitution of letters she effects the second exile of the queen.
8. The queen and her child find shelter in another country.
9. Husband, wife, and child are eventually reunited.

This story is preserved in medieval French, English, Latin, German, and Spanish versions. It appears in England first in the *Vitae Duorum Offarum* and a later version in Trivet's *Chronique Anglo-Normande* was the source of Chaucer's *Man of Law's Tale* and Gower's tale of Constance in *Confessio Amantis*, book II, 587 ff. The story is preserved also in *Emaré*, and elements from it appear in *Sir Triamour*, *The King of Tars*, and *Sir Eglamour*. Many versions have hagiographical features; the heroine is innocent and virtuous throughout, and is an example of humble piety.

The Crescentia Story (Crescentia)[2]

1. A brother-in-law or steward tries to make love to a lady while her husband is away.
2. He is rejected, and when her husband returns, accuses her of adultery.

[1] On the Constance story see A. B. Gough, *The Constance Saga* (Palaestra XXIII, Berlin 1902); *Emaré*, ed. E. Rickert. EETS, ES 99 (1908, repr. 1984), pp. xxxii–xlviii; M. Schlauch, *Chaucer's Constance and Accused Queens* (1927, repr. New York, 1969); N. D. Isaacs, 'Constance in Fourteenth Century England', *NM*, 59 (1958), 260–77.

[2] On the Crescentia story see E. A. Greenlaw, 'The Vows of Baldwin', *PMLA*, xxi (1906), 575–636; L. A. Hibbard, *Mediaeval Romance in England* (1924, repr. New York, 1960), pp. 12–22; *Le Bone Florence of Rome*, ed. C. F. Heffernan (Manchester, 1976), pp. 3–17.

3. The lady is exiled.
4. Another unsuccessful lover revenges himself by murdering the child of the people who have given her shelter, and incriminates her by means of a bloody dagger.
5. The lady flees, and escapes rape by a sailor or merchant.
6. She receives the gift of healing, and her former persecutors come to her for help.
7. She makes them confess, and is reunited with her husband.

This cycle is named after the heroine of the mid-twelfth century German version of the story contained in the *Kaiserchronik*, probably the oldest surviving European version of the story. It differs from **Constance** in having a would-be seducer, usually a brother-in-law, as villain, in the second exile, and in the absence of children. A legendary element is introduced by the lady's gift of healing. The story is adapted as a Miracle of the Virgin, and as an exemplum. **Crescentia** is best preserved in Middle English in *Le Bone Florence of Rome*, where the heroine is a pattern of Christian endurance and virtue. The *Gesta Romanorum* and Hoccleve have versions of the story, and elements of it are combined with those of **Constance** in *The Earl of Tolous* and *Sir Triamour*.

The Eustace Story (**Eustace**)[1]

1. A man is required to choose between present and future happiness, and chooses the latter.
2. He leaves home and possessions, and goes wandering with his wife and children (usually twins).
3. His wife is carried off by sailors, and his children by wild beasts; his last bag of treasure is stolen.
4. His wife is forced to marry, but the marriage is unconsummated. She usually inherits vast possessions when her second husband dies.
5. The sons are rescued and reared by foster parents, usually separately.
6. The family is reunited.

This story is thought to be Oriental in origin, but it became

---

[1] On **Eustace** see G. H. Gerould, 'Forerunners, Congeners and Derivatives of the Eustace Legend', *PMLA*, xix (1904), 335–448; L. Braswell, 'Sir Isumbras and the Legend of Saint Eustace', *Med. Stud.*, xxvii (1965), 128–51.

associated with the legend of Eustace, or Placidas, the Roman general who was converted while hunting, by a vision of a stag with a crucifix between its antlers. As part of the hagiographical reworking, Eustace and his family undergo martyrdom after their reunion. Ælfric translated a Latin *vita* of Eustace in the tenth century,[1] there are numerous English and French lives of St. Eustace, and the story provides the framework of *Sir Isumbras*, where, however, there are three children rather than twins. Elements from **Eustace** occur in other ME romances, including *Sir Eglamour* and *Sir Torrent of Portyngale*, and the theme of the redemptive and purifying power of suffering links it with *Robert of Sicily, Sir Gowther*, and *Sir Amadace*.

The relation between the Crescentia and Constance cycles is especially close, since both deal with persecuted and calumniated wives, though the agents of the persecution differ. The structural similarities between the Constance and Crescentia stories and the Eustace story are also obvious, for all three cycles deal with the trials of an innocent person, separation from a spouse, wandering, and final reunion. The Octavian story is not alone in combining motifs from these different sources; the French romance, *La Belle Hélène de Constantinople*,[2] for example, belongs to the Constance cycle, but has clearly drawn on the Eustace story for its account of the lost children, and a group of ME tail-rhyme romances (including, besides *Octovian, Sir Isumbras, Emaré, Le Bone Florence of Rome, The Earl of Tolous*, and *Sir Triamour*) shows differing combinations of motifs from these story types.

The Octavian story (Octavian)

The wife of Octavian, Emperor of Rome, bears him twin sons (1). The emperor's wicked mother (2) accuses her of infidelity (3), and provides false evidence by inducing a youth to lie in the empress's bed while she is asleep (4). The empress meanwhile has a prophetic dream which heralds her ruin and

[1] See Braswell, 128-9.

[2] For a summary of this unedited work, see A. H. Krappe, *Romania*, lxiii (1937), 324-53. It preserves more closely than the Octavian story does typical **Constance** features such as self-mutilation, the incestuous father, the substitute letters, and the **Eustace** concentration on the parent rather than the children.

the loss of her children (5). The emperor exiles his wife and children, and she and her infant sons are abandoned in a forest (6). As she rests by a spring (7) the two children are stolen separately by wild animals; the first is stolen by an ape, rescued by a knight, captured by robbers, and sold to a palmer called Clement; the second is carried off by a lioness, and captor and prey are then carried off by a griffin (8). The lioness fights and kills the griffin, then suckles the child. The empress recovers this child, and accompanied by the lioness (9), they journey by sea to the Holy Land, where the empress finds shelter and rears her child (10). The other child is brought up in Paris, shows no talent for trade (11), and when a Saracen army attacks Paris, performs great feats of arms and wins the love of a Saracen princess (12). With her help, Clement, the foster-father, steals the Sultan's marvellous horse (13). The emperor Octavian comes to assist the king of France, but both emperor and son are taken prisoner by the Saracens. The child who is reared in the Holy Land enters the service of a king, and subsequently, accompanied by his mother and the faithful lioness, rescues the Christian prisoners, and effects the reunion of his parents. At the feast which follows, the other brother is recognized, and the entire family is reunited (14).

1. *The birth of twins*: Compare **Eustace** 2, where there are usually two children; three occur in a few derivatives, including a Breton ballad and *Sir Isumbras*. In **Constance** 5 usually only one child is born. Most of the instances cited by Gough (*Constance Saga*, 16) involving two children have derived this feature from another source, often **Eustace**.

2. *The wicked mother-in-law*: Compare **Constance** 6. The mother-in-law as persecutor of the calumniated wife is common in folk-tale and appears also in the Swan Children story, of which *Chevalere Assigne* is a ME version.[1] The emperor is not absent, as in the typical form of **Constance** 5, and the device of the substitute letters is not used.

3, 4. *The charge of infidelity*: This is a conflation of **Constance** 6 and **Crescentia** 2. In most versions of **Constance**, the mother-in-law's charge is the primitive one of monstrous or animal offspring (cf. *La Belle Hélène, Emaré*). In **Octavian**

---

[1] On the Swan Children story see Schlauch, *Chaucer's Constance*, pp. 78-85.

she charges the empress with adultery, asserting in FO and SO that the birth of twins is in itself a proof of guilt, and substantiating the charge in all versions by the device of the pretended lover. The first of these alleged proofs reflects the widespread popular belief that a man could beget only one child at a time (compare *Lai le Freine* and *Chevalere Assigne*);[1] the accusation is reinforced from **Crescentia** 2, in some versions of which the thwarted lover places a man in the queen's bed. Here, however, the thwarted lover is replaced as villain by the mother-in-law from **Constance**. The pretended lover is in some versions a leper, cripple or dwarf, as in the ballad of *Sir Aldingar*, and the French Charlemagne romance *La Reine Sibille* (compare the lowly *kokes knaue* of NO and SO); in other versions he is, more plausibly, a young knight, as in *The Earl of Tolous* and *The Avowynge of King Arthur*.

5. *The dream*: A prophetic dream in which animals attack a hero or heroine occurs in various romances; in **Octavian** it may be derived from some version of **Crescentia**. In the English ballad of *Sir Aldingar*, the calumniated queen dreams she is attacked by a griffin, in *The Earl of Tolous*, the absent emperor dreams that his wife is attacked by two wild bears (who correspond to the two would-be lovers).[2]

6. *The forest*: Compare **Constance** 3. In some versions both flights (**Constance** 3, 7) are into a forest, in some the lady journeys across the sea. **Octavian** has both a forest exposure (6) and a journey by sea (10).

7, 8. *The theft of the children*: In **Eustace** 3, the father fords a river carrying one child; while he is returning for the other, both children are carried off separately by wild animals. In some versions such as *Guillaume d'Angleterre*, the thefts take place by the sea, in other versions at a stream, and in the Spanish romance *Cifar* one child is stolen while the father sleeps by a well.

In the many derivatives of the story, the kidnapping animals vary, but a lion and a wolf occur commonly (see Gerould, 'The Eustace Legend', 375). The appearance of a griffin as

---

[1] In both these romances, women who accuse others of adultery, because they give birth to twins, are themselves punished by bearing more than one child. In *Chevalere Assigne* this gives the mother-in-law her chance to launch the typical **Constance** 6 charge.

[2] See the note on 160–71.

a kidnapping beast is unusual, and probably originated in an early version of **Octavian**. It recurs in *Sir Eglamour* and *Sir Torrent of Portyngale*, both of which probably borrowed it from an English version of **Octavian**, and in the Italian *Uggeri il Danese*, which derived it from the story of Drugiolina in *Fioravante*, another **Octavian** derivative. The double theft of one child by a lioness and a griffin in most versions of **Octavian** is curious, since it is not paralleled in **Eustace**. It may reflect some forms of **Eustace** in which three children are stolen; in *Sir Isumbras*, for example, a lion carries off one son, a leopard the second, an eagle carries off treasure, and a unicorn the last child.[1]

9. *The recovery of one child by his mother; the faithful lioness*: The early recovery of one child by his mother is not a feature of **Eustace** or its derivatives. It serves here to re-establish the situation of **Constance 8**, where the mother rears a child in a foreign land.

The account of the faithful lioness has been derived from some other source. The lioness serves two functions in **Octavian**. She suckles the infant and follows the empress when she regains her child; later (14), she fights by the side of the now grown child, and thus helps reunite the family. The first of these services repeats the ancient tradition of animals suckling exposed children (cf. the she-wolf in another twin story, that of Romulus and Remus); the same motif occurs in a modified form in *Chevalere Assigne*, where a hind suckles the abandoned children. The second employs the motif of the grateful lion. Stories of a grateful lion occur in saints' legends and in romances; in *Guy of Warwick* 4144 ff., and *Ywain* 2597 ff., the hero rescues a lion which is attacked by a dragon, and the grateful beast follows him, and fights by his side, as the lioness later does with young Octovian. In **Octavian**, however, there is no reason for such devotion, other than the maternal feelings of the nurturing lioness. The English versions introduce the additional motif of the lion's kinship with those of royal blood (see the note on 349).

10. *The journey by sea to Jerusalem and the education of*

---

[1] In her edition of *Sir Eglamour of Artois*, EETS 256 (1965), p. xxxiv, F. E. Richardson suggests that in **Octavian** the kidnapping motif has been merged with that of the theft of treasure by a bird.

the child: Compare **Constance** 7, 8, **Crescentia** 5, and **Eustace** 3. The episode in FO (absent in the English versions) in which the empress escapes rape by one of the sailors, is paralleled in both **Eustace** and **Crescentia**, where it is a common feature. The means of escape—the protection of the lioness—is, however, an FO introduction. The education of the child is derived from **Constance** 8, since it is only in **Constance** that the mother in exile has a child with her. In some versions of **Constance** the mother lives in poverty (cf. *La belle Hélène, Emaré*), in others she lives in comfort.

11. *One child is raised by a foster-parent*: In versions of **Eustace** the children sometimes are reared by the same foster-father (*Cifar*), sometimes in the same village (*Eustace*), and sometimes far apart (*Die Gute Frau*). The **Octavian** account of the upbringing of Florent resembles another Eustace story, *Guillaume d'Angleterre*, where the children shrink from the trades of their foster-fathers.

12. With the account of the military prowess of Florent, and later of young Octovian, familiar elements of romance (Saracen wars, single combat with a giant, etc.) become dominant. The Saracen princess who loves a Christian and is baptized for his sake, occurs in other romances, notably *Bevis* and *Sir Ferumbras*. The episode where Clement steals the sultan's wonderful horse (13) has apparently been derived in forms of **Octavian** from the *Reine Sibille* story which belongs to the Crescentia cycle.[1] It displays Clement's nerve and cunning, but the capture of the horse serves no useful function in the war.

14. The final reunion of all the family at a feast is paralleled in **Eustace** 6, but the questioning which leads to the identification of Florent is common in forms of **Constance** (see Gough, *The Constance Saga*, p. 19) and is probably derived from there.

VI. TREATMENT

The preceding discussion shows that the main features of the Octavian story are derived from a group of story types which, with various rearrangements, substitutions, and additions of

[1] See A. H. Krappe, 'Florent et Octavian', *Romania*, lxv (1939), 359-73.

motifs, provide the narrative framework for a number of other ME romances, saints' lives, and legends. The distinction between these literary kinds is not always clear, and in the later ME period the production of anthologies designed to satisfy the growing taste for edifying material which would entertain as well as instruct, and romances that would instruct as well as entertain, further encouraged the blurring of categories and the homogenization of different literary kinds.[1] Romance motifs may become attached to legend, as when the motif of the Saracen princess who converts for the love of a Christian (cf. *Bevis, Sir Ferumbras*, and *Octovian*) is incorporated into the life of Becket. Legendary material can be reworked as romance, as in the case of *Sir Isumbras*, and romances which are pious and exemplary in varying degrees occur side by side with overtly didactic and exemplary material in compilations like Ff. 2. 38 and the Lincoln Thornton.[2]

In their studies of ME romance, Mehl and Schelp relate a number of romances with a strongly didactic character to the exemplary tradition represented by saints' legends.[3] Like the legends, these romances offer patterns of Christian conduct in their stories of faith, piety, and resignation in the face of undeserved suffering (cf. **Constance** and **Crescentia**), or illustrate the regenerative power of suffering (cf. **Eustace**). Schelp sees the exemplary impulse emerging, but not central, in an early romance like *Havelok*, and highly developed or dominant in a group of later romances including *Sir Isumbras, Robert of Sicily, Sir Gowther, Sir Cleges, Emaré*, and *Le Bone Florence of Rome*. Mehl includes this latter group and

---

[1] *Robert of Sicily*, an exemplary story about a pseudo-historical figure, offers a good example of the difficulties of classifying some of this material. It is often described as a romance, and the scribe of Ff. 2. 38 copied it among the romances of his 'entertainment' section, yet it was viewed either as an exemplary story or as a legend by various of the compilers of the manuscripts containing it. It occurs most frequently in manuscripts which are religious and didactic in character. In the Vernon MS, its exemplary character is pointed out by the heading: 'Her is of Kyng Robert of Cicyle, Hou pride dude him begyle'. In Oxford, Trinity College MS D. 57 it is titled *Sancti Cicilie Vita Roberti*.

[2] Thus Robert Thornton's copy of the *Earl of Tolous*, a romance about chaste and faithful love, is followed by a *Vita Sancti Christoferi* 'to þe heryng or þe redyng of þe which storye langes [gr]ete mede and it be don with deuocion'.

[3] D. Mehl, *The Middle English Romances of the Thirteenth and Fourteenth Centuries* (London, 1968); H. Schelp, *Exemplarische Romanzen im Mittelenglischen* (Palaestra 246, Göttingen, 1967).

others in his 'homiletic romances', where religious and moral themes dominate and the action has an exemplary pattern.

Romances of this kind may be distinguished from the much larger group in which an exemplary or homiletic impulse is apparent, but is not the major shaping force; it is, rather, subordinated to a central action controlled by one of the classic patterns of romance involving hero, combat, and love. Within this group, to which NO belongs, the strength of the homiletic urge can vary greatly, even between versions of the same romance. Even within the small and closely-related group formed by the extant French and English versions of the Octavian story, shifts of focus and emphasis reflect the interests and talents of the various redactors, and NO is the most didactic version of the story. The Octavian story is a complex one, because it is a composite: it combines one version of the story of a persecuted and innocent wife with the romance theme of the exiled or dispossessed hero winning recognition, glory, and a bride by prowess in arms. The combination is not simply sequential; it is, rather, as if a second romance— the exiled hero story—has been grafted into an already complicated basic story.

The persecuted wife story, with all its potential for exemplary treatment, has thus been displaced from the central position in the poem in all versions, but it provides the narrative frame which initiates and concludes the romance action which is the new focus of attention; one of the two children stolen in the framing story becomes the hero of the central action, and the other reappears with his mother at the end, to resolve the central action, to vindicate the calumniated lady, and to reunite the family.[1] There is no sustained effort in FO to exploit the pathetic and exemplary potential of the unfortunate lady, and in SO she is further reduced to a silent and shadowy figure.[2] One of the most interesting

[1] The most serious structural defect in NO is the weakening of this double resolution through the reunion of emperor and one son at an earlier point (see the note on 1125–60). This was probably an archetypal corruption.

[2] FO does, however, develop a **Eustace** feature in its purgation of the pride and credulity of the emperor. He has learned that he was overhasty and credulous in condemning his wife, and almost every appearance he makes in FO is accompanied by an expression of grief (for extended treatments of this see FO 1627 ff., FO 5127 ff.). NO preserves one manifestation of this feature at 1149–57.

features of NO, however, is its reorganization of the opening narrative, clearly in order to allow its author extended and coherent treatment of the empress as an exemplary model within an action full of dramatic events and exotic detail.

FO is three times as long as NO and two and one half times as long as SO, so substantial revision and condensation was called for in producing the English versions, if FO is a reliable representative of their source, as I believe it is. NO and SO clearly tell the same story, but the differences between them in organization, focus, and style are striking. The action is, inevitably, complicated, especially following the exile of the empress when her twin sons are stolen separately by different animals, and, after a bewildering series of transfers from one kidnapper to another, end up, the one in the possession of his mother in Jerusalem, the other a foster-child in Paris. SO preserves the sequence of events in FO, but reduces them to a series of brief and disjointed episodes, linked by calls to attention (SO 299-300), or announcements of change of time and place (SO 425-6, SO 661-6). NO simplifies the whole sequence by announcing the theft of both children (328-48) and then, reversing the order of FO and SO, deals first with the child who is recovered by the empress, and their journey to Jerusalem (349-531), and then with the child who is bought by Clement and taken to Paris (532-C756). This simple but intelligent change preserves continuity first in the history of the empress (1-531), next in the history of Florent and his upbringing in Paris (532-C756), and finally allows a natural and easy transition to the attack of the sultan on Paris, and Florent's rise to glory.

This rearrangement of the sequence of events makes the empress the central figure in the first third of NO, and the author carefully develops her as an exemplary figure, emphasizing by various innovations her reversal of fortune, the pathos of her situation, and her pious resignation to the will of God. In FO the empress conceives after fifteen years of marriage, but beyond that we learn little about husband and wife. The author of NO, however, stresses the love and tenderness between husband and wife, the emperor's unreproachful grief that he has no heir, and the lady's desire to relieve his sorrow.[1] The conception and birth of twins come as an answer to prayer and to her pious proposal that they dedicate an abbey for this intention. None of this occurs in FO or the other extant versions of the story.

When surprised with the pretended lover, the empress in FO protests her innocence (FO 265 ff.), and when they are about to burn her, protests again, and calls on her husband to honour his promise to protect her (FO 341 ff.). This has been altered in NO. The author heightens the drama and the pathos of the lady's situation by having her father, the King of Cala-bire, unwittingly condemn her to death by burning. Follow-ing this, at 247 ff., the lady begs leave to pray, expresses resignation to her fate, and is shown to be a model of Christian selflessness by praying only that her children may be baptized; abandoned in the forest, she prays again at 319 ff. for divine succour. Finally, at 388 ff., after the loss of both children, she prays again at length, considers the sorrows that have come to her in a spirit of pious resignation, attributes them to her own sinfulness, and resolves on a life of pilgrimage and penance.[2] The thrice-renewed prayers in times of crisis re-inforce the exemplary pattern introduced here by the author of NO, and his treatment of the empress has a simplicity, an earnestness and a commitment of sympathy that makes this one of the most attractive parts of the romance.

When he turned to the story of young Florent, however, the NO poet abandoned edification for simple adventure, and trimmed and modified his source to produce a robust and colourful narrative enlivened by some broad comic strokes. The story of the calumniated queen in fact involves the exile of two infant princes, but NO, like FO, wisely concentrates on a single hero, Florent, whose noble blood asserts itself, despite his humble upbringing in Paris by the good-hearted bourgeois, Clement. F&O, the longer French version of the

[1] The relationship of mutual affection and respect presented here contrasts markedly with the treatment of the barren marriage motif in *Sir Gowther*, where the duke displays a callous brutality towards his wife (*Gowther* 53-56) which pro-vokes her to a reckless prayer for a child by any means.

[2] The NO poet further insists on the edifying aspects of the opening narrative by repeated references to God's providence working in the events he describes. There are eight references to God, God's grace, and God's will in this first third of the romance, compared with seven in the remaining two-thirds.

romance, shows the disastrous consequences of dissipating attention from a single hero by building up the story of his twin, and duplicating episodes; SO shows an inclination to do the same by its last-minute inflation of the role of young Octovian in the battle where he presumably frees his father, brother and other worthies (SO 1603 ff.), although all too characteristically, it omits this important detail. While FO treats with relish the sensational figures and incidents which fill this part of the romance—the Saracen sultan menacing Paris, his giant champion and would-be lover of the beautiful and spirited Saracen princess—it also shows a sustained interest in such topics as the conflict of knightly and bourgeois values, speculation on the nature of love, analysis of feeling, and the question of the dominance of birth or breeding in the shaping of character. NO preserves many of the persons and incidents, but shows no real interest in the topics raised in FO. The discursiveness and courtly elements are eliminated, the love story is much modified and simplified, and the fairly sophisticated social comedy of the prosperous bourgeois Clement and his shrewd rejection of knighthood and all its trappings has been vulgarized.

As a dispossessed prince, Florent's situation is much like that of Havelok, but it receives very different treatment. Havelok's nobility emerges through his exemplary character, and the charity, humility, and courage he displays in miserable circumstances. His royal status is manifested by supernatural signs, and he is clearly divinely appointed for great things. Florent, on the other hand, stands out from the society in which he is reared because he is ill-adapted to cope with it; he is both uninterested and incompetent in the trades to which Clement tries to set him. His nobility is manifested by the natural predilection for knightly pursuits he shows in the falcon and horse episodes, by a talent for fighting, and by the ability to fall instantly in love with the Saracen princess. These reveal stereotypical knightly rather than royal attributes, and the author of NO, unlike the SO poet,[1] shows no disposition to remodel Florent into a more exemplary figure.

Both English versions have been justly praised for their

[1] On the possible influence of *Havelok* on the treatment of Florent in SO, see my edition, p. 105, note on 985–1056.

genre scenes of bourgeois life, and for the realistic middle-
class values asserted by Clement.[1] But I think it is the case
that here, and here only, the SO poet offers a livelier and
more appealing picture. In SO, for whatever reasons, Clement
is a butcher;[2] there are numerous references to this occupation, and SO conveys some real sense of a bustling lower
middle-class world of trade. The NO poet outshines him in
the handling of non-realistic material, whether it be his
reworking of the opening of the romance, or the well-paced
accounts of Florent's exploits and wooing of the Saracen
princess.

Neither of the English versions preserves much of the tone
of FO, but while SO settles for a sketchy, breathless, and
confused summary of events in this part of the romance, NO
has eliminated extraneous characters and episodes, simplified
the action, and organized what it retains in a series of well-
developed and lively episodes, touched sometimes by a crude,
comicbook-like extravagance of detail.[3] In the treatment of
the Saracen princess's love for Florent, the lady's troop of
high-born attendants disappears; so do the long passages of
introspective analysis of feeling. Instead, the lady has a single
confidante, Olyue, and the two engage in detailed and practi-
cal discussion of how to manage matters so that the lovers
meet. Changes of style and substance like this are directed towards producing a piece of work which is shorter and simpler
than its sources, but solidly realized and self-consistent. The
author of NO has produced an unsophisticated but successful

---

[1] See, for example, D. Pearsall, 'The Development of Middle English Romance',
Med. Stud., xxvii (1965), 111.

[2] On Clement as a butcher, see my edition of SO, p. 34, and p. 99, note on
398. The frequent references to his trade in SO were probably encouraged by the
fame of the butchers of Paris. They formed one of the most ancient and important of the merchants' guilds. See also the note on 646–57.

[3] The giant in NO, for example, terrorises the people of Paris by leaning over
the walls to threaten them (696–701). A more elaborately developed stroke of
grotesque humour is introduced by the NO poet in his reworking of a detail in FO
2046 ff., where the giant promises the Saracen princess to bring her the King of
France as a love token, in exchange for a kiss. In NO this becomes a promise of
the King of France's head (678 ff.), and when, instead, Florent defeats and
beheads the giant, he carries the head to the lady, remarking (915 ff.) that her
lover is more or less fulfilling his promise by having a head delivered, though not
that of the King of France. The lady relishes and makes further play with this
joke (924–6). See also the note on 915–29.

popular romance where the same energy informs the moral earnestness of the treatment of the exemplary elements, the comic-grotesque elements, and the presentation of the action-filled story.

SELECT BIBLIOGRAPHY

1. *Manuscripts containing Octovian (NO)*
Cambridge, University Library, MS Ff. 2. 38.
Lincoln, Dean and Chapter Library, MS. 91.

2. *Texts*
Athelston, ed. A. McI. Trounce, EETS 224 (1951, repr. 1984).
The Awntyrs off Arthure at the Terne Wathelyn, ed. R. Hanna, Manchester, 1974.
La Belle Hélène de Constantinople, A. H. Krappe, *Romania*, lxiii (1937), 324-53. (A summary of the unedited OF romance.)
Le Bone Florence of Rome, ed. C. F. Heffernan, Manchester, 1976.
Cambridge University Library MS Ff. 2. 38, Introduction by F. McSparran and P. R. Robinson, London, 1979.
The Earl of Toulouse, ed. W. H. French and C. B. Hale, in *Middle English Metrical Romances*, 2 vols., 1930, repr. New York, 1964.
English Writings of Richard Rolle, ed. H. E. Allen, Oxford, 1931.
Florent et Octavian de Rome, P. Paris, *Histoire Littéraire de la France*, XXVI, Paris, 1873, 303-35. (A summary of the romance, with notes on the manuscripts.)
Guy of Warwick (Auchinleck, Caius), ed. J. Zupitza, EETS, ES 42, 49, 59 (1883-91, repr. as one vol. 1966).
Guy of Warwick (Ff. 2. 38), ed. J. Zupitza, EETS, ES 25, 26 (1875, 1876, repr. as one vol. 1966).
The 'Liber de Diversis Medicinis', ed. M. S. Ogden, EETS, OS 207 (1938, rev. repr. 1969).
Libro delle Storie di Fiorovante, ed. P. Rajna, Bologna, 1872.
Lybeaus Desconus, ed. M. Mills, EETS 261 (1969).
Morte Arthure, ed. E. Björkman, Heidelberg, 1915.
Octavian, ed. M. Mills, in *Six Middle English Romances*, London, 1973.
Octavian, ed. G. Sarrazin (Altenglische Bibliothek, 3), Heilbronn, 1885. (Cited as Sarrazin.)
Octavian, ed. K. Vollmöller (Altfranzösische Bibliothek, 3), Heilbronn, 1883, repr. 1967. (Cited as FO.)
Octovian Imperator, ed. F. McSparran (Middle English Texts 11), Heidelberg, 1979. (Cited as SO.)
I Reali di Francia, ed. G. Vandelli, Bologna, 1872, repr. 1947.
Richard Coeur de Lion, ed. K. Brunner (*Wiener Beiträge zur englischen Philologie*, xlii), Vienna, 1913.
The Romance of Emaré, ed. E. Rickert, EETS, ES 99 (1908, repr. 1984).
The Romance of the Emperor Octavian, ed. J. O. Halliwell (Percy Society, xiv), London, 1844.

The Romance of Octavian, Emperor of Rome, J. J. Conybeare, Oxford, 1809. (A summary with extracts and translations of FO.)
Sir Beues of Hamtoun, ed. E. Kölbing, EETS, ES 46, 48, 65 (1885-94, repr. as one vol. 1973).
Sir Eglamour of Artois, ed. F. E. Richardson, EETS 256 (1965).
Sir Ferumbras, ed. S. J. Herrtage, EETS, ES 34 (1879, repr. 1966).
Sir Gawain and the Green Knight, ed. J. R. R. Tolkien and E. V. Gordon, 1925, 2nd edn., ed. N. Davis, Oxford, 1967, corrected repr. 1972.
Sir Gowther, ed. M. Mills, in *Six Middle English Romances*, London, 1973.
Sir Launfal, ed. A. J. Bliss, London, 1960.
The Thornton Manuscript, Introductions by D. S. Brewer and A. E. B. Owen, 1975, rev. edn., London, 1977.
The Thornton Romances, ed. J. O. Halliwell (Camden Society, xxx), London, 1844, repr. 1970.
Yorkshire Writers, Richard Rolle of Hampole, ed. C. Horstman, 2 vols., London, 1895.
Ywain and Gawain, ed. A. B. Friedman and N. T. Harrington, EETS 254 (1964, repr. 1981).

3. *Literary Studies and Articles*

Baugh, A. C., 'Improvisation in the Middle English Romance', *Proceedings of the American Philosophical Society*, 103 (1959), 418-54.
—— 'The Middle English Romance: Some Questions of Creation, Presentation, and Preservation', *Speculum*, xlii (1967), 1-31.
Bordman, G., *Motif-Index of the English Metrical Romances* (FF Communications lxxix, 190), Helsinki, 1963.
Braswell, L., 'Sir Isumbras and the Legend of Saint Eustace', *Mediaeval Studies*, xxvii (1965), 128-51.
Brunner, K., 'Middle English Metrical Romances and Their Audience', in *Studies in Medieval Literature in Honor of Professor Albert Croll Baugh*, ed. MacEdward Leach, Philadelphia, 1961, 219-27.
Eule, R., *Untersuchungen über die nordenglische Version des Octavian*, Halle, 1899. (Cited as Eule.)
Gerould, G. H., 'Forerunners, Congeners, and Derivatives of the Eustace Legend', *PMLA*, xix (1904), 335-448.
Gough, A. B., *The Constance Sage* (Palaestra, 23), Berlin, 1902.
Greenlaw, E. A., 'The Vows of Baldwin', *PMLA*, xxi (1906), 575-636.
Hibbard, L. A., *Mediaeval Romance in England*, 1924, repr. New York, 1960.
Krappe, A. H., 'Florent et Octavian', *Romania*, lxv (1939), 359-73.
—— 'Une Version Noroise de la Reine Sibille', *Romania*, lvi (1930), 585-8.
Kratins, O., 'Treason in the Middle English Metrical Romances', *PQ*, xlv (1966), 668-87.
Mehl, D., *The Middle English Romances of the Thirteenth and Fourteenth Centuries*, London, 1968.

Pearsall, D., 'The Development of Middle English Romance', *Mediaeval Studies*, xxvii (1965), 91–116.

Schelp, H., *Exemplarische Romanzen im Mittelenglischen* (Palaestra, 246), Göttingen, 1967.

Schlauch, M., *Chaucer's Constance and Accused Queens*, 1927, repr. New York, 1969.

—— 'The Man of Law's Tale', in *Sources and Analogues of Chaucer's Canterbury Tales*, ed. W. F. Bryan and G. Dempster, Chicago, 1941, 155–206.

Streve, P., *Die Octaviansage*, Halle, 1884.

Strong, C., 'History and Relations of the Tail-Rhyme Strophe in Latin, French and English', *PMLA*, xxii (1907), 371–420.

Trounce, A. McI., 'The English Tail-Rhyme Romances', *MÆ*, i (1932), 87–108, 168–82; ii (1933), 34–57, 189–98; iii (1934), 30–50.

4. *Linguistic and Bibliographic Studies*

Breul, K., review of G. Sarrazin, *Octavian, Englische Studien*, ix (1886), 456–66.

Brunner, K., *Die englische Sprache* II, Tübingen, 1962. (Cited as Brunner.)

Campbell, A., *Old English Grammar*, Oxford, 1959, corrected repr., 1974. (Cited as Campbell.)

Dobson, E. J., *English Pronunciation 1500–1700*, 2 vols., Oxford, 1957, 2nd edn., 1968. (Cited as Dobson.)

—— 'ME Lengthening in Open Syllables', *TPS 1962* (1963), 124–48.

Hodnett, E., *English Woodcuts 1480–1535* (*Illustrated Monographs*, xxii, Bibliographical Society), London, 1935 (for 1934).

Jordan, R., *Handbuch der mittelenglischen Grammatik*, 1925, 2nd ed., rev. H. Ch. Matthes, Heidelberg, 1934. (Cited as Jordan.)

Kaiser, R., *Zur Geographie des mittelenglischen Wortschatzes* (Palaestra, 205), Leipzig, 1937. (Cited as Kaiser.)

Keiser, G. R., 'A Note on the Descent of the Thornton Manuscript', *Transactions of the Cambridge Bibliographical Society*, vi (1976), 346–8.

—— 'Lincoln Cathedral Library MS 91: Life and Milieu of the Scribe', *Studies in Bibliography*, 32 (1979), 158–79.

Kristensson, G., *A Survey of Middle English Dialects 1290–1350: the six northern counties and Lincolnshire* (*Lund Studies in English*, 35), Lund, 1967. (Cited as Kristensson.)

Luick, K., *Historische Grammatik der englischen Sprache*, Stuttgart, 1964.

McIntosh, A., Review of M. Ogden, *Liber de Diversis Medicinis*, *RES*, xv (1939), 336–8.

—— review of G. Kristensson, *A Survey of Middle English Dialects 1290–1350*, *MÆ*, xxxviii (1969), 210–16.

—— 'The Textual Transmission of the Alliterative *Morte Arthure*', in *English and Medieval Studies*, ed. N. Davis and C. L. Wrenn, London, 1962, 231–40.

Mead, H. R., 'A New Title from de Worde's Press', *The Library*, 5th Series, ix (1954), 45–49.

Mustanoja, T. F., *A Middle English Syntax*, I, Helsinki, 1960. (Cited as Mustanoja.)

Owen, A. E. B., 'The Collation and Descent of the Thornton Manuscript', *Transactions of the Cambridge Bibliographical Society*, vi (1975), 218–25.

Samuels, M. L., *Linguistic Evolution with special reference to English*, London, 1972.

Stanley, E. G., 'Some Notes on *The Owl and the Nightingale*', *English and Germanic Studies*, vi (1957), 30–63.

Stern, K., 'The London "Thornton" Miscellany', *Scriptorium*, xxx (1976), 26–37, 201–18.

Strandberg, O., *The Rime-Vowels of Cursor Mundi*, Uppsala, 1919. (Cited as Strandberg.)

5. Works of Reference

Altfranzösiches Wörterbuch, ed. A. Tobler and E. Lommatzsch, Berlin, 1925–.

A Catalogue of the Manuscripts preserved in the Library, Cambridge, 1857.

Dictionary of the Older Scottish Tongue, ed. W. A. Craigie and A. J. Aitken, Chicago, 1931–. (Cited as *DOST*.)

Dictionnaire de l'ancienne Langue Française, ed. F. Godefroy, Paris, 1881–1902.

English Dialect Dictionary, ed. J. Wright, London, 1898–1905.

A Manual of the Writings in Middle English 1050–1400, J. E. Wells, New Haven, 1916, and Supplements 1–9, 1919–1951.

A Manual of the Writings in Middle English 1050–1500, ed. J. Burke Severs, Fascicule 1, I. Romances, New Haven, 1967. (Based upon the preceding item.)

Middle English Dictionary, ed. H. Kurath, S. M. Kuhn, J. Reidy, *et al.*, Ann Arbor, 1952–. (Cited as *MED*.)

Oxford English Dictionary, ed. J. Murray, H. Bradley, W. Craigie, *et al.*, London, 1888–1933. (Cited as *OED*.)

Revised Medieval Latin Word-List, rev. and ed. R. E. Latham, London, 1965.

Woolley, R. M., *Catalogue of the Manuscripts of Lincoln Cathedral Chapter Library*, London, 1927.

The sawdge of bretayne thane bishoppes and other

... thann to Glastenbury. At Glasstynnbury bishop ...

To bery thare the bolde kynge. and brynges to y' erthe ...

With all worschipe and worthe. that any kyng scholde ...

Thus belles thay ryngge. and Requiem synges ...

Doses messe and matyns. Cet monumento notes ...

Poligrono ionoste in thare firste copre ...

Contyficalar and platter. in fjoronse bethe ...

Anteo and buffoporio in thare dule cotes ...

Codenttyffor Englande. and claspande thare handes ...

lawe langenoffande: and lokeande to shone ...

All bete busteste in blake. by dar and other ...

That schokede at the sepulture. Cet fildede tere ...

What now do worschefull a cyphte. seen in thare tyme ...

thus endes kyng Arthure. as Auctors Alegges ...

That was of Ectors blode. the kynge son of Troye ...

And off Sr Pryamos the pryncc. prayssede in erthe ...

... thethen brochte the bretons. all his bolde eldyrs ...

In to bretayne the brode. as þe bruytte tellys + Explicit

THE TEXTS

The texts have been transcribed from photographs, and collated with the manuscripts. The punctuation and capitalization are modern, and the occasional arbitrary use of capitals within the line in both manuscripts is ignored. The letters *i* and *j* represent respectively the minim *i* and the long-tailed *j* of the manuscripts, while capital *I* and *J*, which are not differentiated in the manuscripts, are distributed here according to function. In L, Thornton regularly uses *y* in the function of *þ*, but it is here printed as *þ*; the scribe of C distinguishes *þ* and *y*. The character *ȝ* usually represents English *ȝogh*, and is so printed; in L it also occasionally represents long-tailed *z* (as in *Sarazenes*), and is then printed as *z*. The distribution of *u* and *v* in the manuscripts is preserved here. The abbreviations used in both texts have been expanded without notice in accordance with the scribes' general practice when the words, or similar words, are written in full. Emendations to words are enclosed in square brackets, and the manuscript reading is given in the footnotes; angle brackets enclose letters partly visible on the damaged folios of L.

L

Curls on final *m* and *n*, the stroke through *ll* in final position and occasionally in the sequence *lle*, and the stroke through final *h* have all been ignored, as being merely flourishes with no grammatical significance. A common mark of abbreviation in the manuscript is ⌐ or ⌐, indicating an omitted nasal in such forms as *hy̅* (used frequently), *su̅* 472, *wo̅dirly* 538. Beside these, however, we find the following forms with both nasal consonant and the mark of contraction: *rañe* 43, *sa̅men* 64, *heue̅ns* 259, *swoñynge* 343, *woñe* 748, *woññe* 778, *soñe* 'sun' 777, *ĉomes* 847, *bowñe* 934, *bro̅une* 936, *[b]aro̅ns* 1531, *ĉomen* 1539, *ño̅men* 1540, *soñe* 'soon' 1611. In addition *nane* 44, *sowdane* 670, 956, *bryne* 755, and *whene* 1260, occur with a terminal curl or stroke above *n* followed by final *e*. The various other occurrences of these words elsewhere in *Octovian* do not have a double nasal, and I have therefore ignored these marks of abbreviation as probably an arbitrary feature of Thornton's orthography. It is possible that he found contracted forms of these words in his exemplar, and simultaneously expanded and reproduced them, as he did in the case of *honowre* 1092 (see fn. to text). In three cases where the mark of contraction occurs before the lengthening group –*nd*, I have expanded it (*founde* 951, *wounde* 952, *grounde* 1316); *fownde* occurs three times elsewhere, *grounde* or *grownde* seven times beside *gronde* twice, and *wonde* occurs three times.

C

The abbreviations in C presented no difficulties. The flourish which occurs sometimes on final *d*, and the stroke through *h* in the sequence *ght* have been disregarded. A large and distinctive backward curl on long-tailed final *r*, which occurs less than twenty times in the text of *Octovian*, has been expanded as *e*. An interesting feature of scribal practice is the use of different marks of contraction to represent *m* and *n*; *m* is indicated by a straight stroke over the preceding letters and *n* by a curved stroke with a dot under. The use of this mark in *Mountmertrõs* C811 confirms that the penultimate letter (ambiguous elsewhere) is *n* rather than *u*.

OCTOVIAN

f. 90rb

Lytyll and mykyll, olde and yonge,   1
Lystenyth now to my talkynge,
Of whome y wyll yow [k]ythe;
Jhesu lorde, of heuyn kynge,
Grawnt vs all hys blessynge   5
And make vs gladd and blythe.

f. 90va

Sothe sawys y wyll yow mynge
Of whom þe worde wyde can sprynge,
Yf ye wyll lystyn and lythe;
Yn bokys of ryme hyt ys tolde   10
How hyt befelle owre eldurs olde,
Well oftynsythe.

Sometyme felle aventure,
In Rome ther was an emperowre,
In romans as we rede;   15
He was a man of grete fauour,
He leuyd in yoye and gret honour,
And doghty was in dede.
In turnament and yn fyght
Yn the worlde was not a bettur knyght   20
Then he was vndur wede.
Octavyan hys name hyght;
He was a man of moche myght,
And bolde at euery nede.

An emperes he had to wyfe,   25
The feyrest þat myght bere lyfe:
These clerkys seyn soo.
Sevyn yere togedur had þey ben
Wyth yoye and game þem betwene,

---

1 *Large L rubricated, three lines deep*   3 kythe] lythe

LINCOLN 91

Here Bygynnes The Romance off Octovyane

f. 98va Mekyll and littill, olde and ȝynge,   1
Herkyns all to my talkynge,
Of whaym I will ȝow kythe;
Jhesu fadir, of heuen kynge,
Gyff vs all thy dere blyssynge   5
And make vs glade and blythe.
For full sothe sawis I will ȝow synge
Off whaym þe worde full wyde gan sprynge,
And ȝe will a stownde me lythe;
In þe bukes of Rome als it es tolde,   10
How byfelle amange oure eldyrs olde,
Full ofte and fele sythe.

f. 98vb Somtym byfell ane auenture,
In Rome þer was ane emperoure,
Als men in romance rede;   15
He was a man of grete fauoure
And leuede in joye and grete honoure,
And doghety was of dede.
In tornament nor in no fyghte
In þe werlde þer ne was a bettir knyghte   20
No worthier vndir wede.
Octouyane was his name thrugheowte;
Euirylke man hade of hym dowte
When he was armede one stede.

f. 99ra Ane emprice he hade to wyffe,   25
One of fayreste þat was one lyffe:
Thus thies clerkes sayne vs so.
Seuen ȝeres had þay samen bene
With joy and gamen þam bytwene,

1 *Large* M *rubricated, four lines deep*

And othur myrthys moo.   30
Tho the sevyn yerys were all goon
Chylde myght they gete noon
That tyme betwene them twoo,
That aftur hym hys londys schulde welde;
Therfore grete sorowe drewe þem to elde,   35
Yn herte he was full woo.

The emperowre, on a day,
In hys bedd as he lay
Wyth hys lady bryght,
He behelde hur feyre lere   40
That was bryght os blossom on brere,
And semely in hys syght.
A sorowe to hys herte ranne
That chylde togedur þey myȝt noon han,
Hys londe to ye[m]e and ryght.   45
Be hys lady as he sete,
For woo hys chekys waxe all wete,
That was so hende a knyght.

When the lady can hyt see,
Chaunge sche dud hur feyre blee   50
And syghyd wondur sare;
Sche felle on kneys hym agayne,
And of hys sorowe sche can hym frayne,
And of hys mekyll care:
'For yf that hyt were yowre wylle,   55
Yowre counsell for to schewe me tyll
Of yowre lyuys fare;
Ye wott y am youre worldys fere,
Youre thoght to me ye myght dyskeuyr,
Youre comfort were the mare.'   60

In hys armes he can hur folde
And hys cownsell to hur tolde,
And of hys hertys wownde:
'Now haue we sevyn yere togedur byn,

f. 90vb (at line 46 area)

45 yeme] yeue

And oþir myrthis moo.   30
The seuen ȝere were comen and gone,
Bot child togedir had þay none
Getyn bytwene þam two,
þat aftir þam þair land moghte welde
When þat þay drewe till elde,   35
And forthi in hert þam was full woo.

And als þe emperoure satt appon a daye
In his chambir, hym to playe
With his lady bryghte,
He byhelde hir faire lyre   40
Was whyte so blossome on þe brere,
That semly was of syghte.
A sorow þan to his herte þer rane
Forthi þat þay childir hade nane,
Thaire landis to rewle one ryghte.   45
And by his lady so als he satte,
For sorowe his chekes wexe all wate,
That was so hende a knyghte.

Bot when þe lady þat gan aspye,
All chaunged þan hir bryghte blyee   50
And scho syghede full sore;
Scho felle hir lorde one knees agayne,
And of his sorow scho gan hym frayne,
And of his mekyll care:
'Sir,' scho sais, 'if it were ȝour will,   55
Ȝoure concelle for to schewe me till
And of ȝour lyffes fare;
Ȝe wote I ame ȝoure werldes fere,
Opyn ȝour herte vnto me here,
Ȝoure comforthe may be þe mare.'   60

Þan in his armes he gan hir folde
And all his sorow he to hir tolde,
And all his hertis wonde:
'Now hafe we seuen ȝere samen bene,

36 forthi in hert þam] forthi þam in hert þam; full] *interlined, caret after* was

And we no chylde haue vs betwen,   65
And here we schall not leue but a stownde.
Y wott not how thys londe schall fare
But leue in warre, in sorowe and care,
When we are broght to grownde.
Therfore y haue so mekyll thoght   70
That when y am to bedd broght
Y slepe but selden sownde.'

Than answeryd that lady bryght,
'Syr, y can yow rede aryght:
Yf yow nothyng to ylle.   75
A ryche abbey schall we make
For owre dere lady sake,
And londys geue thertylle.
Sche wyll prey hur sone feyre
That we togedur may haue an heyre,   80
Thys londe to welde at wylle.'
They let make an abbey thoo;
The lady was wyth chyldren twoo,
As hyt was Goddys wylle.

Wyth chylde waxe the lady thore;   85
Grete sche was wyth peynys sore,
That was bothe hende and free;
Tyll tyme felle þat hyt was soo
The lady had menchyldren two,
That semely were to see.   90
Tythyngys come to the emperowre
As he lay in hys towre:
A gladd man was hee.
Two maydenys þe errande hym broght—
Wythowt gyftys yede they noght: 95
Eyther he gafe townys three.

The emperowre was full blyþe of mode;
To hys chapell swythe he yode
And thanked God of hys sonde.
Yerly when the day can sprynge,   100
A preest he dud a masse synge;

f. 91ra

And hase no chylde vs bytwene;   65
For fay we sall hythen fownde.
And I ne wote how þis land sall fare
Bot lyfe in werre and in kare,
When we are broghte to grownde.
Therefore I hafe so mekyll thoghte   70
þat when I am to bedde broghte
I slepe bot littill stownde.'

And þan answerde þat lady bryghte,
'Sir, I kan rede ȝow full ryghte:
Gyffe ȝow nothynge ill.   75
A ryche abbaye schall ȝe do make
For oure swete lady sake,
And landis gyffe þeretill.
And scho will pray hir son so fayre
That we may samen gete an ayere,   80
This land to welde with skyll.'
An abbaye þan he gerte wyrke soo,
And sone he gatt knauechildire two,
Als it was Goddis wyll.

With childe þan ȝode þat lady þore;   85
Full grete scho wexe with paynnes sore,
That was so faire and free;
Till þe tym felle þat it was soo
The lady hade knauechildir two,
That semly weren to see.   90
Tythande come to þe emperoure
þere he laye in his ryche towre:
A full glade man was hee.
Two maydynes hym þe bodworde broghte—
Withowttyn gyftes ȝede þay noghte: 95
Aythire hadde townnes three.

The emperoure rosse with mylde mode
And till his chambir he hym ȝode,
And thankes God his sande.
Erly are þe daye gan sprynge,   100
He did a pryste his messe to synge;

Hys modur there he fonde.
'Sone,' sche seyde, 'y am blythe
That the emperes schall haue lyue,
And leue wyth vs in londe;   105
But moche sorowe deryth mee
That Rome schall wrong heyred bee,
In vnkynde honde.'

'Modur,' he seyde, 'why sey ye soo?
Now haue we menchyldren two,   110
Ythankyd be Goddys wylle!'
'Nay,' sche seyde, 'sone myne,
Ther ys neuyr neyþyr of þem thyn:
That lykyth me full ylle.
For thou myght no chylde haue,   115
Thy wyfe hath take a cokys knaue;
That wyll y proue be skylle.'
A sorowe to the emperowrs herte ranne,
That worde cowde he speke noon,
But yede awey full stylle.   120

To hys chapell forthe he yode
And at hys masse stylle he stode,
As man that was in care.
The emperowrs modur let calle a knaue
And hym behett grete mede to haue— 125
A thowsande pownde and mare.
To the chaumbur the knaue toke þe way,
There as the emperes in chyldebedd lay,
All slepte that there were;

f. 91rb   For why they had wakyd longe   130
In peynys, and in sorowe stronge,
Or sche were delyuyrd thare.

'Haste the, knaue, wyth all thy myght

His modir þore he fande.
'Sone,' scho said, 'I am full blythe
That þe empryse sall haf hyre lyfe,
And lyffe with vs in lande;
Bot mekyll sorowe dose it me
That Rome sall wrange ayerde bee,
And jn vncouthe hande.'

'Modir,' he sayse, 'why saye ȝe soo?
Haffe I noghte knauechildir two?
I thanke it Goddes will!'
'Nay, certis,' scho said, 'sone myn,
Wete þou wele þay are noghte thyn,
And þat lykes me full ill.
For þou myghte no childir haue,
Scho hase takyn thy kokes knaue;
I will it proue thurgh skyll!'
A sorowe þere to his herte gan goo,
þat wordis moghte he speke no moo,
Bot ȝod awaye full still.

Till his chapelle forthe he ȝode
Full sory at his messe he stode,
Als man þat was in kare.
His modir jwhils garte calle a knaue
And highte hym grete gyftis to hafe—
A thowsande pownde or mare.
To the chambir bothe þay tuk þe waye,
There þe empryce in childbed laye,
All slepede þat were there;
For scho had wakyd ryghte longe
In paynes, and in thoghte full stronge,
Or scho delyuered ware.

Than said þat lady to þat knaue,
'Hye þe faste þi golde to hafe,
þou schall be rewarde þis nyghte.
Haste þe tyte with all thi myghte

f. 99va

105

110

115

120

125

130

135

112 said] *interlined, caret after* scho

Preuely that thou were dyght,
And that thou were vncladd;   135
Softly be hur yn thou crepe
That þou wake hur not of hur slepe,
For seke sche ys bestadd!'
Hastyly was the knaue vncladd,
In he went, as sche hym badd,   140
Into the ryche bedde;
And euyr he drewe hym away,
For the ryches that he in lay—
Sore he was adredd.

The emperowrs modur awey went than,   145
To hur sone swythe sche wan
At masse there as he stode.
'Sone,' sche seyde, 'thou trowest not me;
Now thou mayste the sothe see.'
To the chaumbur wyth hur he yode.   150
When he sawe that syght than
Sorowe to hys herte ranne,
And nerehonde waxe he wode.
The knaue he slewe in the bedd:
The ryche clothys were all bebledd   155
Of that gyltles blode.

Euyr lay the lady faste aslepe;
A dylfull sweuyn can sche mete,
That was so swete a wyght.
Sche thoght sche was in wyldyrnes,   160
Yn thornes and in derkenes,
That sche myght haue no syght.
There come fleyng ouyr the stronde
A dragon, all wyth fyre brennand,
That all the londe was bryght;   165
In hys palmes all brennyng bloo
Vp he toke hur chyldren twoo,
And away he toke hys flyght.

When the lady can awake
A dylfull gronyng can sche make: 170

Preuely þat þou were dyghte,
And þat þou were vnclede;
Softely by hir þou jn crepe
þat scho ne wakyn of hir slepe,   140
For full seke es scho bystadde!'
Whatte for lufe and whatt for drede
Into þe ladyes beedd he ȝede,
He dyd als scho hym badd;
Bot euir he droghe hym ferre awaye,   145
For þe rechese þat scho jn laye—
Full sore þan was he drade.

The emperours modir away ȝode þan
And till hir son full tite scho wan,
There he att his messe stode.   150
'Son,' scho saide, 'þou trowed noghte me;
Come forthe, þou sall þe sothe now see.'
With hir to chambir he ȝode.
Bot when þe emperoure sawe þat syghte
For sorowe no worde speke he ne myghte,   155
For he wexe nerhande wode.
A scharpe baselarde owte he droghe,
þat giltles knaue þere he sloghe:
Alle was byblede with blode.

Ay lay þat lady faste and slepee;   160
A dolefull sweuenynge gan scho mete,
Scho was a wofull wyghte.
Hir thoghte scho was in wyldyrnes,
In thornes and in thyknes,
þat scho myghte hafe no syghte.   165
And þer come flyande ouir þe strande
A dragon, all full bryghte birnande,
þat all schone of þat lyghte;
In his palmes alle byrnand so
Vp he tuke hir childir two,   170
And away he tuke his flyghte.

Therewith þe lady bygan to wake;
A dolefull gronyng gan scho make

The lasse was hur care.

The emperowre toke vp the grome,
The herre in hys honde he nome:
The hede smote of thare.
He caste hyt ageyne into the bedd,   175
The ryche clothys were all bebledd,
Of redd golde there they ware.
The grete treson that þere was wroght,
The lady slept and wyste hyt noght:
Hur comfort was the mare.   180

Wordys of thys were spoke no moo
Tyll the emperes to churche was goo,
As lawe was in lede.
The emperowre made a feste, y vndurstonde,
Of kyngys that were of farre londe,   185
And lordys of dyuers stede.
The kyng of Calabur, wythowt lees,
That the ladys fadur was,
Thethur was he bede.
All they semblyd on a day,   190
Wyth myrthe, game and wyth play,
Whan the lady to churche yede.

Kyngys dwellyd then all in same:
There was yoye and moche game
At that grete mangery,   195
Wyth gode metys them amonge,
Harpe, pype and mery songe,
Bothe lewte and sawtre.
When the sevyn nyght was all goon
Wyth allkyn welthe in that won,   200
And mery mynstralsy,
Ther was neuyr so ryche a getherynge
That had so sory a pertynge,
I wyll yow telle forwhy.

And scho syghede full sare.
The emperoure to þe knaue wente,   175
þe hede vp by þe hare he hente
And caste it till hir thare.
The lady blyschede vp in þe bedde
Scho saw þe clothes all byblede,
Full mekyll was hir care.   180
Scho bygan to skryke and crye
And sythen in swonynge for to ly:
Hirselfe scho wolde forfare.

Wordis of this were spoken no mo
To þat lady to þe kirke solde go,   185
Als þe lawe was in þat lede.
The emperoure made a full riche feste
Of kynges and dukes þat were honeste,
Of many and dyuirse stede.

f. 100ra The kynge of Calabre, allas,   190
That the lady fadir was,
Thedir þan gan he bede.
Alle were þay sampnede appon a daye,
With grete solace and mekill playe,
To þe kyrke that lady 3ede.   195

And þere duellyn þe kynges samen,
With joy and myrthe and mekill gamen
At þat mawngery,
With gud myrthis þam emange,
Harpes, fethils and full faire songe,   200
Cytoles and sawtrye;
Till þe seuenyghte was gone
With alkyn welthis in þat wone,
Of myrthis and mynstralsye.
Was neuir so riche a gedirynge   205
That hadd so sary a partynge:
I sall 3ow tell forwhy.

178 blyschede] *preceded by deleted* blyssed blyshh h   187 full] *followed*
by deleted r   204] mynstralsye] *second* y *written over* e

Grete dele hyt ys to telle   205
On the nynthe day what befelle:
Lystenyth, and ye schall here!
The emperowre to chaumbur yode,
All the kyngys abowte hym stode,
Wyth full gladd chere.   210
The emperowre seyde, there he can stonde,
Soche auenture felle in that londe

f. 91vb Of a lady in that yere,
Wyth soche a treson was take and teynt;
He askyd wh[at] maner jugement   215
That sche worthy were.

When the emperowre had hys tale tolde,
The kyng of Calabur answere wolde—
He wyste not what hyt mente.
He seyde, 'Hyt ys worthy for hur sake   220
Wythowt the cyté a fyre to make,
Be ryghtwyse yugement;
When þe fyre were brennyng faste,
Sche and hur two chyldren þerin to be caste,
And to dethe to be brente.'   225
The emperowre answeryd hym full sone:
'Thyn own doghtur hyt hath done:
Y holde to thyn assent.'

There was dele and grete pyté;
A feyre they made wythowt the cyté,   230
Wyth brondys brennyng all bryght.
To the fyre they ledd þat lady thare—
Two squyers hur chyldren bare,
That semely were in syght;
In a kyrtull of scarlett redd,   235
In the fyre to take hur dedd,
Redy was sche dyght.
The kyng of Calabur made euyll chere,
For dele he myȝt not stonde hys doghtur nere;
There wept both kynge and knyght.   240

215 what] when

Grete dole forsothe it es to telle
Oppon þe haghten daye byfell:
Herkyns, and ȝe may here!   210
The emperoure to þe chambir ȝode,
All þe lordes abowte hym stode,
With full mery chere.
The emperoure said, 'I vndirstande
Swylke a nawntir fell in þis lande   215
By a lady to ȝere,
That was ouirtaken with swylk a treson;
I aske juggement of þis with reson
Of hir whate worthy were?'

When þe emperoure his tale hade tolde,   220
The kyng of Calabire answere wolde—
He ne wyste whate it bement.
He said, 'It es worthi for hir sake
Withowtten þe ceté a fyre to make,
With rightwyse juggement;   225
And when þe fyre es byrnand faste,
Hir and hir childir in it to caste,
Till þay to þe dede be bryntte.'
The emperoure answeres to hym sone:
'Thyn awen doghetir hase it done: 230
I holde to thyn assent.'

f. 100rb

There was dole and grete peté;
A fyre þay made withowtten þe ceté,
With brondes byrnande bryghte.
To þe fyre þay ledde þat lady thare—   235
Two sqwyers hir childir bare,
þat semly weren of syghte;
In a kirtyll of sckarlett rede,
Into þe fyre to take hir dede,
All redy was scho dyghte.   240
The kynge of Calabire made euyll chere,
He ne myghte for sorowe stande hir nere;
Bothe wepede kynge and knyghte.

234 byrnande] y *corrected from* r

The lady sawe no bettur redd
But that sche schulde be dedd
That day vpon the fylde.
Wyth sory hert, the sothe to telle,
Before þe emperowre on kneys sche felle   245
And bothe hur hondys vphelde.
'Grawnt me, lorde, for Jhesu sake,
Oon oryson that y may make
To hym that all may welde,
And sythen on me do yowre wylle: 250
What dethe þat ye wyll put me tyll,
Therto y wyll me ȝelde.'

The lady on hur kneys hur sett,
To Jhesu Cryste full sore sche wepte:
What wondur was hyt þogh she were woo.   255
'Jhesu,' sche seyde, 'kynge of blysse,
Thys day thou me rede and wysse,
And heuene qwene alsoo.
Mary, mayden and modur free,
My preyer wyll y make to thee   260
For my chyldren twoo;
As thou lett them be borne of mee,
Grawnt that they may crystenyd bee,
To dethe or that they goo.'

Kyngys and qwenys abowte hur were;   265
Ladys felle in swownyng there,
And knyghtys stode wepande.
The emperowre hur lorde stode hur nere,
The terys tryllyd downe on hys lere,
Full sory can he stande.   270
The emperowre spake a worde of pyté:
'Dame, thy dethe y wyll not see
Wyth herte nothur wyth hande.'
The emperowre gaf hur leue to goo
And wyth hur to take hur chyldren two,   275
And flee owt of hys londe.

The lady þan, þe sothe to telle,
Byfore hir lorde one knees scho felle,   245
And bothe hir handis vphelde.
Scho sayde, 'My lorde, for Jhesu sake,
Graunt me ane orysoune to make
Till hym þat alle sall wellde,
And þen of me ȝe do ȝoure wyll: 250
The dede þat I am ordeynede till,
Therto I will me ȝelde.'
The emperoure graunted hir righte so,
Ilke a man þan was full woo,
That were þat day in þe felde.   255

Than þe lady hir one knes þer sette,
Till Jhesu Cryste full sore scho grette:
No wondir þoghe hir ware wo.
'Now, lorde,' scho sayd, 'of heuens blysse,
This day þou me rede and wysse,   260
And heuen qwene also.
Mary, mayden and modir free,
My prayere make I to the
For my childir two;
Als þou lete þam be borne of me,   265
Helpe þat þay crystened may be,
Or þat þay to þe dede goo.'

f. 100va   Than lordis þat abowte hyr ware,
And ladyes, felle in swonyng thore,
And knyghttes stode wepande.   270
The emperoure stode by hyr full nere,
The teris trykylde one his lyre
That wele nere [ne] myghte he stande.
Than spake he wordis of gret peté,
And sayde, 'Thi dede will I noghte see   275
With herte nor ȝitt with hande.'
The emperoure gafe hire leue to goo
And take with hir hir childir two,
And flemed hir of his lande.

The emperowre gaf hur fowrty pownde
Of florens that were rownde,
In yeste as we rede;
And betoke hur knyghtys twoo,   280
And gaf hur þe golde and badd hur goo,
Owt of hys londe to lede.
The knyghtys the chyldren bare
There the hye weyes ware,
And forthe full swythe they yede.   285
The kyngys from the parlement,
Eche man to hys own londe went:
For sorowe ther hertys can blede.

Tho the lady come to a wyldurnes
That full of wylde bestys was,   290
The wode was grete and streyght.
The knyghtys toke hur þere þe chyldren twoo,
And gaf hur the golde and badd hur goo
The way þat lay forthe ryght.
They badd hur holde þe hye strete   295
For drede of wylde beestys for to mete,
f. 92rb   That mekyll were of myght.
Ageyne they went wyth sory mode;
The lady aloon forthe sche yode,
As a wofull wyght.   300

So had sche wepte there beforne
That the ryght wey had sche lorne—
So moche sche was in thoght—
Ynto a wode was veryly thykk,
There cleuys were and weyes wyck,   305
And hur wey fonde sche noght.
Yn a clyff vndur an hylle
There sche fonde a full feyre welle,
In a herber redy wroght,
Wyth olyfe treys was the herber sett;   310
The lady sett hur downe & wepte,
Further myght sche noght.

The emperoure gafe hir fowrty pownde
Of florence þat were riche and rownde,
In romance als we rede;
And he bytaghte hir knyghtes two,
And bad þat þay solde with hir goo,
Owt of his lande to lede.   285
Two sqwyers hir childyr bare
In stede þer þay were neuir are,
And intill vncouthe thede.
When scho was flemyd þat was so gent,
Ilke a lorde to hys lande es went: 290
For sorow þaire hertes gan blede.

When þis lady was in a wyldirnes,
That full thyke of wylde bestes bysett was,
And all wylsom it semed to syghte,
Thay hir bytaghte hir childir two,   295
Gafe hir hir golde, and bad hir go:
A stye þer laye full ryghte.
They bade hir holde þe hye strete
For drede with whilde bestes to mete,
That mekill weren of myghte.   300
And agayne þay went with sory mode,
And allone þat lady forthe scho ȝode,
Als a full wafull wyghte.

Scho hade so wepede þer byforne
That scho þe ryghte way hase sone forlorne—   305
So mekill was hir thoghte—
And jnto a wode was ferly thykke,
f. 100vb   There dales weren depe and cleues wykke,
þe ryghte waye fonde scho noghte.
In a greue vndir ane hill   310
Scho found a welle full faire and schille,
And ane herbere þerby was wroghte,
With faire trees it was bysette;
The lady sett hir down and grette,
For ferrere scho ne moghte.   315

293 bestes] *interlined, caret after* wylde   294 wylsom] w *written over another*
letter, perhaps a   305 forlorne] *at end of next line, marked for insertion*

The lady by the welle hur sett,
To Jhesu Cryste sore sche grett:
No further myght sche gone.   315
'Lorde kynge,' sche seyde, 'of heuyn blys,
Thys day þou me rede and wysse:
Full weyle y am of won.
Mary modur, maydyn free,
My preyer wyll y make to the,   320
Thou mende my sorowfull mone.
So full y am of sorowe and care
That thre dayes are goon and mare,
That mete ete y noon.'

Be that sche had hur chyldren dyght,   325
Hyt was woxe derke nyght,
As sche sate be the welle.
In the erber downe sche lay
Tyll hyt was dawnyng of the day,
That fowlys herde sche ȝelle.   330
There came an ape to seke hur pray,
Hur oon chylde sche bare away
On an hye hylle.
What wondur was thogh sche were woo?
The ape bare the chylde hur froo: 335
In swownyng downe sche felle.

In all the sorowe that sche in was,
There come rennyng a lyenas,
f. 92ᵛᵃ   Os wode as sche wolde wede.
In swownyng as the lady lay,   340
Hur wodur chylde sche bare away,
Hur whelpys wyth to fede.
What wondur was þogh sche woo ware?
The wylde beestys hur chyldyr away bare:
For sorowe hur herte can blede.   345
The lady sett hur on a stone
Besyde the welle, and made hur mone,
And syghyng forthe sche yede.

Bot by þe welle scho sett hir down,
Scho gret and cryede with sory sown,
For scho was lefte allone.
'Now, lorde,' scho said, 'if it be þi will,
In þis wode late me nott spylle,   320
For full will I am of wone.
Mary, mayden, qwene of heuen,
I pray þe herkyn to my steuen
And mend my carefull mone.
So full I am of pyn and wo   325
That thre dayes es gon and mo,
þat mete ne ete I none.'

And by þat scho had hir childir dyghte,
By þat þan wexe it euen myrk nyghte,
Als scho satt by þe welle.   330
So jn þat herbere down scho laye
Till it was lyghte on þe toþir day,
That fowlles herde scho þan synge and ȝelle.
Thare come an ape to seke hir pray,
Hir one childe scho bare awaye   335
Vp heghe appon ane hyll.
What wondir was ȝif hir were wo
When hir child was fro hir so?
In swonynge doun scho felle.

And in all þe sorow þat scho in was,   340
Ryghte so com rynnande a lyones,
Of wode als scho wolde wede.
In swonynge als þe lady laye,
Hyr oþir childe scho bare awaye,
f. 101ra   Hir whelpes with to feede.   345
Whate wonndir was þofe hyr were wo?
Awaye were borne hir childir two:
In swoghe scho lay for drede.
Bot for it was a kynge sone jwysse,
The lyones moghte do it no mys,   350
Bot forthe þerwith scho ȝede.

342 wede] *preceded by deleted* wende

There came a fowle þat was feyre of flyght,
A gryffyn, he was callyd be ryght,   350
Ouyr the holtys hore.
The fowle was so moche of myght
That he wolde bare a knyght,
Well armyd thogh he ware.
The lyenas wyth þe chylde vp toke he,   355
And into an yle of the see
Bothe he them bare.
The chylde slept in þe lyenas mowthe,
Of wele nor wo noþyng hyt knowyth,
But God kepe hyt from care!   360

Whan þe lyenas had a fote on londe
Hastyly sche can vpstonde,
As a beste þat was stronge and wylde.
Thorow Goddys grace þe gryffyn she slowe,
And sythen ete of the flesche ynowe   365
And leyde hur downe be the chylde.
The chylde soke the lyenas,
As hyt Goddys wylle was,
Whan hyt the pappys feled.
And when the lyenas began to wake,   370
Sche louyd þe chylde for hur whelpys sake,
And therwyth sche was full mylde.

Wyth hur fete sche made a denne
And leyde the lytull chylde theryn,
And kepte hyt day and nyght.   375
And when þe lyenas hungurd sore
Sche ete of the gryffyn more,
That afore was stronge and wyght.
As hyt was Goddys owne wylle,
The lyenas belafte the chylde stylle: 380
The chylde was feyre and bryght.
The lady sett hur on a stone
Besyde the welle, and made hur mone,
As a wofull wyght.

'Jhesu,' sche seyde, 'kynge of blys,   385

f. 92vb

There come a fewle full faire of flyghte,
A gryffone, sayse þe buke, he hyghte,
Ouir þose holtes so hare.
The fewle þan was so mekill of myghte   355
That esyly myghte he bere a knyghte,
Alle armed þofe he ware.
The lyones with þe childe tuke he,
And intill ane jle of the see
The gryffone bothe þam bare.   360
The child slepid in þe lyones mouthe,
Of wele ne wo it ne kouthe,
Bot God kepid it fro kare.

And whane þe lyones gatt fote on lande
Full styfly þan gan scho vpstande,   365
Als beste bothe stronge and whilde.
The gryffone thurgh Goddis grace scho sloghe,
And of þat fewle scho ete ynoghe
And layde hir by þat childe.
The childe sowkyde þe lyones,   370
Als it Goddis will was,
When it þe pappes felide.
The lyones gan it wake
And lufe it, for hir whelpes sake,
And was þerwith full mylde.   375

With hir feete scho made a dene,
That lyttill childe jn broghte scho þen,
And kepede hym day and nyghte.
And ay when hir hungirde sore
Scho ȝode and ete of þe gryffone more,   380
þat are was mekill of myghte.
And thus als it was Goddis will,
The lyones byleues þore styll
With þat barne so bryghte.
f. 101ʳᵇ The lady þat was leued allone   385
To Jhesu Criste scho made hir mone,
Als a full wofull wyghte.

Scho sais, 'Jhesu, kyng of alle,

Thys day þou me rede and wysse:
Of all kyngys thou art flowre.
As y was kyngys doghtur and qwene,
And emperes of Rome haue bene,
Of many a ryche towre,   390
Thorow þe lesyng þat ys on me wroght
To moche sorowe y am broght,
And owt of myn honowre.
The worldys wele y haue forlorne,
And my two chyldren be fro me borne: 395
Thys lyfe y may not dewre.

'Lorde, the sorowe that y am ynne
Well y wot hyt ys for my synne:
Welcome be thy sonde!
To the worlde y wyll me neuyr yeue,   400
But serue the, lorde, whyll y leue,
Into the Holy Londe.'
Downe be an hylle þe wey she name
And to the Grekeysch see sche came,
And walkyd on the stronde.   405
Beforne hur an hauen þere she sye,
And a ceté wyth towrys hye,
All redy there sche fonde.

When sche come to the ryche towne
A schyppe sche fonde all redy bowne,   410
Wyth pylgrymys forthe to fare;
Sche badd the schyppman golde and fee
In hys schypp that sche myght bee,
Yf hys wylle ware.
A bote they sende ouyr the flode   415
To the lady there sche stode,
A wyght man in hur bare.
By the maste þey badd hur sytte;
Of hur wo myght noman wytt,
But euyr sche wept full sare.   420

With carefulle herte to þe I calle
That þou be my socoure.   390
Als I was kyngis doghetir and qwene,
And emprice of Rome hase bene,
And many a riche towre,
And thorowe þe lessynges es one me wroghte,
Till mekill sorow þus am I broghte,   395
And owte of myn honoure.
This werldes blysse hafe I forlorne,
And my two childir er fro me borne:
This lyfe may I noghte dowre.

'This sorowe, lorde, þat I am jn   400
Full wele I wote es for my syn:
Welcome be alle thi sande!
To þe werlde will I me neuir gyffe,
Bot serue the, lorde, whills I may lyfe
Into þe Holy Londe.'   405
And ouir an hill þe waye scho name
And to þe Grekkes se scho came,
And welke appon þe strande.
And byfore hir an hauen scho seghe,
And a ceté with towris full heghe,   410
A redy waye þere scho fand.

Whan þe lady com þan to þat town
A schipe scho fond all redy bowne,
With pylgremes for to fare;
Scho bedd þe schipmen golde and fee   415
In þat schipp þat scho moghte be,
If þat þaire willes it were.
A bote þay sente appone þe flode
To þe lady right þer scho stode,
A wyghte man jn hir bare.   420
And by þe maste þay badde hir sytt;
There myghte no man hir sorowe wete,
And ay scho wepede sare.

411 *Line misplaced in MS where it follows 405*   418 þay] y *corrected*
from n

The schypp come be an yle syde,
The schyppman bade þem þere abyde:
'Fresche watur haue we none.'
Besyde them was a roche hye,
A well feyre welle there they sye   425
Come strykyng ouyr a stone.
Two men to the londe they sente,
Vp by the streme they wente,
The welle they fonde anone.
A lyenas lay in hur denne   430
And was full fayne of þo two men,
Anon sche had them slon.

So long on ankyr can they ryde,
The two men for to abyde,
Tyll none was on the day.   435
Twelue men anon can they dyght
Wyth helmes and hawberkys bryght,
To londe than wente they.
They fonde the lyenas denne,
A manchylde lyeng therynne   440
Wyth the lyenas to pley.
Sometyme hyt soke the lyenas pappe,
And sometyme they can kysse and cleppe:
For fere they fledd away.

They yede and tolde what þey sye: 445
They fonde on the roche on hye
A lyenas in hur denne;
A manchylde therin lay
Wyth the lyenas to play,
And dedd were bothe ther men.   450
Than spake the lady mylde:
'Mercy, lordyngys, that ys my chylde,
On londe ye let me renne!'
The bote they sente ouyr the flode,
To londe allone the lady yode: 455
Sore wepeyd the schypman than.

The schippe come sayland by an jle syde,
The maystir badd þat þay sold byde: 425
'For fresche watir hafe we nane.'
Bysyde þam was a roche on hye,
A welle streme þare þay see
Come rynnande ouir a stone.
Two men to þe lande þay sent,   430
Heghe vpe ouir þat roche thay went,
The welle þay found anone.
The lyones laye in hir dene
And was full blythe of þo two men,
And full sone scho had þam slayne.   435

So lange one ankir gan þay ryde,
Thies two men for to habyde,
Till none was of the daye.
Than gan twelue men þam dyghte
With helme and with hawberke bryghte,   440
And till þe lande wente þay.
The lyones fonde þay in hir dene,
A knauechilde laye sowkand hir þen
And gan with þe lyones to playe.
Vmwhile þe childe sowkede hir pappe,   445
Vmwhile gan þay kysse and clappe:
For drede þay fledde awaye.

Thay tolde þe wondir þat þay seghe,
And þat þay fonde on þe roche on heghe
A lyones in hir den;   450
A knauechilde þerin laye,
Therewith þe lyones gan hir playe,
And dede were bothe þaire men.
Than spake þat lady so mylde:
'Mercy, syrris, þat es my childe,   455
One land ȝe late me rynn!'
A bote þay sett appon þe flode,
The lady vnto þe lande þer ȝode:
Full sore wepide þay þen.

---

427 þam] m *corrected from* n   432 þay] *interlined, caret after* welle

When sche came on the roche on hyght,
Sche ranne whyll sche myght,
Wyth full sory mode.
The lyenas, thorow Goddys grace,   460

When sche sye the ladyes face,
Debonerly stylle sche stode.
Thorow the myght of Mary mylde
Sche suffurd hur to take vp þe chylde,
And wyth the lady to þe see she yode.   465
When þe schypmen þe lyenas sye,
The londe durste þey not come nye:
For feere they were nye wode.

Some hente an oore and some a sprytt
The lyenas for to meete,   470
Owt of ther schyppe to were.
The lady ynto the schyp wente,
Thyrty fote the lyenas aftur sprente,
Ther durste no man hur yn bere.
There men myght game see,   475
Fowrty men lepe ynto the see,
So ferde of the lyenas they were.
By the lady þe lyenas downe lay
And wyth the chylde can sche play,
And no man wolde sche dere.   480

They drewe vp seyle of ryche hewe;
The wynde owt of þe hauyn þem blewe
Ouyr the wanne streme.
The furste londe that they sye
Was a ceté wyth towrys hye,   485
That hyght Jerusalem.
As glad they were of that syght
As fowlys be of daylyght,
And of the sonne leme.
When hyt was ebbe and not flode,   490
The schypmen and þe lady to londe yode
Into that ryche realme.

When scho com on þat roche on heghe,   460
Scho ran ywhils þat scho myght dreghe,
With full sory mode.
The lyones, thurgh Goddis grace,
When scho sawe þe lady face,
Full debonorly vp scho stode.   465
Thurgh þe myghte of Mary mylde
Scho sufferd þat lady to tak hir childe,

f. 101vb   And scho forthe with hir ȝode.
Bot when þe schippmen þe lyones seghe
The land durste þay noghte com neghe: 470
For drede þay were nere wode.

Sum hent an ore and som a sprete
The wylde lyones for to mete,
And þaire chippe for to werre.
The lady intill þair chippe þay hente,   475
Thritty fote aftir þe lyones sprente,
Durste no man jn hir bere.
There was þan bot lyttill glee,
For many lepped into þe see,
So ferde of hir þay were.   480
Bot by þe lady downe scho laye
And with þe childe bygan to playe,
And to no man wolde scho dere.

They droghe vp saile of riche hewe;
The wynd þam owte of hauen blewe   485
Ouir þat wan streme.
The fyrste lande þan þat þay seghe
Was a ceté with towres full heghe
That hyghte Jerusalem.
Als blythe were þay þan of þat syghte   490
Als es þe fowlles, when it es lighte,
Of þe dayes gleme.
When it was ebbe and no flode,
The lady to þe lande þan ȝode
Into þat riche rewme.   495

473 lyones] *followed by deleted* for lyones   492 *Line written vertically*
in r.h. margin and marked for insertion

Ouyr all þe cyté wyde and longe
Of þys lady worde þer spronge,
That þere on londe was lende;   495
How sche had a lyenas
Broght owt of wyldurnes;
The kynge aftur hur sende.
The kynge bad hur lett for noþynge,
And the lyenas wyth hur brynge   500
To the castell there nerehonde.
When þat sche before hym come,
For the emperyce of ryche Rome
Full well he hur kende.

The kynge frayned hur of hur fare,   505
And sche hym tolde of moche care,
As a wofull wyght.
Wyth hys quene he made hur to dwelle,
And maydenys redy at hur wylle,
To serue hur day and nyght.   510
The chylde þat was so feyre and free
The kynge let hyt crystenyd bee:
Octauyon he hyght.
When the chylde was of elde
That he cowde ryde and armys welde,   515
The kynge dubbyd hym knyght.

The lyenas that was so wylde
Sche leuyd wyth the lady mylde:
Hur comfort was the more.
The lady was wyth the quene,   520
Wyth myrthe and game þem betwene,
To couyr hur of hur care.
Eche oon seruyd hur day and nyght,
To make hur gladd wyth all þer myght,
Tyll hyt bettur ware.   525
In Jerusalem can þe lady dwelle;
And of hur odur chylde y can yow telle
That the ape away bare.

Ouir alle þe ceté wyde and longe
Of þat lady the worde þan spronge,
þat þore one lande was lente;
And how scho hade a lyones
Broghte owte of wyldirnes.   500
The kyng aftir hir sente;
He bad scho solde lett for nothynge,
And þe lyones with hir brynge.
To þe castelle es scho went.
When scho byfore þe kynge þer come,   505
He kende hir for þe emprice of Rome
And by þe hande he hir hente.

f. 102ra   The kyng þan frayned of hir fare;
Scho tolde hym of hir mekill care
And of hir grete vnryghte.   510
He garte hir duelle with þe qwene stille,
Scho hadd maydyns redy to will,
To serue hir bothe daye and nyghte.
The childe þat was so faire and fre
The kyng did it crystened for to be: 515
Octouyane it highte.
When þe childe was of elde
That he couthe ryde and armes welde,
The kyng dubbede hym to knyghte.

The lyones þat was so wilde   520
Belefte with þe lady and þe childe:
Hir comforthe was the more.
The lady byleued with þe qwne,
With joye and blysse þam bytwene,
To couyre hir of hir care.   525
Ilke man hir plesyde day and nyghte,
To make hir glade with all þair myghte,
Vnto hir bettir were.
In Jerusalem thus gan scho duelle;
Of hir oþir childe now will I telle   530
That þe ape awaye bare.

507 þe] *interlined, caret after* by

Now comyþ þe ape þat was wylde
þorow þe forest wyth þe chylde,   530
Be the holtys hoore;
As þe ape come ouyr þe strete
Wyth a knyght can sche meete,
That chylde as sche bare.
There faght þe kny3t wondur longe   535
Wyth þe ape þat was so stronge,
Hys swyrde brake he thare.
The ape then awey ranne,
The kny3t þere þe chylde wanne,
And on hys way can he fare.   540

Forþe rode þe kny3t wyth þe chylde þen,
And yn þe foreste he mett owtlawys ten,
That moche were of myght.
The kny3t 3yt was neuyr so wo
For hys swerde was brokyn yn two,   545
That he ne my3t wyth them fyght.
Thogh þe kny3t were kene and þro
The owtlawys wanne þe chylde hym fro,
That was so swete a wyght.
The kny3t was woundyd so þat day   550
Vnnethe hys hors bare hym away,
So delefully was he dyght.

The owtlawys set þem on a grene,
And leyde þe lytyll chylde þem betwene:
The chylde vpon them loghe.   555
The maystyr owtlawe seyde then:
'Hyt were grete schame for hardy men
Thys chylde here and we sloghe.
I rede we bere hyt here besyde
To a ryche cyté wyth grete pryde,   560
f. 94ra   And do we hyt no woghe;
Hyt ys so feyre and gentyll borne
That we my3t haue therforne
Golde and syluyr ynoghe.'

529 *Large N rubricated, four lines deep*

Now comes þe ape þat was wilde
Thurgh þe forest with þe childe,
Ouir þe holttis so hare;
Als þe ape come ouir a strete   535
With a knyghte so gan scho mete,
Als scho þe childe bare.
Thore faghte þe knyght wondirly longe
Agayne þe ape styffe and stronge,
His swerde so brake he there.   540
The ape leued þe childe and away ran,
The knyght þe child son vp wan,
And with it forthe gan fare.

Forthe with þe child þe knyght went þan,
In þe wode mett he owtlawes tene,   545
That mekill weryn of myghte.
Ʒitt was neuir þe knyghte so wo
For his swerde was brokyn in two,
That he myghte nothyng fyghte.
If all þe knyghte were kene and thro   550
Those owtlawes wan þe child hym fro,
þat was so swete a wyghte.
þe knyghte was wondid, forsothe to saye,
Vnnethes his horse bare hym awaye,
So dulefully was he dyghte.   555

Those owtlawes sett þam on a grene,
þe child þay laide þam bytwene,
And it faste on þam loghe.
þe maystir owtlawe spake þen:
'Grete schame it were for hardy men   560
If þay a childe sloghe.
I rede we bere it here besyde
To þe se with mekill pride,
And do we it no woghe;
It es comyn of gentill blode: 565
We sall hym selle for mekill gude,
For golde and syluir enoghe.'

f. 102rb appears at line 548 in the left margin.

532 *Large* N *rubricated, four lines deep*   553 saye] *interlined, above deleted*
sayne, *with caret*

Then two of þem made þem yare   565
And to þe cyté þe chylde þey bare,
That was so swete a wyght.
Ther was no man þat the chylde sye
But þat þey wepte wyth ther eye:
So feyre hyt was be syght.   570
A burges of Parys came þem nere
That had be palmer sevyn yere,
Clement the Velayn he hyght.
'Lordyngys,' he seyde, 'wyll ye þys chylde selle?'
'Ye, who wyll vs golde and syluyr telle,   575
Floryns brode and bryght.'

For fowrty pownde þe chylde selle þey wolde;
Clement seyde, 'Longe ye may hym holde
Or ye hym selle may.
Y swere yow, lordyngys, be my hode,   580
I trowe ye can full lytyll gode,
Soche wordys for to say.
Golde and syluyr ys to me full nede,
Twenty pownde y wyll yow bede,
And make yow redy paye.'   585
The chylde þey to Clement yolde;
Twenty pownde he them tolde,
And wente forthe on hys way.

When Clement had þe chylde boght;
A panyer he let be wroght,   590
The chylde yn to lede;
A nurse he gate hym also,
Into Fraunce wyth hym to go,
The chylde for to fede.
f. 94ʳᵇ   Home he toke the wey full ryght   595
And hastyd hym wyth all hys myght;
That was hys beste rede.
Burgeys of Parys were full fayne;
Many wente Clement agayne:
A sklauyn was hys wede.   600

                578 ye] y   579 ye] y

Two owtlawes þan made þam ȝare,
To þe Grekkes se þay it bare:
þay couthe þe way full ryghte.   570
It was no man þat it seghe
þat þay ne wepid with þaire eghe:
So faire it was of syghte.
A burgesse of Pareche com þan nere
Had bene a palmere seuen ȝere,   575
Clement þe Velayne he hyghte.
'Sirris,' he said, 'will ȝe þis child selle?
The golde will I for hym telle,
Florence bothe brode and bryghte.'

For fourty pound hym selle þay wolde;   580
He said, 'Full lange may ȝe hym halde
Are ȝe hym so selle may.
Gode men,' he said, 'be my hode,
I trowe ȝe kan ful littill gude,
Swilke wordis for to saye.   585
Golde and siluir es me bot nede,
Bot twentty pownd I will ȝow bede,
And mak ȝow redy paye.'
The childe þay vnto Clement ȝolde,
And twentty pownde he þam tolde,   590
And went forthe one his waye.

Clement hase þe childe boghte,
A payneȝere did he to be wroghte,
The childe jn forthe to lede;
A noresche gatt he hym also,   595
Into Fraunce with hym to go,
That ȝong childe for to fede.
Home he tuke þe way ful ryghte
And hastede hym with all his myghte,
And vnto Paresche he ȝede.   600
The burgesche of Paresche wer ful fayne;
Full many went Clement agayne:
A slavyne was his wede.

f. 102ᵛᵃ

582 so] *interlined, caret after* hẏm

They callyd Clement and kyssyd hym all,
And broght hym home to hys halle;
Hys wyfe þerof was blythe.
Sche askyd hym the ryght dome
How he to the chylde come,   605
He tolde hur full swythe:
'In Jerusalem there y hym gete,
For þere wolde y hym not lete:
The sothe y wyll the kythe.'
The wyfe answeryd wyth herte mylde: 610
'Hyt schall be myn own chylde!'
And kyssyd hyt many a sythe.

'Dame,' seyde Clement, 'whyll y palmer was,
Thys chylde y gate wyth my flesche
In the hethen thede;   615
Into þys londe y haue hym broght,
For why þat þou wylt greue þe noght
Full ryche schall be thy mede.'
The wyfe answeryd wyth herte fre:
'Full welcome, syr, hyt ys to me,   620
Full well y schall hym fede;
And kepe hym wyth my chylde
Tyll that he come of elde,
And clothe them yn oon wede.'

Clement than was full blythe,   625
And let crysten hym full swythe,
Hyt was [not] taryed that nyght.
In the jeste as hyt ys tolde
The ryght name he hym calde:
Florent be name he hyght.   630
Whan þe chylde was sevyn yere olde
Hyt was feyre, wyse and bolde,
The man that redyth aryght.
Thorow þe realme of Fraunce wyde and longe
Of þys chylde the worde spronge,   635
So feyre he was be syght.

f. 94va

627 was not taryed] was taryed

Thay haylse[d] Clement and kyssed hym alle,
And broghte hym till his awen haulle;   605
His wyfe was glade and blythe.
Scho hym fraynede þe ryght dome
How he to þe childe come,
He tolde hir also swythe:
'In þe Holy Lond I hym gatt   610
And þore I wold hym noghte lett:
þe sothe I will the kythe.'
His wyfe ansuerde with herte mylde:
'He sall be myn awen childe!'
Scho kyste hym ful oftesythe.   615

Clement saide to his wyfe tho,
'Sen þe childe es getyn so
In þe hethen thede,
And now es it to þis land broghte,
I pray the, dame, þat þou greue þe noghte,   620
And riche sall be thi mede.'
'Sir,' scho said, with wordis free,
'Full welecom es it vnto me,
Full faire sall I hym fede;
And 3eme hym with oure awen child   625
f. 102vb   To þat he come of helde,
And clothe þam in one wede.'

Clement was þerof full blythe.
He garte crysten þe child ful swythe,
It was not duellid þat nyghte;   630
And als it es in romance tolde
The right name þat þay it callde:
Florent þe child hyghte.
And when þe child was seuen 3ere olde
He was bothe wysse, faire and bolde,   635
The man þat redis righte.
Alle þe rewme wyde and longe
Worde of þe childe spronge,
So was he faire to syghte.

604 haylsed] haylsest   627 *Line misplaced in MS where it follows 625 as*
last line in the column

Euyr the burges and hys wyfe
Louyd the chylde as ther lyfe:
To them he was full dere.
Tyll þe chylde was sevyn yere olde and more,   640
The burges set hym to lore
To be a chaungere.
Clement toke the chylde oxen two,
And bad hym to the brygge go
To be a bochere;   645
To lerne hys crafte for to do—
And hys kynde was neuyr therto,
Soche games for to lere.

As Florent to the brygge can go,
Dryuyng forthe hys oxen two,   650
He sawe a semely syght:
A squyer, as y schall yow telle,
A jentyll fawcon bare to selle,
Wyth fedurs folden bryght.
Florent to the squyer yede,   655
Bothe hys oxen he can hym bede
For the fawcon lyght;
The squyer therof was full blythe
For to take the oxen swythe,
And gave hym the fawcon ryght.   660

f. 94vb   The squyer þerof was full gladd
When he þo oxen taken had,
And hyed owt of syght.
And Florent to fle was full fayne—   664
He wende he wolde haue had hys hawk agayn—
And ranne wyth all hys my3t.
Home he toke þe ryght way
To Clementys hows, as hyt lay,
And yn he went full ryght.
He fedde þe hawke whyll he wolde,   670
And sythen he can hys fedurs folde,
As þe squyer had hym tey3t.

665 hawk] k *partly lost in binding*;   agayn] *at end of next line, marked for*
insertion   672 hym] hym hym

Euir þe burgesse and his wyfe   640
Loffed þe childe als þaire lyfe:
With þam he was full dere.
When he was tuelue ȝere olde and more,
He sett his owun son to þe lore
To be a chawndelere;   645
And Florent bytaughte he oxen two,
And bad hym ouir þe bryge go
Vnto a bouchere,
To lere his crafte for to do—
Als hym was neuir of kynd þerto,   650
To vse swylke mystere.

Als Florent ouir þe brygge gan go,
Dryvand on his oxen two,
A semely syghte sawe he:
A sqwyere bare, als I ȝow telle,   655
A gentill fawcon for to selle,
That semly was to see.
Florent to þe sqwyere ȝede,
And bothe his oxen he gan hym bede
For þat fowle so fre;   660
þe sqwyere þerof was full glade,
He tuke þe oxen als he hym bade:
Florent was blythe in ble.

The sqwyere hasted hym to go

Clement came yn full sone:
'Thefe, where haste þou my oxen done,
That y the begyfte?'   675
Grete dele myȝt men see thore:
Clement bete þe chylde sore,
That was so swete a wyght.
'Wyth odur mete shalt þou not leue
But þat þys glede wyll þe yeue,   680
Neythur day ne nyght.'
As sore beton as þe chylde stode
Ȝyt he to the fawcon yode,
Hys fedurs for to ryght.

The chylde þoght wondur thore   685
That Clement bete hym so sore,
And mekely he can pray:
'Syr,' he seyde, 'for Crystys ore,
Leue, and bete me no more,
But ye wyste well why.   690
Wolde ye stonde now and beholde
How feyre he can hys fedurs folde,
And how louely they lye,
f. 95ra   Ye wolde pray God wyth all your mode
That ye had solde halfe your gode,   695
Soche anodur to bye.'

The burgeys wyfe besyde stode,
Sore sche rewyd yn hur mode
And seyde, 'Syr, thyn ore!
For Mary loue, þat maydyn mylde,   700
Haue mercy on owre feyre chylde
And bete hym no more!
Let hym be at home and serue vs two,
And let owre odur sonys go
Eche day to lore.   705
Soche grace may God for þe chylde haue wroȝt,
To a bettur man he may be broght
Than he a bocher were.'

Aftur all thys tyme befelle,

Clement fowrty pownde can telle   710
Into a pawtenere.
Clement toke hyt chylde Florent,
And to the brygge he hym sente,
Hys brothur hyt to bere.
As þe chylde þorow þe cyté of Parys yede,   715
He sye where stode a feyre stede,
Was stronge yn eche werre;
The stede was whyte as any mylke,
The brydyll reynys were of sylke,
The molettys gylte they were.   720

Florent to the stede can gone,
So feyre an hors sye he neuyr none
Made of flesche and felle.
Of wordys þe chylde was wondur bolde,
And askyd whedur he schoulde be solde;   725
The penyes he wolde hym telle.
f. 95rb   The man hym louyd for thyrty pownde,
Eche peny hole and sownde:
No lesse he wolde hym selle.
Florent seyde: 'To lytull hyt were!   730
But neuyr þe lees þou schalt haue more.'
Fowrty pownde he can hym telle.

The merchaund þerof was full blythe
For to take the money swythe,
And hastyd hym away.   735
Chylde Florent lepe vp to.ryde,
To Clementys hows wyth grete pryde
He toke the ryght way.
The chylde soght noon odur stalle,
But sett hys stede yn the halle   740
And gaue hym corne and haye.
And sethyn he can hym kembe and dyght
That euery heer lay aryght,
And neuyr oon wronge lay.

Clement comyth yn full sone: 745
'Thefe,' he seyde, 'what haste þou done?

What haste thou hedur broght?'
'Mercy, fadur, for Goddys peté!
Wyth þe money that ye toke me
Thys horse haue y boght.'   750
The burges wyfe felle on kne þore:
'Syr, mercy,' sche seyde, 'for Crystys ore,
Owre feyre chylde bete ye noght!
Ye may see, and ye vndurstode,
That he had neuyr kynde of þy blode,   755
That he þese werkys hath wroght.'

Aftur þys hyt was not longe
In Fraunce felle a werre stronge;
An hondryd thousande were there ylente.
f. 95va   Wyth schyldys brode and helmys bry3t,   760
Men þat redy were to fyght,
Thorowowt þe londe þey went.
They broke castels stronge and bolde,
Ther my3t no hye wallys þem holde,
Ryche townys they brente.   765
All the kyngys ferre and nere
Of odur londys, þat Crysten were,
Aftur were they sente.

Octauyon, the emperour of Rome,
To Parys sone he come,   770
Wyth many a mody knyght.
And oþur kyngys kene wyth crowne,
All they were to batell bowne,
Wyth helmys and hawberkys bryght.
In Parys a monyth þe oost lay,   775
For they had takyn a day
Wyth the sowdon moche of myght.
The sowdon wyth hym a gyaunt bro3t,
The realme of Fraunce durste no3t
Agenste hym to fyght.   780

The sowdon had a doghtur bryght,

757 *Large* A *rubricated, three lines deep*   771 Wyth] *followed by deleted* a

Marsabelle that maydyn hyght,
Sche was bothe feyre and fre,
The feyrest þynge alyue þat was
In Crystendome or hethynnes,   785
And semelyest of syght.
To þe kynge of Fraunce þe maydyn sende
To lye at Mountmertrons þere nerehonde,
From Parys mylys thre,
At Mountmertrons besyde Borogh Larayn,   790
That stondyþ ouyr the banke of Sayne,
For auentours wolde sche see.

f. 95vb   The kyng of Fraunce þe maydyn hy3t,
As he was trewe kyng and kny3t,
And swere hur be hys fay,   795
That she must sauely come þerto;
Ther schulde no man hur mysdo
Neythur be nyght ne day.
The mayde þerof was full blyþe,
To the castell sche went swythe   800
And sevyn nyghtys þere sche lay;
For sche thoght yoye and pryde
To see þe Crystyn knyghtys ryde,
On fylde them for to play.

The gyauntys name was Aragonour,   805
He louyd þat maydyn paramour,
That was so feyre and free;
And she had leuyr drawyn bene
Than yn hur chaumbur hym to sene:
So fowle a wyght was he.   810

f. 103ra

'Merueylle þerof thynkes mee.   665
If þou and alle thi men will blyn,
I will vndirtake to wynn
Paresche þat stronge ceté;
Bot Mersabele þan weedde I will.'
Sayd þe sowdane, 'I halde þertill   670
With thi þat it so bee.'

Arageous, appon þat same daye,
To þe Mount Martyn þer þe lady laye
The waye he tuke full ryghte.
And hir hade leuir dede to hafe bene   675
Than hym in hir chambir to hafe sene:
So fulle he was of syghte.

The gyaunt came to Mountmertrons on a day,
For to comfort þat feyre may,
And badd hur blythe bee;
He seyde: 'Lemman, or y ete mete,
The kyngys hed of Fraunce y wyll þe ge[te], 815
For oon cosse of the.'

Than spake þe mayde mylde of mode
To þe gyaunt þere he stode
And gaf hym answere:
'The kyngys hed when hyt ys broȝt, 820
A kysse wyll y warne þe noght,
For lefe to me hyt were.'
The gyaunt armyd hym full well
Bothe yn yron and yn stele,
Wyth schylde and wyth spere; 825
Hyt was twenty fote and two
Betwyx hys hedd and hys too:
None hors myȝt hym bere.

f. 96ra

The gyaunt toke the ryȝt way
To þe cyté of Parys as hyt lay, 830
Wyth hym went no moo.
The gyaunt leynyd ouyr the walle
And spake to the folkys all
Wordys kene and thro;
And bad þem sende hym a knyght 835
To fynde hym hys fylle of fyght,
Or the londe he wolde ouyrgo;
And he ne wolde leue alyfe
Man, beste, chylde ne wyfe,
But þat he wolde þem brenne and slo. 840

All the folke of that cyté
Ranne that gyaunt for to see,
At the walle there he stode;
As farre as they sye hys blee
They were fayne for to flee: 845

811 a day] *at end of next line, marked for insertion* 815 gete] *final letters lost in binding* 817 mode] *at end of next line, marked for insertion*

He sayse: 'Leman, kysse me belyue,
Thy lorde me hase þe graunte to wyefe,
And Paresche I hafe hym hyghte;   680
And I hete the wittirly
The kynges heuede of Fraunce certanely,
Tomorowe or it be nyghte.'

The mayden sayse with mylde mode
To þe geaunte þer he stode   685
And gaffe hym this answere:
'The kynges heuede if þou me brynge,
Than sall þou hafe thyne askynge,
For full lefe to me it were.'
Thane armede þe geaunt hym ful wele   690
Bothe in jryn and in stele,
With helme and schelde and spere;
It was twenty fote and twoo
Bytwyxe his crown and his too:
There myghte none horse hym bere.   695

The geaunte tuke þe ryghte waye
Vnto Paresche þat ilke daye,
With hym wente no moo;
He lenede hym ouir þe towne walle,
And thus he spake þe folke with alle   700
Wordis kene and throo.

f. 103rb He badde þay solde send owte a knyghte
þat myghte hym fynde his fill of fyghte,
Ore he þat londe wolde ouirgoo.
þerin solde he noþir leue one lyffe   705
Beste ne man, childe ne wyffe,
That he ne sold þam bryne and sloo.

Than all þe folke of þat ceté
Rane þe geaunte for to see,
At þe bretage þare he stode;   710
Bot als ferre als þay myghte hym se or ken
Faste awaywarde gan þay ryn:

700 folke] forkle

For fere þey were nye wode.
Owt went armyd knyghtys fyue,
They þoght to auentour þer lyue;
The gyaunt thoght hyt gode.
Full hastely he had þem slayne,   850
Ther came neuyr oon quyk agayne
That owt at the yatys yode.

Chylde Florent askyd hys fadur Clement
Whodur all that people went,
That to the yatys dud renne.   855
Clement tolde Florent hys sone:

For ferde þay were nere wode.
There wente owte armede knyghtes fyve
And sayd þay wolde auenture þair lyfe;   715
The geaunte thoghte it gode.
Full hastyly he hase þam slayne,
Skapede neuir one qwykke agayne
That owte vnto hym ȝode.

When he had slayne the knyghtes fyve,   720
Agayne to þe walles gan he dryve
And ouir þe bretage gan lye.
'Kynge Dagaberde of Fraunce,' he sayde,
'Come thiselfe and fyghte a brayde
For thi curtasye,   725
For I will with none oþir fyghte;
Thi heuede I hafe my leman highte
Scho salle me kysse with thi.
And if þou ne will noghte do so,
Alle this ceté I will ouirgo: 730
Als dogges þan sall þay dy!'

Grete dole it was þan for to see
The sorowe þat was in þat ceté,
Bothe with olde and ȝonge;
For þer was noþir kynge ne knyghte   735
þat with þat geaunt þan durste fyghte,
He was so foulle a thynge.
And ay jwhills Arageous with his staffe
Many a grete bofete he gaffe
f. 103ᵛᵃ   And þe walles down gan he dynge.   740
And þan gane alle þe pepille crye
Vnto God and to mylde Marye,
With sorowe and grete wepynge.

Florent þan askede his fadir Clement
Whate alle þat petous noyes þan ment,   745
And whedir þe folke so faste ren.
Clement saide: 'My dere sone,

743 wepynge] *interlined, above deleted* sygheynge   745 þat] *superscript*
t *written over* e;   petous] ppetous

'Soche a gyaunt to þe walle ys come'—
The chylde harkenyd hym then—
'Sone but yf he may fynde a man
That he may fyght hys fylle vpon,　　　　860
Thys cyté wyll he brenne,
And sythen thys londe ouyrgone:
Quykk wyll he leue noon
Alyue that ys therynne.'

'Fadur,' he seyde, 'sadull my stede,　　　865
And lende me somedele of your wede,
And helpe that y were dyght!
Yf that hyt be Goddys wylle,
I hope to fynde hym hys fylle,
Thogh he be stronge and wyght.'　　　　870
Clement seyde, 'And þou oon worde more speke,
Thys day y wyll thy hedd breke,
I swere, be Mary bryght!'
'For nothynge, fadur, wyll y byde,
To the gyaunt wyll y ryde　　　　　　875
And proue on hym my myght.'

f. 96ʳᵇ

A geaunte to þe walles es wone,
Hase slayne fyve of oure men;
Oure kynges hede hase he highte   750
The sowdan doghetir, þat es so bryghte,
For scho solde kysse hym then.
There es no man dare with hym fyghte,
Forthi, my dere sone, hase he tyghte
This ceté to breke and bryne.'   755

'Now, fadir,' he sayde, 'I hafe a stede;
Wanttes me nothynge bot wede,
Nowe helpes þat I were dyghte!
A, lorde, why euir þus many men hym drede,
Me thynke I myghte do alle his nede,   760
And I were armede ryghte.'
Sayse Clement: 'And þou þerof speke,
I trow I sall thyn hede breke;
For had þou of hym a syghte
For all þis ceté [n]olde þou habyde,   765
Bot faste awaywarde wold þou ryde:
He es so fowle a wyghte.'

'A, fadir,' he said, 'takes to none ille,
For with þe geaunt fighte I wille,
To luke if I dare byde;   770
And bot I tittir armede be,
I sall noghte lett, so mote I the,
That I ne salle to hym ryde.'
Clement saide: 'Sen þou willt fare,
I hafe armoures, swylke als þay are,   775
I sall þam lene þe this tyde;
Bot þis seuen ȝere sawe þay no sone.'
'Fadir,' he sayd, 'alle es wonne,
Ne gyffe I noghte a chide!

'Bot fadir,' he sayde, 'I ȝow praye   780
That we ne make no more delaye
Bot tyte þat I ware dyghte;

f. 103vb

765 nolde] wolde

For sorowe Clementys herte nye braste
When he on Florent hacton caste—
The chylde was bolde and kene—
An hawberke aboue let he falle,   880
Rowsty were the naylys all
And hys atyre bedeene.
Clement broght forthe schylde and spere
That were vncomely for to were,
All sutty, blakk and vnclene.   885
A swyrde he broght the chylde beforne
That sevyn yere afore was not borne,
Ne drawe, and that was seene.

Clement the swyrde drawe owt wolde,
Gladwyn hys wyfe schoulde þe scabard holde,   890
And bothe faste they drowe;
When the swyrde owt glente,
Bothe to the erthe they wente:
There was game ynowe.
Clement felle to a benche so faste   895
That mowth and nose all tobraste,
And Florent stode and loghe.
Hyt ys gode bowrde to telle
How they to the erthe felle,
And Clement lay yn swoghe.   900

Chylde Florent yn hys onfayre wede,
When he was armyd on a stede

f. 96va

For I wolde noghte for þis ceté,
That anoþir man before me
Vndirtuke that fyghte.'   785
'Nay, nay,' saise Clement, 'I vndirtake
þat þer will none swylke maystres make,
Noþir kynge ne knyghte.
Bot God, sone, sende þe grace wirchipe to wyn,
And late me neuir hafe perelle þerin,   790
To þe dede if þou be dyghte.'

For sorowe Clement herte nere braste
When he one hym an actone caste—
The childe was bolde and kene—
Ane hawberke abowne lete he falle,   795
Full ruysty weren þe mayles alle
And alle his atyre bydene.
Clement broghte forthe schelde and spere
That were vnsemly for to were,
Soyty and alle vnclene.   800
A swerd he broghte þe child byforne
þat seuen [ȝere] byfore had noghte bene borne,
Ne drawen, and that was sene.

Clement drewe þe swerd bot owte it nolde,
Gladwyn his wyfe sold þe schawebereke holde,   805
And bothe righte faste þay drewe;
And when þe swerde owte glente
Bothe vnto þe erthe þay went:
Than was þer gamen ynoghe.
Clement felle to þe bynke so faste   810
þat mouthe and nese al tobraste,
And Florente stode and loghe.
Grete gamen it es to telle
How þay bothe to þe erthe felle,
And Clement laye in swoghe.   815

Child Florent in his vnfaire wede,
f. 104ra   Whane he was armede on his stede

802 seuen ȝere byfore] seuen byfore   809 ynoghe] *preceded by deleted* yng

Hys swyrde ydrawyn he bare;
Hys ventayle and hys basenett,
Hys helme on hys hedd sett: 905
Bothe rowsty they were.
Bothe Clement and hys wyfe
Louyd the chylde as þer lyfe,
For hym þey wept full sore.
To Jhesu Cryste faste can þey bede   910
To sende hym grace well to spede:
They myght do no more.

For hys atyre þat was so bryght,
Hym behelde bothe kynge and knyȝt,
And moche wondur thoght.   915
Many a skorne there he hent
As he thorow the cyté went,
But therof roght he noght.
The people to þe wallys can go
To see þe batell betwene þem two,   920
When þey were togedur broght.
Clement hys fadur wo was he
Tyll he wyste whych schulde maystyr be,
Gladd was he noght.

f. 96vb   The chylde came to þe yatys sone,   925
And bad þe portar them ondone
And opyn them full wyde.
All þat abowt þe chylde stode
Laghed as they were wode,
And skornyd hym that tyde.   930
Euery man seyde to hys fere:
'Here comyth an hardy bachelere,
Hym besemyth well to ryde;
Men may see be hys bre[ny]e bryght
That he ys an hardy knyght,   935
The gyaunt to abyde.'

The gyaunt vpryght can stonde

923 be] *at end of next line, marked for insertion*   934 brenye] breme

His swerde with hym he bere;
His auentayle and his bacenete,
His helme appon his heued was sett   820
And bothe full soyty were.
Bothe two, Clement and his wyfe,
Luffede þe childe als þaire lyfe,
For hym þay wepede sore.
To Jhesu Criste full faste þay bede   825
Lene hym grace wele for to spede:
Thay myghte do hym no more.

For his atyre þat was vnbryghte,
Hym byhelde bothe kyng and knyghte,
And mekill wondir þam thoghte.   830
Many a skornefull worde he hent
Als he thurghe þe ceté went,
Bot þerof gafe he noghte.
Than gane þe folke to þe walles goo
To see þe batelle bytwyx þam two,   835
When þay were samen broghte.
His fadir Clement full sory was he
To þat he wyste wheþir maystir solde be,
And glade ne was he noghte.

Florent came to þe ȝates full sone,   840
And bade þe portere swythe vndone
And open þe ȝates wyde.
All þat abowte þe ȝates stode
Loughe so faste þay were nere wode,
And skornede hym that tyde.   845
Ilk a man sayde to his fere:
'Here comes a doghety bachelere,
Hym semes full wele to ryde;
Men may see by hys brene bryghte
That he es a nobylle knyghte,   850
The geaunt for to habyde.'

Bot þan þe geaunt vpryghte gan stande

831 he] *followed by deleted* hade   842 ȝates] *followed by deleted and*
expuncted whyd

And toke hys burdon yn hys honde,
Of stele that was vnryde;
To the chylde smote he so   940
That þe chyldys shylde brake yn two
And felle on euery syde.
The chylde was neuyr ȝyt so wo
That hys schylde was brokyn yn two:
More he thoght to byde.   945
To þe gyaunt he smote so sore
That hys ryȝt arme flye of þore:
The blode stremyd wyde.

Clement on þe wallys stode,
Full blythe was he yn hys mode   950
And mende can hys chere:
'Sone, for that y haue seene
Thy noble stroke þat ys so kene,
To me art þou full dere;
Now me thynkyth yn my mode   955
Thou haste well besett my gode,
Soche playes for to lere.
Jhesu, that syttyth yn trynyte,
f. 97ᵐᵃ   Blesse the fadur that gate the,
And þe modur þat þe dud bere!'   960

Chylde Florent yn hys feyre wede
Sprange owt as sparkyll on glede,
The sothe y wyll yow say.
He rode forthe wyth egur mode
To the gyaunt there he stode: 965
There was no chyldys play.
The gyaunt to the chylde smote so
That hys hors and he to grounde dud go;
The stede on kneys lay.
Clement cryed wyth egur mode: 970
'Sone, be now of comfort gode,
And venge the yf thou may!'

And tuke his burdone in his hande,
That was of stele vnryde;
And to þe childe he smote so   855
That his schelde brake in two
And felle one aythire syde.
Than was þe childe neuir so wo

f. 104rb Als when his schelde was in two,
Bot more he thoghte to byde;   860
And to þe geaunt he smote so sore
That his righte arme flowe of þore:
The blode stremyde þan full wyde.

Than Clement appon þe walles stode,
And full blythe he wex þan in his mode   865
And gan amende his chere,
And said: 'Son, I hafe herde, I wene,
Thi nobill dynt þat es so kene;
With me þou arte full dere.
Now thynke me righte in my mode   870
That þou hase wele bysett oure gude,
Swylke lawes for to lere.'

Childe Florent in his vnfaire wede
Spronge als sparke dose of glede,
The sothe I will ȝow saye.   875
And rode hym forthe with egre mode
To þe geaunt righte þer he stode:
Was þore no childes playe.
The geaunt smote to þe childe so
þat childe and horse to þe grownde gan go;   880
The stede one knes laye.
Than cryede Clement with sory mode,
And said: 'Sone, be of comforthe gude
And venge the if þou maye!'

869 dere] *preceded by deleted* w

As euyll as the chylde farde,
When he Clementys speche harde,
Hys harte beganne to bolde.   975
Boldely hys swyrde he lawght,
To the gyaunt soche a strok he raght
That all hys blode can colde.
He hytt the gyaunt on þe schouldur boon
That to the pappe the swyrde ranne: 980
To grounde can he folde.
Thus hyt was, þorow Goddys grace,
The gyaunt swownyd yn that place,
In geste as hyt ys tolde.

The kyngys on the wallys stode;   985
Whan the gyaunt to grounde yode
All gladd they were;
All the people at the chylde loghe,
How he the gyauntys helme ofdroghe
And hys hedd he smote of there.   990
The chylde lepe vpon hys stede
And rode awey a gode spede;
Wyth them spake he no more.
The chylde toke the ryght way
To Mountmertrons þere the mayde lay,   995
And the hedd wyth hym he bare.

When he came to þe maydyns halle
He fonde the boordys couyrde all,
And redy to go to mete.
The maydyn that was so mylde of mode,   1000
In a kyrtull there sche stode,
And bowne sche was to sete.
'Damysell,' he seyde, 'feyre and free,
Well gretyth thy lemman the
Of that he the behete.   1005
Here an hedd y haue the broght,
The kyngys of Fraunce ys hyt noght:
Hyt ys euyll to gete.'

f. 97rb

And als ill als the childe ferde,   885
When he þe speche of Clement herde,
His herte bygan to bolde.
Boldly his swerde vp he laghte,
And to þe geaunt a stroke he raughte
þat all his blode gan colde.   890
The childe hym hitt one þe schuldir bone
That to þe pappe þe swerde gan gone,
And þe geaunt to þe grounde gan folde.
And thus it felle, thorow Goddes grace,
He slewe þe geaunt in that place,   895
In bukes als it es tolde.

The kynges appon þe walles stode;
When þe geaunt to þe grounde ȝode,
f. 104va   The folke full blythe þay were;
Alle þe folke at the childe loughe,   900
How he the geaunt hede ofdroghe
When he hade smetyn hym thore.
The childe leppe vp appon his stede
And rode awaye wele gude spede;
With þam spekes he no more.   905
The childe toke þe ryghte waye
To þe castelle þer þe mayden laye,
And the hede with hym he bare.

When he come to þe mayden haulle
He founde the burdes couerde alle,   910
And þam bowne to the mete;
The mayden þat was mylde of mode,
In a surkott in hyr haulle scho stode,
And redy was to hir sette.
'Damesele,' said Florent, 'faire and free,   915
Wele now gretis thi leman the
Of þat he the byhete.
Lo, here an heuede I hafe þe broghte,
The kynges of France ne es it noghte,
For it were full euylle to gete!'   920

904 And] *preceded by deleted* Ar

The byrde bryght as golde [b]ye
When sche the gyauntys hedd sye,   1010
Well sche hyt kende.
'Me thynkyth he was trewe of hete;
The kyngys when he myght not gete
Hys own that he me sende.'
'Damysell,' he seyde, 'feyre and bryght,   1015
Now wyll y haue þat þou hym hyght.'
And ouyr hys sadull he leynyd.
Oftesythys he kyste that may,
And hente hur vp and rode away,
That all the brygge can bende.   1020

Crye and noyse rose yn the towne;
Sone ther was to batell bowne
Many an hardy knyght,

f. 97va Wyth sperys longe and schyldys browne;
Florent let the maydyn adowne   1025
And made hym bowne to fyght.
Hur skarlet sleue he schare of then,
He seyde, 'Lady, be thys ye shall me ken,
When ye me see by syght.'
Soche loue waxe betwene þem two   1030
That the lady wepte for wo,
When he ne wynne hur myght.

Chylde Florent yn onfeyre wede
Sprange owt as sparkyll on glede,
The sothe for to say;   1035
Many hethen men that stownde
In dede he broght to þe grounde:
There was no chyldys play.
When Florent beganne to fownde,
Wythowt any weme of wownde,   1040
To Parys he toke the way.
The hethyn men were so fordredd,
To Cleremount wyth þe mayde þey fledd
There the sowdon lay.

That mayden brighte als golden bey
When scho þe geaunt heued sey,
Full wele scho it kende,
And sayde, 'He was ay trewe of his hete;
When he þe kynges heuede myght not gete   925
His owen he hase me sende.'
'Damesele,' he sayde, 'faire and bryghte,
Now wolde I hafe þat þat ȝe hym highte.'
And ouir his sadylle he lende.
Full oftesythes he kyssede þat maye,   930
And hent hir vpe and wolde awaye,
Bot þay alle þe brigge did fende.

Crye and noyse rose in thate towne,
And sone þay ware to þe batelle bowne,
Full many an hardy knyghte,   935
With speres longe and swerdes broune;
And Florent lete þe mayden downe
And made hym bowne to fyghte.
Hyre surkotte sleue he rofe of þen
And sayde, 'By this ȝe sall me kene,   940
When ȝe se me by syghte.'
Swylke lufe wexe bytwix þam two
That lady grett, so was hir wo,
That he ne wyn hir myghte.

Childe Florent in his vnfaire wede   945
Full many a Sarezene made he to blede,
The sothe I will ȝow saye.
Many a hethyn man in a stownde
He made to lygge appon the grownde:
Was þer no childes playe.   950
When Florent thoghte þat he wold founde,
Withowtten oþir weme or wounde,
To Paresche he tuke the waye.
The hethyn men were so adrede,
To Cleremont with the may þay flede   955
There þe sowdane laye.

f. 104vb

In hur fadur pauylon   1045
There þey let the maydyn downe,
And sche knelyd on knee.
The sowdon was full blythe,
To hys doghtur he went swythe
And kyssyd hur sythys thre.   1050
He set hur downe on a deyse,
Rychely, wythowt lees,
Wyth grete solempnyte.
Sche tolde hur fadur and wolde not layne
How Araganour þe gyaunt was slayne: 1055
A sory man was he.

'Leue fadur,' sche seyde, 'thyn ore,
At Mountmertrons let me be no more,
So nere the Crysten to bene.
In soche auenture y was today   1060
That a rybawde had me borne away,
For all my knyghtys kene;
Ther was no man yn hethyn londe
Myght sytte a dynte of hys honde,
The traytur was so [b]reme.   1065
As oftyn as y on hym thenke
Y may nodur ete nor drynke,
So full y am of tene.'

When þe sowdon þes tythyngys herde
He bote hys lyppys and schoke hys berde,   1070
That hodyus hyt was to see;
He swere be egur countynawns
That hange he wolde þe kyng of Fraunce
And brenne all Crystyante.
'I schall neythur leue on lyue   1075
Man ne beste, chylde ne wyue,
Wyth eyen that y may see.
Doghtur, go to chaumbur swythe,
And loke þou make þe glad and blythe;
Avengyd schalt thou be.'   1080

f. 97vb (in left margin)

                    1065 breme] preme

And jn hir fadir paveleone
Thore lyghttede þe mayden down,
And knelede appon hir knee.
Than was þe sowdane wondir blythe   960
And to his doghetir went he swythe,
And kyssed hir sythes thre.
He sett hir downe appon þe dese,
That full riche was, withowttyn lese,
With grete solempnyte.   965
Scho tolde hir fadir and wilde nott layne
How Arageous þe geaunt was slayne:
A full sorye man was he.

Scho saide, 'Leue fadir, thyn ore,
At þe Mont Martyn late me lye no more,   970
So nere Crysten men to bene.
In swylke ane auenture I was þis daye,
A rebawde me hade nere borne awaye
Fro alle myn knyghttes kene;
Thore was no man of hethen londe   975
That myghte a dynt stonde of his honde,
þat he ne fellede þam bydene.
Als ofte als I appon hym thynke
I may noþir ete nor drynke,
So full I ame of tene.'   980

Bot when þe sowdane þis tythande herde
He [bote] his lippes and schoke his berde
That grymly was to see;
And swore with hedouse contenance
That he sulde hange þe kynge of Frauncce   985
And bryne alle Cristyante.
And þat he sulde noþir leue one lyue
Man, beste, childe no wyfe,
With eghene þat he myghte see.
'Doughetir,' he said, 'go to þi chambir,   990
And luke þou make full glade chere;
Thow salle wele vengede be.'

f. 105ra

982 He bote his] He his

Full rychely was þe chaumbur spradd,
Therto was the maydyn ladd
Wyth maydenys that sche broght.
On softe seges was sche sett,
Sche myght nodur drynke ne ete,   1085
So moche on hym sche thoght,
Odur whyle on hys feyre chere,
And of the colour of hys lere:
Sche myght forgete hym noght.
Stylle sche seyde wyth herte sore: 1090
'Allas, wyth my lemman þat y ne were,
Where he wolde me haue broght.'

On hur bedd as sche lay
To hur sche callyd a may
Full preuely and stylle;   1095
The maydyn hyght Olyvan,
The kyngys doghtur of Sodam,
That moost wyste of hur wylle.
Sche seyde: 'Olyuan, now yn preuyté,
My councell wyll y schewe the,   1100
That greuyth me full ylle:
On a chylde ys all my thoght
That me to Parys wolde haue broȝt,
And y ne may come hym tylle.'

Olyuan answeryd hur tho: 1105
'Sethyn, lady, ye wyll do so,
Drede ye no wyght.
I schall yow helpe bothe nyght and day,
Lady, all that euyr y may,
That he yow wynne myght.   1110
Ȝyt may soche auentour be,
Lady that ye may hym see
Or thys fourtenyght.
At Mountmertrons y wolde ye were,
The sothe of hym þere shulde ye here,   1115
Be he squyer or knyght.'

f. 98ra

Full richely was hir chambir sprede,
And thedir jn was þat lady lede
With birdis þat scho broghte.   995
One softe seges was hir sete,
Bot myghte scho noþir drynke ne ete,
So mekill scho was in thoghte,
Sumtyme one his faire chere,
And one his coloure, and one his lyre: 1000
Scho myghte forgete hym noghte.
Full stylle scho saide, with hert sore:
'Allas, þat ne with my lemane [I] wore,
Whedir he wolde me hafe broghte.'

One hir bede righte als scho laye   1005
Scho callede vnto hir a maye
Full preualy and stylle;
That mayden highte Olyuayne,
þat was full faire of blode and bane,
And moste wiste of hir wille.   1010
Scho saide: 'Olyue, in preuaté,
My concelle I will schewe to the,
That greues me full ille:
For one a childe es alle my thoghte
That me to Paresche wolde hafe broghte,   1015
And I ne maye come hym tylle.'

Olyue hir answers tho,
And sais: 'Lady, sen ȝe will so,
Ne drede ȝow for no wyghte.
For I sall helpe ȝow þat I may,   1020
Bothe by nyghte and by day,
That he wynn ȝow myghte.
Ȝitt may swylke auenture be,
At ȝoure will ȝe may hym see
Or this daye fowrtene nyghte.   1025
At þe Monte Martyne I wolde ȝe were,
There salle ȝe somewhate of hym here
Wheþir he be sqwyere or knyghte.'

f. 105rb (aligned to line 1020 area)

1003 lemane I wore] lemane wore   1016 ne] *interlined, caret after* I

The Crysten men were full blythe
When þey sye Florent on lyue,
They wende he had be lorne.

The Cristyn men þan were full blythe
When þay sawe Florent on lyfe,   1030
þay wende he hade bene lorne.
And when he come nere the ceté
Agayne hym wente kynges thre,
And þe emperoure rode byforne,
And to þe palayse þe childe was broghte.   1035
Full riche atyre þay for hym soghte
Of golde and syluir schene.
Men callede hym Florent of Paresche,
For thus in romance tolde it es,
þoghe he þer were noghte borne.   1040

And Clement, for þe childes sake,
Full faire to courte þay gan take
And gaffe hym full riche wede;
One softe seges was he sett
Amonge grete lordes at þe mete,   1045
And seruede of many riche brede.
The childe was sett with grete honowre
Bytwixe þe kynge and þe emperoure,
His mete þay gan hym schrede.
He was so curtayse and so bolde   1050
þat alle hym louede, ȝonge and olde,
For his doghety dede.

Noghte longe aftir, als I ȝow saye,
The childe solde be knyghte þat oþir daye:
No lengir wolde þay habyde.   1055
His atyre of golde was wroghte;
Byfore þe emperoure þe childe was broghte,
f. 105va   A kyng one aythir syde.
The kyng of Fraunce byfore hym ȝode
With mynstralles full many and gode,   1060
And lede hym vp with pryde.
Clement to þe mynstralles gan go
And gafe some a stroke and some two:
There durste noghte one habyde.

1029 *Large* T *rubricated, three lines deep*

The chylde was set wyth honour 1120
Betwyx the kyng of Fraunce and þe emperour,
Sothe wythowten lees.
The emperour the chylde can beholde,
f. 98rb   He was so curtes and so bolde,
But he ne wyste what he was; 1125
The emperour thoght euyr yn hys mode
The chylde was comyn of gentyll blode,
He thoght ryght as hyt was.

Clement so sorye was þat daye   1065
For alle þaire costes þat he solde paye,
That he gane wepe wele sore.
And whills þe kynges dauwnsede in þe halle,
Clement tuke þaire mantills alle
And to his howse þam bare.   1070
Than the kynges gan þaire mantills myse,
And jlke man askede aftir his,
Where þay bycomen were,
Than swore Clement: 'By Goddes daye,
For ȝoure mete moste ȝe paye,   1075
Or ȝe gete þam no more.'

Thereatt all þe kynges loghe;
There was joye and gamen ynoghe
Amonges þam in the haulle.
The kynge of Fraunce with hert ful fayne   1080
Said: 'Clement, brynge þe mantils agayne,
For I sall paye for alle.'
Clement þoreof was full blythe
And home he rane alsso swythe
To his owen haulle;   1085
And to þe palays he mantils bare
And bade þam take þam alle þare,
And downe he lette þam falle.

The burdes were sett and couerd alle,
Childe Florent was broghte into þe haulle   1090
With full mekill presse.
The childe was sett with gret honowre
Bytwyxe þe kyng and þe emperoure,
Sothe withowtten lese.
The emperoure gan þe childe byholde,   1095
He was so curtayse and so bolde,
Bot he ne wiste what he was;
And euir he thoghte in his mode
The childe was comen of gentill blode,
f. 105vb   Hym thoghte righte als it was.   1100

1092 honowre] *with superfluous mark of contraction above* ow   1093 By-
twyxe] *second* y *not completed*

When the folke had all eton,
Clement had not all forgeton,   1130
Hys purce he openyd thore.
Thyrty florens forthe caste he:
'Haue here for my sone and me,
I may pay for no more.'
Clement was so curtes and wyse,   1135
He wende hyt had ben merchandyse,
The pryde that he sawe thore.
At Clement logh the kyngys all,
So dud the knyghtys yn þat halle,
And chylde Florent schamyd sore.   1140

The emperour than spekyth he
To Florent, that was feyre and fre,
Wordys wondur stylle:
'Yonge knyght, y pray the,
Ys he thy fadur, telle þou me?'   1145
The chylde answeryd þertylle:
'Syr, loue y had neuyr hym to
As y schulde to my fadur do,
In herte ne yn wylle.
Of all the men þat euyr y sye,   1150
Moost yeuyth my herte to yow trewly:
Syr, take hyt not yn ylle.'

The emperour let calle Clement there;
He hym sett hym full nere
On the hygh deyse.   1155
He bad hym telle the ryght dome
How he to the chylde come,
The sothe wythowten lees.
'Syr, þys chylde was take yn a forest
From a lady wyth a wylde beest,   1160
In a grete wyldurnes;
And y hym boght for twenty pownde,
Eche peny hole and sownde,
And seyde my sone he was.'

f. 98va (marginal note beside line 1157)

When þe folke all had eten,
Clement hade noghte forgetyn,
His purse he openede thore.
Thritty florence forthe keste he,
And said: 'Hafe here for my son and me,   1105
I may paye for no more!'
Clement was curtaise and wyse,
He wend alle had bene marchandyse,
The pryde that he sawe thore.
At Clement loghe the knyghtes alle,   1110
So did þe kynges in þe haulle,
Childe Florent schamede full sore.

Than spekes þe emperoure anone ryghte
To Florent, þat was faire and bryghte,
Wordis full wondir stille,   1115
And said: '3onge knyghte, telle þou me
If 3one man thyn owen fadir be.'
The childe answerde hym till:
'Sir, lufe hade I neuir hym too
Als I solde to my fadir doo,   1120
Neuir in herte ne wille.
Bot of alle the men þat euir sawe I,
Moste lufes myn herte 3owe sekirly:
Syr, takes it to none ille.'

The emperoure did calle Clement þere   1125
And made hym come and sytt hym nere,
Oppon the heghe dese.
He bade hym telle þe righte dome
How he to þe childe come,
Sothe withowtten lese.   1130
'Sir,' he said, 'þis childe was taken in a foreste
Fro a lady with a wylde beste,
In ane grete wildirnes;
And I hym boghte for thritty pownde,
Euirylke peny bothe hole and rownde,   1135
And sayde myn owen he was.'

The emperour than was full blythe   1165
Of that tythynge for [to] lythe,
And thankyd God almyght.
The emperour felle on kne full swythe
And kyste the chylde an hondryd sythe,
And worschyppyd God full ryght;   1170
Well he wyste, wythowt lees,
That he hys own sone was;
All gamyd, kyng and knyght.
The chyldys name was chaungyd wyth dome,
And callyd hym syr Florent of Rome,   1175
As hyt was gode ryght.

The emperour was blythe of chere,
The terys traylyd downe on hys lere;
He made full grete care.
'Allas,' he seyde, 'my feyre wyfe,   1180
The beste lady that euyr bare lyfe,
Schall y hur see no more?
Me were leuyr then all the golde
That euyr was vpon molde,
And sche alyue wore.'   1185
The emperour gaue Clement townys fele,
To leue yn ryches and yn wele,
Inowe for euyrmore.

On a nyght as the chylde yn bedd lay
He thoght on hys feyre may,   1190
Mekyll was he yn care.
The chylde had nodur reste ne ro
For thoght how he myȝt come hur to,
And what hym beste ware.
The chylde þoght, for þe maydyns sake,   1195
A message that he wolde make,
And to the sowdon fare;
On the morne he sadulde hys stede
And armyd hym yn ryche wede;
A braunche of olefe he bare.   1200

f. 98vb (marginal, at line 1190)

Than was þe emperoure joyefull and blythe
Of his tales for to lythe,
And thanked God almyghte.
The emperoure felle one knes als swythe   1140
And kyssede þe childe full fele sythe,
Thoghe he ne wiste whate he highte;
f. 106ra   For full wele he trowede, withowtten lese,
His owen sone that he was;
Alle gamnes, bothe kyng and knyghte.   1145
The childes name was chaungede with dome,
Thay callede hym þan Florent of Rome,
Als it was full gude ryghte.

The emperoure was so blythe of chere
That the teris trekelide one his lyre;   1150
He made þan full grete care,
And said, 'Allas, my faire wyfe,
The beste lady þat was one lyfe,
Salle I hir see no mare?
Me ware leuir þan alle þe golde   1155
þat euir was appon Cristyn molde,
Wyste I one lyue scho ware.'
The emperoure gafe Clement welthis fele,
To lyfe in reches and in wele,
Aye nowe for euirmore.   1160

Als Florent one an nyghte in bede laye
He thoghte one Marsabele, þat faire maye,
And full mekill he was in kare.
The childe had noþir riste ne ro
For thoghte how he myghte com hir to,   1165
And whate þat hym beste ware.
The childe thoghte, for þe mayden sake,
A message þat he wolde make,
And to þe sowdane fare;
And sone þe childe did sadill his stede   1170
And armede hym in full riche wede;
A braunche of olyue he bare.

Hýt was of messengerys the lawe
A braunche of [o]lefe for to haue,
And yn ther honde to bere.
For the ordynaunce was so,
Messengerys schulde sauely come and go,   1205
And no man do them dere.
The chylde toke þe ryght way
To Cleremount as hyt lay,
Wyth hym hys grete heere.
At þe halle dore he reynyd hys stede,   1210
And on hys fete yn he yede,
A messengere as he were.

Than spake þe chylde wyth hardy mode
Before the sowdon þere he stode,
As a man of moche myght: 1215
'The kynge of Fraunce me hedur sende
And byddyþ þe owt of hys londe þou wynd,
Thou werryst ageyn þe ryght;
Or he wyll brynge agenste the
Thyrty thousande tolde be thre,   1220
Wyth helmys and hawberkys bryght;
Eche knyȝt schall thyrty squyers haue,
And euery squyer a foteknaue
Worthe an hethyn knyght.'

f. 99ra   Than began the sowdon to speke,   1225
There he sate at hys ryche mete,
Amonge hys knyghtys kene:
'The kyng of Fraunce shall welcome be;
Agenste oon he schall haue thre,
I wot wythowten wene,   1230
That also fayne are of fyght
As fowle of day aftur nyght,
To schewe ther schyldys schene.
To proue tomorne, be my lay,
I wyll neuyr set lenger day,   1235
Than schall the sothe be sene.'

For þat was þat tym messangere lawe
A brawnche of olyue for to schewe,
And it in hand to bere.   1175
For þe ordynance þan was so,
Messangers solde sauely come and go,
And no man solde þam dere.
The childe takes þe heghe waye
To Cleremont, þare þe sowdan laye   1180
With alle his grete here.
And at þe haulle dore he reyngened his stede,
And one fote in he ȝede,
Messangere als he were.

Than spekes þe childe with hardy mode,   1185
f. 106rb Byfore þe sowdane þere he stode,
Als man of mekill myghte:
'The kynge of Fraunce me hedir sende
And byddis the owte of his lande wende,
For þou werreys agayne þe righte;   1190
Or he wille brynge agayne the
Twentty thowsande tolde by thre,
With helmes and hawberkes bryghte;
And ilke a knyghte sall thritty sqwyers hafe,
And ilke a sqwyere a foteknaue   1195
Worthe an heythen knyghte.'

Than the sowdane bygane to speke,
Als he satt at his riche mete,
Amonge his knyghttes kene:
'The kynge of Fraunce welecome sall be;   1200
Euir agayne on I sall brynge thre,
Weite he withowtten wene,
That als fayne bene for to fyghte
Als fowle es of dayes lyghte,
To schewe þaire scheldes schene.   1205
To prove tomorowe, by my laye,
I kepe to take no langere daye,
Than salle þe sothe be sene.'

1177 Messangers] *second letter has been corrected and could be* a *or* e
1201 on] *interlined, caret before* I

Than spekyth þe mayde wyth mylde mode
To feyre Florent there he stode,
That was so swete a wyght:
'Messengere, y wolde the frayne   1240
Whedur he be knyght or swayne,
That ys so moche of myght,
That hath my fadurs gyaunt slayne,
And rauyschyd me fro Borogh Larayn,
And slewe there many a knyght.'   1245
Thogh sche monyd hym to ylle,
Ʒyt were hyt mykull yn hur wylle
To haue of hym a syght.

'Lady,' he seyde, 'nodur lesse nor more
Than yf hyt myselfe wore;   1250
Syth þou wylt of me frayne,
Thou schalt me knowe yn all þe heere,
Thy sleue y wyll bere on my spere,
In the batell playne.'
All they wyste ther by than   1255
That he was the same man
That had the gyaunt slayne.
Wythowt ony odur worde
f. 99ʳᵇ   All they start fro the borde,
Wyth swyrdys and knyuys drawyn.   1260

Florent sawe none odur bote
But þat he muste fyght on fote
Agenste the Sarsyns all;
And euyr he hyt them amonge
Where he sawe the thykest thronge: 1265
Full fele dud he the[n] falle.
Some be the armys he nome
That all the schouldur wyth hym come,
The prowdyst yn the halle;
And some soche bofettys he lente,   1270
That the hedd fro the body wente,
As hyt were a balle.

1266 then] them

Than spekes þat may with mylde mode
To faire Florent þare he stode,   1210
That was so swete a wyghte:
'Messengir, I wolde the frayne
Wheþir he es knyghte or swayne,
That es so mekill of myghte,
That hase my fadir geaunt slayne,   1215
And wolde hafe rauesched me fra Borow Lerayne,
And slewe þer many a knyghte.'
Alle þoghe scho neuenede hym with ille,
Full mekill was it þan hir wille
Of hym to hafe a syghte.   1220

'Lady,' he sayse, 'he es noþir lesse ne moree
Than it I myselfe wore;
Sythe ȝe will of hym frayne,
Ȝe sall hym knawe thurgh alle þe here,
Ȝoure sleue he wille hafe on his spere,   1225
In þe batelle al playne.'
Withowtten any more worde,
Ilke man stirte vpe fro þe borde,
With swerdes and knyues drawen;
For alle þay wiste wele by þan   1230
þat he it was, þat ilke man,
þat hade þe geaunt slayne.

Than Florent sawe no bettir bote
Bot nedely hym tydes to fighte one fote
Agayne þe Sarazenes alle;   1235
And euir he hitt þam amange
Where he sawe þe gretteste thrange:
Full many he did to falle.
Sum by þe armes he nome
That the schuldir with hym come,   1240
The prowdeste in the haulle;
And some he swilke a boxe lent,
þat þe heued fro þe body went,
Als it were a foteballe.

f. 106va

1211 so] *interlined, caret after* was   1219 it] *interlined, caret after* was

Whan hys swyrde was ybrokyn,
A sarsyns legge hath he lokyn,
Therwyth he can hym were.   1275
To the grounde he dud to go
Sevyn skore, and somedele moo,
That hethyn knyghtys were.
The chylde made hym wey full gode
To hys stede there he stode,   1280
Tho myght hym no man dere.
The chylde toke the ryght way
To the cyté of Parys as hyt lay,
Thorowowt all the heere.

The Crysten men were full blythe   1285
When they sye Florent come alyue:
They wende he lorne had bene.
When he come nye the cyté
Agenste hym rode kyngys thre,
And the emperour rode them betwene.   1290
The folke presyd hym to see,
Euery man cryed: 'Whych ys he?'
f. 99va   As they hym neuyr had sene.
To the pales was he ladd,
And tolde them how he was bestadd   1295
Amonge the Sarsyns kene.

'Lordyngys, loke þat ye ben yare
To the batell for [to] fare,
And redy for to ryde.
Tomorne hyt muste nede be sene   1300
Whych ys hardy man and kene;
We may no lenger byde.'
The folke seyde they were blythe
To wynde to the batell swythe,
In herte ys noght to hyde.   1305
A ryche clothe on borde was spradde
To make the chylde blythe and gladd,
A kynge on aythur syde.

1298 to] that

And when his swerde broken was,   1245
A mete forme he gatt, par cas,
And þerewith he gan hym were;
And to þe grounde sone garte he go
Ten score, and somdele mo,
That heythen knyghtes were.   1250
Florent made a waye ful gode
To his stede righte þer he stode,
There myghte no man hym dere;
And home he takes þe righte waye
Vnto Parische als it laye,   1255
Thurgheowte þe heythen here.

Than were þe Crysten folke full blythe
When þay sawe Florent one lyue:
Thay wende he lorne hade bene.
And whene he come nere the ceté   1260
Agayne hym went kynges thre,
The emperoure rode bytwene.
Alle þe folke pressede hym to se,
Ilke a man fraynede: 'Whilke es he?'
Als þay hym neuir hade sene.   1265
Vnto þe palese he was ledde,
He tolde þam alle how he had spede
Amonge þe Sarazens kene.

'Lordynges,' he saide, 'lukes ȝe be ȝare
Vnto þe batelle for to fare,   1270
f. 106ᵛᵇ   And redy for to ryde.
Tomorowe moste it nede be sene
Who es hardy man and kene;
No lengere ne may we byde.'
The folke sayde þat þay were blythe   1275
To wende to þat batelle swythe,
In her[t]e es noghte to hide.
A riche clothe one þe borde was sprede
To make þe childe bothe blythe and glade,
A kyng one aythir syde.   1280

1277 herte] herde; h *written over* e

On the morne when hyt was daylyght,
The folke can them to batell dyght,   1310
All that wepyn myght welde.
There men myght see many a knyght
Wyth helmys and wyth hawberkys bryght,
Wyth sperys and wyth schylde.
Wyth trumpys and wyth moche pryde,   1315
Boldely owt of the borowe þey ryde
Into a brode fylde;
The downe was bothe longe and brode
There bothe partyes odur abode,
And eyther on odur behelde.   1320

Marsabelle, the maydyn fre,
Was broght the batell for to see
To Mountmertrons ouyr Seyn.
Florent hur sleue bare on hys spere,
In the batell he wolde hyt were,   1325
And rode forthe yn the playne;
f. 99vb For that men schulde see by than
That he was that ylke man
That had the gyaunt slayne;
And also for the maydyn free,   1330
That sche schulde hys dede see;
Therof sche was fayne.

That whyle was moche sorowe yn fyȝt
When þe batell began to smyte
Wyth many a greuys wounde.   1335
Fro þe morne, þat day was lyght,
Tyll hyt was euyn derke nyght,
Or eythur party wolde fownde.
Florent can euyr among þem ryde
And made þere many a sore syde,   1340
That afore were softe and sownde.
So moche people to dethe yode
That the stedys dud wade yn blode
That stremyd on the grounde.

One þe morowe when þe daye was lyghte,
The folke þam to þe batelle dyghte,
Alle þat wapen moghte welde.
There men myghte se many a wyghte
With helmes schene and hawberke bryghte,   1285
With spere and als with schelde.
With trompes and with mekill pryde,
Full boldly owt of borowe þay ryde
Vnto a full brode felde;
The felde was bothe longe and brode   1290
þore bothe þe partyes one habode,
And aythere oþir byhelde.

Marsabele, þat mayden fre,
Was broghte þat batelle for to see
To þe Mont Martyne appon Seyne.   1295
Florent hir sleue did on his spere
For in þe batelle he wolde it bere,
And forthe he rode in þe playne;
For þat men solde wele se þan
That he it was, þat ilke man,   1300
That haued þe geaunt slayne;
And also for þat mayden free
Was broghte þat batelle for to see;
þereof scho was full fayne.

Than was þere mekill sorow [and] syte   1305
When þe batells bygan to smytte
With many a grymly wonde.
Fro morow, þat þe daye was lyghte,
To it was euen and dirke nyghte,
Or owthir partye wolde fownde.   1310
Florent gan euir amonges ryde
And made þore many a sory syde,
þat ore was hale and sownde.
So many folke þore to þe dede ȝode
That stedis wode in the blode   1315
That stremyd one the grounde.

f. 107ra (in left margin, aligned with "So many folke þore...")

1305 and] in

There men myght see helmys bare, 1345
Hedys þat full feyre ware,
Lay to grounde lyght.
The Crystyn party become so th[ynne]
That þe fylde þey my3t not wynne,
All arewyd hyt kynge and knyght. 1350
Florent smote wyth herte gode,
Thorow helme ynto þe hed hyt wode,
So moche he was of myght.
Thorow Godys grace, and Florent there,
The Crysten men þe bettur were 1355
That day yn the fyght.

The partyes were ydrawe away,
And takyn was anodur day,
That þe batell schulde bee.
Florent rode toward Borough Larayn, 1360
Be the watur banke of Seyne,
Moo auenturs for to see.
The maydyn whyte as lylly flowre
Lay yn a corner of hur towre,
That was ferly feyre and free. 1365
Florent sche sye on fylde fare,
Be the sleue that he bare
Sche knewe that hyt was he.

Then spekyth þe mayde wyth mylde mode
To Olyuan, that be hur stode, 1370
And knewe hur preuyté:
'Olyuan, how were beste to do
A worde þat y my3t speke hym to?
Iwysse, then wele were me.'
Sche seyde, 'Lady, we two 1375
Allone wyll be the reuer go,
There as he may yow see.
Yf he yow loue wyth herte gode,
He wyll not let for the flode,
For a full gode stede hath he.' 1380

f. 100ra

1348 thynne] than   1377 may] *followed by deleted* h

Thore men myghte see helmes bare,
And heuedis þat full faire waree,
Full lawe to þe grownde þan lyghte.
The Cristen men bycome so thyn   1320
That the felde myghte þay noghte wyn,
Alle cryede bothe kyng and knyghte.
Than Florent smote with herte so gude,
His swerde thurghe þaire helmes wode,
So mekyll he was of myghte.   1325
Thurghe Goddes grace, and Florent thore,
The Cristen men þe bettir wore
That ilke daye in þe fyghte.

The parties ere withdrawen awaye,
And taken there es anoþir daye,   1330
That the batelle sulde be.
Florent rode to Borow Lerayne,
Besyde þe watir banke of Sayne,
For auenturs wolde he see.
The mayden whitt als lely floure   1335
Laye in a kirnelle of a towre,
Was ferly faire and fre.
Florent scho sawe on þe felde fare,
By hir sleue þat he bare
Scho knewe wele þat it was he.   1340

Than spekes þat may with mylde mode
To Olyue, þat byfore hir stode,
þat wyste hir preuaté,
And saide: 'Howe were it beste to do
A worde þat I myghte speke hym to?   1345
Iwysse, than wele were me.'
Scho saide, 'Lady, we one two
By þe reuir banke sall go,
That he may vs see.
If he ȝow lufe with hert gude,   1350
He lettes nothyng for þe flode,
A full gude horse haues he.'

Forthe went the maydyns two;
Be the reuer syde can they goo,
Themselfe allone that tyde.
When Florent sawe þat swete wyght
He sprange as fowle dothe yn flyght,   1385
No lenger wolde he byde.
The stede was so wondur gode
He bare the chylde ouyr the flode,
Hymselfe well cowde ryde.
Grete yoye hyt was to see þem meete   1390
Wyth clyppyng and wyth kyssyng swete,
In herte ys not [to] hyde.

'Lady,' he seyde, 'well ys me
A worde þat y may speke wyth the,
f. 100rb   So bryght þou art of hewe;   1395
In all þys worlde ys noon so fre,
Why ne wyll ye crystenyd be
And syth of herte be trewe?'
Sche seyde, 'Yf þat ye myght me wynne,
I wolde forsake all hethyn kynne   1400
As thogh y them neuyr knewe;
And syth ye wolde me wedde to wyfe,
I wolde leue yn Crysten lyfe,
My yoye were euyr newe.'

'Lady,' he seyde, 'wythowt fayle,   1405
How were beste yowre counsayle
That y yow wynne myght?'
'Certys, ye neuyr wynne me may
But hyt were on that ylke day,
That ye haue take to fyght;   1410
That ye wolde sende be the flode,
Wyth men þat crafty were and gode,
A schyppe þat well were dyght.
Whyll þat men are at þat dere dede,
That whyle myȝt men me awey lede   1415
To yowre cyté ryght.

1392 not to hyde] not hyde   1414 men] e obscured by blot

Forthe þan went theis maydenes two;
Owte of the castelle gan þay goo
By the reuere syde.   1355
When Florent sawe þat swete wyghte
He sprent als any fowle of flyghte,
No lengir þen wolde he byde.
His horse he was full wondir gude
And bare hym smertly ouir þe flode,   1360
Hymselffe couthe full wele ryde.
It was grete joye to se þam mete
With haulsynge and with kyssynge swete,
In herte es noghte to hyde.

'Lady,' he sayde, 'full wele es mee   1365
A worde þat I may speke with the,
So bryghte ert þou of hewe;
In alle this werlde es non so free
Forwhi þat þow wolde cristenede be,
And sythen of herte be trewe.'   1370
'Sir, if þat þou myghte me wyn,
I wolde forsake all my kyn
Als I þem neuir knewe;
Sythen þou wolde wedde me to wyfe,
I wolde lyue in Cristen lyfe,   1375
My joye solde euir be newe.'

'Lady,' he sayde, 'withowtten fayle,
Howe were þan thi beste consaile
That I the wynn myghte?'
'Sertes, ȝe me neuir wyn ne maye   1380
Bot if it were þat ilke daye,
That ȝe hafe tane to fyghte;
That ȝe wolde send vp by þe flode
Men þat bene styffe and gude,
And a schippe þat wele were dyghte.   1385
And ywhills þe folke weren at þaire dede,
That thay me myghte awaye lede
Into ȝoure ceté full ryghte.

1375 lyfe] *preceded by deleted* lyue

f. 107rb

'My fadur hath a noble stede,
In the worlde ys noon so gode at nede
In turnament ne yn fyght;
Yn hys hedd he hath an horne,   1420
Schapon as an vnycorne,
That selkowth ys be syght.
Syr, yf þat ye hym myght wynne,
There were no man yn hethyn kynne
That hym wythstonde myght.'   1425
Florent kyste that feyre maye
And seyde: 'Lady, haue gode day,
Holde that ye haue hyght!'

f. 100ᵛᵃ   Florent ynto the sadull nome
And ouyr the reuer soon he come,   1430
To Parys he toke the way.
He ne stynt ne he ne blanne
To Clementys hows tyll þat he came,
Hys auenturs to say.
He tolde hym of the noble stede   1435
That gode was at euery nede,
And of that feyre maye.
'Sone,' seyde Clement, 'be doghty of dede,
And certys þou schalt haue þat stede
To-morne, yf that y may.'   1440

On the morne, when hyt was daylyȝt,
Clement can hymselfe dyght
As an onfrely feere;
He dud hym ynto þe hethen ooste
There þe prees was althermoost,   1445
A Sarsyn as thogh he were.
To the pauylown he can hym wynne
There þe sowdon hymselfe lay ynne,
And breuely can he bere;
Full well he cowde þer speche speke,   1450
And askyd þem some of ther mete;
The sowdon can hym here.

'My fadir has a nobille stede,
In þe werlde es none so gude at nede   1390
In tornament no in fyghte;
In his heuede he hase an horne,
Es schapen als an vnycorne,
That selcouthe es of syghte.
Sir, if þou myghte þat stede now wyn,   1395
There were no man in heythen kynn
Agayne the that stande myghte.'
Florent kyssede þat faire maye
And sayd: 'Lady, hafe gud daye,
And holde þat þou hase highte!'   1400

Florent hase his stede nomen
And ouir þat watir es he comen,
To Paresche he tuke the waye.
He wolde neythir stynte ne blyn
Bot home to Clement gan he wyn,   1405
His awntirs for to saye;
And tolde hym of þat gude stede
That nobille was in ilke a nede,
And of that faire maye.
And he said: 'Sone, be doghety man of dede,   1410
And certes þou sall hafe þat stede
Tomorowe, gyff þat I maye.'

One þe morne, when þe day was lyghte,
Clement gan hymseluen dyghte
Lyke an vnfrely fere;   1415
And went into þe heythen oste
Thore þe presse was alþirmoste,
A Sarazene als he were.
And to þe paveleone he gan wynn
There þe sowdan hymselfe was jn,   1420
Full brymly he gan bere;
And askede þam sum of þaire mete—
Full wele he couthe þaire speche speke—
The sowdane hymselfe gan here.

f. 107va (margin)

1419 þe] *interlined, caret after* to   1424 selfe] *interlined, caret after* hym

Grete dole þe sowdon of hym þoght,
And soon he was before hym broght,
And wyth hym can he speke.   1455
He seyde he was a Sarsyn stronge
That yn hys oost had be longe,
And had defawte of mete.
'Lorde, þer ys noon hethyn lede
That so well cowde kepe a ryche stede,   1460
Or othur horsys full grete.'

f. 100vb   The sowdon seyde þat ylke tyde:
'Yf þou can a stede well ryde,
Wyth me thou schalt be lete.'

They horsyd Clement on a stede,   1465
He sprang owt as sperkull on gle[de]
Into a feyre fylde.
All that stodyn on ylke syde
Had yoye to see hym ryde,
Before the sowdon they tolde.   1470
When he had redyn coursys three,
That all had yoye þat can hym see,
The sowdon hym behelde.
Downe he lyght full soon
And on a bettur was he done;   1475
Full feyre he can hym welde.

Grete yoye þe sowdon of hym þoȝt,
And bad hys feyre stede forþe be broȝt,
And Clement shall hym ryde.
When Clement was on þat stede   1480
He rode away a full gode spede:
No lenger wolde he byde.
When he was redy forþe to foun[de]:
'Beleue þere,' he seyde, 'ye heþen hou[nde],
For ye haue lorne yowre pryd[e]!'   1485
Clement toke the ryght way
Into Parys as hyt lay:
Full blyþe was he that tyde.

1466 glede] *final letters lost in binding*   1478 broȝt] *at end of next line,*
marked for insertion   1481 a] *interlined, caret after away*   1483-5 *final*
letters of these lines cannot be read

Grete dole þe sowdane of hym thoghte,   1425
And sone he was byfore hym broghte,
And with hym gan he speke.
He saide he was a Sarazene stronge
And jn his oste hade bene full longe,
And hade grete fawte of mete.   1430
'Sir, þere es no man in heythen thede
That bettir kane ryde and kepe a stede,
Or oþir horsses grete.'
The sowdane saide þat ilke tyde:
'If þat þou wele a stede kan ryde,   1435
With me þou sall be lette.'

Thay horsede Clement one a stede,
f. 107vb   He spronge als any sparke one glede
Appone a full faire felde.
Alle þat stode on ilk a syde   1440
Hade joye to se Clement ryde
Byfore the sowdans telde.
And when he hade reden courses thre
Alle had joye þat hym gan see,
The sowdan hym byhelde.   1445
Clement lyghtede down full sone
And one a bettir horse was done;
Full faire he gan hym welde.

Grete joye þe sowdan of hym thoghte,
And badde his owen stede solde be broghte,   1450
And Clement one hym solde ryde.
And when Clement was on þat stede
He rode awaye wele gud spede:
No lengare he wold habyde.
And when he was redy for to fownde: 1455
'Farewele,' he said, 'heythen honde,
For þou hase loste thi pryde!'
Clement tuke hym þe heghe waye
Vnto Paresche als it laye:
Full blythe he was þat tydee.   1460

'Florent, sone, where art thou?
That y þe hyght y haue hyt n[ow];   1490
I haue broght thy stede.'
Florent blythe was that day
And seyde: 'Fadur, yf y leue may,
I wyll the quyte thy mede;

But to the emperour of Rome   1495
Therwyth y wyll hym present sone;
To þe pales ye schall hym lede.
For euyr me thynkyth yn my mode
That y am of hys own blode,
Yf hyt so pouerly myght sprede.'   1500

To the pales the stede was ladde,
And all þe kyngys were full gladd
Theron for to see.
The emperour before hym stode,
Rauyschyd herte and blode,   1505
So wondur feyre was he.
Then spekyth þe chylde of honour
To hys lorde the emperour:
'Syr, thys stede geue y the.'
All that abowte þe chylde stode   1510
Seyde he was of gentull blode:
Hyt myght noon odur be.

Aftur thys the day was nomyn
That þe batell on schulde comyn,
Agenste the Sarsyns to fyght.   1515
Wyth trumpys and wyth moche pryde,
Boldely owt of þe borogh þey ryde,
As men moche of myght.
Florent thoght on the feyre maye,
To batell wente he not that day,   1520
A schyppe he hath hym dyght;
Fro Mountmertrons þere þe lady lay
To Parys he broght hur away,
Ne wyste hyt kynge ne knyght.

1490 now] *final letters lost in binding*

'Florent,' he said, 'whore art þou?
That I þe highte I hafe here now;
I hafe þe broghte þe stede.'
Florent was full blythe þat daye
And saide: 'Fadir, if þat I maye,   1465
I salle þe ȝelde thi mede;
Bot to þe emperoure of Rome
The stede I wolde were present sone;
To þe palesse ȝe hym lede.
For euir me thynke in my mode   1470
That I ame comen of his blode,
So prodly if I moghte spede.'

Than to þe palays þe stede was ledde;
The knyghttes were þan alle full glade
One hym for to see.   1475
The emperour byfore þam stode,
And resceyuede hym with mylde mode,
So wondir faire was hee.

f. 108ra   Florent spake with grete
To his lorde þe emperour: 1480
'Sir, this stede gyffe I t   '
Alle þat euir abowte h
Sayde he was comen
It moghte neuir oþir w

Aftir this þe day   1485
That þe batelle
Agayne þe Sa
With trompes and with n
Boldely owte of bor
Als men of mekill   1490
Florent thoghte
To þe batelle w
A schipe sone ga
Fro Mont Marty
To Paresche he   1495
Wist noþir kyng

1479-1560 *Much of f. 108 is missing; many lines are lost, others are defective*
1485 *Large A rubricated, three lines deep*

That whyle was moche sorowe yn fyȝt,   1525
When þe batell began to smyght
Wyth many a grymme gare;

Fro morne þat hyt was daylyght
Tyll hyt was euyn derke nyght,
Wyth woundys wondur sore.   1530
Forwhy þat Florent was not þere
The hethyn men þe bettur were,
The batell venquyscht þey þore;
Or Florent to þe felde was comyn,
Emperour and kynge were ynomyn   1535
And all that Crysten were.

Florent was of herte so gode
He rode þorow þem, he was wode,
As wyght as he wolde wede.
Ther was no Sarsyn so moche of mayn   1540
That myȝt hym stonde wyth strenkyth agayn,
Tyll they had slayne hys stede.
Of Florent there was dele ynow,
How þey hys hors vndur hym slowe,
And he to grounde yede.   1545
Florent was take yn that fyght;
Bothe emperour, kynge and knyght,
Woundyd they can them lede.

The Sarsyns buskyd them wyth pryde
Into ther own londys to ryde;   1550
They wolde no lenger dwelle.
Takyn they had syr Florawns,
The emperour and þe kyng of Fraunce,
Wyth woundys wondur fele;
Othur Crystyn kyngys moo,   1555
Dewkys, erlys and barons also,
That arste were bolde and swelle;
And ladd them wyth yron stronge,

Hur fete vndur þe hors wombe:
Grete dele hyt ys to telle.   1560

Wyde þe worde sprange of þys chawnce,

That while w
When þe bate
With many a gry
Fro morowe þa   1500
To it euen and my
With wondes wo
And for þat Flore
The heythen folke
The batelle þay ve   1505
Or Florent was to þ
The emperoure and the kyng
And þe Cristen kynges all þat þ

Than Florent smote with herte
And rode thurgh þam als he wer   1510
Of witt als he wolde wede.
Thore was no Sarazene of myghte ne
þat myght with strenghe stande hym agayne,
Whills þat he hade his stede.
Than was of Florent dole ynoghe,   1515
How þay his stede vndir hym sloghe,
And he to þe gronde þan ȝode.
Sir Florent was taken in þat fyghte;
Bothe þe emperoure, kynge and knyghte
Bownden þay gan thaym lede.   1520

[31 (?) lines missing]

How the sowdon was yn Fraunce
To warre agenste the ryght.
In Jerusalem men can hyt here,
How þe emperour of Rome was there   1565
Wyth many an hardy knyght.
Than spekyth Octauyon þe ȝyng
Full feyre to hys lorde the kyng,
As chylde of moche myght:
'Lorde, yf hyt were yowre wylle,   1570
I wolde wynde my fadur tylle
And helpe hym yn that fyght.'

Than spekyth þe kyng of moche myȝt
Full fayre vnto that yong knyght;
Sore hys herte can blede: 1575
'Sone, þou schalt take my knyghtys fele,
Of my londe that thou wylle wele,
That styffe are on stede,
Into Fraunce wyth the to ryde,
Wyth hors and armys be thy syde,   1580
To helpe the at nede.
When þou some doghtynes haste done
Then may þou shewe þyn errande soone;
The bettur may thou spede.'

He bad hys modur make hur yare   1585
Into Fraunce wyth hym to fare:
He wolde no lenger byde.
Wyth hur she ladd the lyenas
That sche broȝt owt of wyldurnes
Rennyng be hur syde.   1590
f. 101ᵛᵇ There men myght see many a kny[ght],
Wyth helmys and wyth hawberkys bryght,
Forthe ynto the strete.
Forthe they went on a day,
The heþyn ooste on the way   1595
All they can them meete.

1591 knyght] *final letters cannot be read*

f. 108rb   ⟨W⟩
          To
          Wh
          Thy
          The   1525

[41 (?) lines missing]

1521-5 *These fragments at the end of f. 108rb*

By the baners that þey bare
They knewe þat þey hethyn ware,
And stylle they can abyde;
They dyȝt þem wyth bren[ye]s bryght　　　1600
And made þem redy for to fyȝt,
Ageyn þem can they ryde.
They hewe þe flesche fro þe bone:
Soche metyng was neuyr none,
Wyth sorow on ylke syde.　　　1605
Octauyon þe yong knyght,
Thorow þe grace of God almyght,
Full faste he fellyd ther pryde.

The lyenas þat was so wyght,
When she sawe þe yong knyght　　　1610
Into the batell fownde,
Sche folowed hym wyth all hur myȝt
And faste fellyd þe folke yn fyȝt:
Many sche made onsownde;
Grete stedys downe sche drowe　　　1615
And many heþen men she slowe,
Wythynne a lytull stownde.
Thorow God þat ys of myȝtys gode,
The Crysten men þe bettur stode;
The hethyn were broȝt to grownde.　　　1620

The Crysten prysoners were full fayne
When þe Sarsyns were yslayne,
f. 102ra And cryed: 'Lorde, thyn ore!'
He ne stynt ne he ne blanne
To þe prysoners tyll þat he wanne,　　　1625
To wete what they were.
The emperour, wythowt lees,
That hys own fadur was,
Bowndon fownde he there;
The kyng of Fraunce and odur moo,　　　1630
Dewkys, erlys and barons also,
Were woundyd wondur sore.

1600 brenyes] brem*us*

f. 108vb

at þay ware.
wtten lese,
r was,
he þore;
nce and oþir mo,   1530
arons also,
en full sore.

1526 *Surviving fragment of f. 108va has a final -e, 4–5 lines before 1526*

Hys fadur was the furste man
That he of bondys to lowse began,
Ye wete, wythowten lees;   1635
And he lowsyd hys brodur Floraunce
Or he dud the kynge of Fraunce,
Ʒyt he wyste not what he was.
Be þat hys men were to hym comyn,
Soon they were fro yrons nomyn,   1640
The pryncys prowde yn prees.
Whan he had done þat noble dede,
The bettur he oght for to spede,
To make hys modur pees.

A ryche cyté was besyde,   1645
Boldely thedur can they ryde
To a castell swythe;
Ryche metys were there ydyght,
Kyngys, dewkys, erlys and knyght,
All were gladd and blythe.   1650
Syth came Octauyon þe yong wyth honour
And knelyd before the emperour,
Hys errande for to kythe;
That ylke tale that he tolde,
Ryche and pore, yong and olde,   1655
Glad they were to lythe.

f. 102rb

He seyde: 'Lorde, yn all þys londe y haue þe soght,
My modur haue y wyth me broght:
I come to make hur pees;
For a lesyng þat was stronge,   1660
Sche was exylyd owt of yowre londe:
I proue that hyt was lees.'
The emperour was neuyr so blythe,
He kyssyd that yong knyght swythe
And for hys sone hym chees.   1665
For yoye that he hys wyfe can see,
Sevyn sythys swownyd he
Before the hye deyse.

firste man
⟨l⟩ousede þan,
n lese;   1535
s broþir Florence
ng of Fraunce,
⟨h⟩ate he was.
⟨a⟩s to hym comen,
s nomen,   1540
in prese.
ne þat nobill dede,
r to spede,
esee.

besyde,   1545
y ryde
swythe;
þore dyghte,
and knyghte,
and blythe.   1550
with grete honoure
e the emperoure,
e he kythe;
þat he þore tolde,
wre, ȝong and olde,   1555
ade þay were to lythe.

in this lande I hafe þe soghte,
modir I hafe with me broghte:
ome to make hir pese.'
The emperoure was neuir so blythe,   1560
Als for to kysse þe childe full swythe
And for his sone hym chese.
'Lorde, for a lessynge þat was stronge
Scho was flemede owt of londe:
I proue þat it was lese!'   1565
For joye þat he his wiefe gan se,
Seuen sythes swonede he
Byfore the heghe dese.

f. 109ra

1563 lessynge] lesesynge

Feyre Florent was full blythe
Of thes tydyngys for to lythe,   1670
And hys modur to see.
Than spekyth þe lady of honowre
To hur lorde the emperour,
Wordys of grete pyté:
'Lorde, yn all þe sorow þat me was wroght,   1675
Thyn own sone haue y wyth me broght
And kepyd hym wyth me.
Thyn odur sone yn a foreste
Was takyn wyth a wylde beste,
That was ferly feyre and fre.   1680
I wot hyt ys Godys grace,
I knowe hym be hys face:
Hyt ys þat yong knyght by the.'

There was moche yoye and game
Wyth clyppyng and wyth kyssyng same;   1685
Into a chaumbur they yode.

f. 102va   Grete yoye þere was also,
The metyng of the brethurn two,
That doghty were yn dede.
A ryche feste þe emperour made þere   1690
Of kyngys þat were farre and nere,
Of many londys thede;
The tale whoso redyth ryght,
The feste lastyd a fourtenyght,
In jeste as we rede.   1695

Marsabelle that feyre maye
Was aftur sente, the sothe to say,
Fro Parys there sche was.
Crystenyd sche was on a Sonday,
Wyth yoye and myrthe and moche play;   1700
Florent to wyfe hur chees.
Soche a brydale þer was there
A ryaller þer was neuyr noon here,
Ye wot wythowten lees.
Florent hymselfe can hur wedd   1705
And ynto Rome sche was ledd,
Wyth pryncys prowde yn prees.

Faire Florent þan was full blythe
Of þat tydandes for to lythe,   1570
His modir for to see.

'Lorde,' scho said, 'for alle þe noye þat me was
                                    wroghte,
Thyn on childe I hafe the broghte
And ȝemede hym euir with me.
Thyn oþir sone in a foreste   1575
Was taken with a wilde beste,
He was bothe faire and fre.
Alle, I wote, es Goddes grace,
I knowe hym by his faire face
That ȝone ȝong knyghte es he.'   1580

Than was þore full mekill gamen
With halsynge and with kyssyngez samen,
Into þe chambir þay ȝede.
And full grete joye þere was also
At þe metyng of þe brethir two,   1585
þat doghety weren of dede.
A riche feste þe emperour mad thare
Of lordes þat were ferre and nere,
And of many a londes lede;
This tale whoso telles ryghte,   1590
The feste lastede a fourtenyghte,
In romance thus we rede.

Marsabele þat faire maye
Was aftir sent, þe sothe to saye,
To Paresche righte þore scho was.   1595
Cristenede scho was on a Sonondaye,
With joye and gamen and mekill playe;
Florent to wyefe hir chese.
Swylke a brydale als was þore
In that ceté was neuir ore,   1600
Ȝe wiete withowtten lese.
Child Florent þore hir gan wedde
And into Rome was scho ledde,
With prynces prowde in prese.

Than hyt befelle on a day
The emperour began to say,
And tolde þe lordys how hyt was.   1710
The ryche kyngys gaue jugement
The emperours modur schulde be brent
In a tonne of brasse.
As swythe as sche þerof harde telle,
Swownyng yn hur chaumbur she felle,   1715
Hur heere of can sche race.
For schame sche schulde be prouyd false,
Sche schare ato hur own halse
Wyth an analasse.

f. 102ᵛᵇ   Therat all the kyngys loghe,   1720
What wondur was þowe þer were no swoghe?
They toke þer leue þat tyde.
Wyth trumpys and wyth mery songe
Eche oon went to hys own londe,
Wyth yoye and wyth grete pryde.   1725
Wyth game and wyth grete honowre
To Rome went the emperour,
Hys wyfe and hys sonys be hys syde.
Jhesu, lorde, heuyn kynge,
Graunt vs all thy blessyng   1730
And yn heuyn to abyde!

1716 of] *followed by deleted* s   1721 swoghe] *at end of next line, marked*
for insertion

And þen byfelle appon a daye   1605
The emperoure bygan for to saye,
And tolde alle how it was.
And alle þan gafe juggement
f. 109rb   That his modir sulde be brynte
In a belle of brasse.   1610
Als sone als scho þerof herde telle,
In swonynge to þe gronde scho felle,
Hir hare of scho gan rase.
For schame þat scho was proued false,
In two scho cutte hir owen halse   1615
With a longe anelase.

And þerat alle þe kynges loghe,
There was joye and gamen ynowghe;
Alle tuke þaire leue that tyde.
With trowmpes and with lowde songe   1620
Ilke a man wente to his owun londe,
With joye and mekill pryde.
With gamen and joye and grete honoure
To Rome þan wente þe emperoure,
His lady by his syde,   1625
And his two sonnes also,
And with þam many one mo,
Home þan gan thay ryde.

And thus endis Octouean,
That in his tym was a doghety man,   1630
With þe grace of Mary free.
Now Jhesu, lorde, of heuen kynge,
Thou gyffe vs alle thi dere blyssynge!
Amen, Amen, par charyte, Amen.   1634

NOTES

1 The form *ȝynge* is confirmed by rhyme, and is required also by rhyme in C1567 (where L is defective) and at 734 (where C is defective). In OE, *ging* was Northumbrian, though the comparative *gingra* occurs in the *Vespasian Psalter* (see Campbell, §176). It cannot be taken here as a distinctive northern form, since it is confirmed by rhyme in romances from other areas (cf. *Lybeaus Desconus* 94, 441, SO 897, 1293, 1804). On its use in non-northern works, see Dibelius, *Anglia*, xxiii (1901), 193.

10 L and H refer here to the *bukes of Rome* as a source; such references occur elsewhere (cf. *Eglamour* 408) and may reflect a popular etymology of *romance*. Here, however, a specific reference to a supposed source may be intended, since Rome is the capital city of the titular hero, Octouyane.

15 Variants of this conventional reference to a source occur also at 282, 353, 631, 896, 1039, 1592. Elsewhere C usually refers to a *jeste* rather than a *romance* as source.

22 *Octouyane*: L, like SO and the title of the lost *Gesta octouiani*, uses the form with *-o-* (< L *octo*) in the second syllable, which is usual in ME. Cf. *Book of the Duchess* 368, *Eglamour* (L) 770, *Speculum Vitae* 40, etc. *Octauyan* and *Octouyane* occur as variants in *Richard Coer de Lion* 6731. C and H have forms with *-a-* (< L *octāvus*), and FO uses *Otheuien(s)*.

27 On the untypical pr. pl. form *sayne* here in C and L (cf. the otiose use in H416), see p. 35 above.

28 L's reading *samen* is probably archetypal, and has been replaced ·in C and H as part of their modernization of forms. L uses the word again in the common ME rhyme sequence *same(n)* : *game(n)* at 196 (with which H181 agrees), and at 1582 (in agreement with C).

31-36 NO preserves the barren marriage motif common to FO and F&O; it occurs also in *Sir Gowther* 46-51. SO 31-46 has replaced it with a different motif, the exhortation to marriage which is used in Chaucer's *Clerk's Tale* and in *Lai le Freine*. See p. 44 above, and note to SO 31-60.

45 L, C, and H all have different readings here, which suggests some difficulty in the archetype. C is closest to what must have been the original reading: *yeme and ryght* 'rule and govern' (cf. *Ywain* 1185: *My landes for to lede and ȝeme*). *ȝeme* in the sense 'rule, govern' is uncommon, and chiefly northern or North Midland. In the sense 'keep, look after' it occurs also in L625 and L1574, where C has *kepe*. Here, however, C, which has occasional difficulties with *m, ni, n* spellings (cf. note on C934) has either perpetuated or introduced the misreading *yeue*, which, though awkward, is intelligible here.

66 L may well preserve the original reading here; *fay* 'doomed to die' was used rather infrequently in ME, and survives longest in Scottish use. *Fownde* in the sense 'depart in death' is rare in ME. Both may have been eliminated in *CH, since C and H have similar lines, though C's version is long and unwieldy.

74-84 NO introduces the building of an abbey to win the intercession of the Virgin Mary with her son. The building of abbeys for various purposes (in memory of the dead, as a penance, to earn grace for the donor) occurs in other romances; cf. *Amis and Amiloun* 2497 ff., *Sir Gowther* 691 ff., *Guy of Warwick* st. 298, etc. On this as part of the reworking of the first part of the romance for didactic purposes, see pp. 63-4.

98 C and H86 agree on the emperor going to his chapel rather than to his *chambir* as in L. This conflicts with C121 where we are told once again, this time in agreement with L, that the emperor went to his chapel and heard mass. L's version makes better sense and is probably archetypal. *CH seems to have been confused by (i) the usual sense of *chambir*, 'bedroom', and the apparent contradiction between the emperor rising and then going to his *chambir*, and (ii) the reference to the priest and mass. On the strength of this *CH has replaced *chambir* 'counsel chamber, reception room' (cf. 211) by the apparently more appropriate *chapell*.

107 The pp. forms *ayerde* (L) and *heyred* (C) are those of the verb *heiren* 'inherit', for which *MED* has only two citations (from Mannyng and *Medulla*).

112-17 The mother-in-law's accusation here resembles that in F&O rather than FO. She suggests both here and in F&O (in this case during the pregnancy) that since the emperor has been unable to beget children, his wife has taken a lover (see further p. 46 above). In both FO and SO the birth of twins becomes the grounds for the accusation of infidelity. See SO 115-32 and note.

C118-19 The rhyme is probably on *ă*, with shortening of long *ā* in *noon*. Strandberg, §122, records similar rhymes in *Cursor Mundi*.

124 ff. The introduction of the pretended lover in the Octavian story is derived from the Crescentia cycle. Cf. its use in *The Earl of Tolous* 709 ff., and see p. 57 above.

133-5 L has here three lines, absent in C and H, which are puzzling. They upset the tail-rhyme sequence and produce a 15-line stanza, and hence seem likely to be a later interpolation; on the other hand they parallel FO 195-8:

> 'Amis,' dist ele, 'or m'entendes,
> Se uos faites mes uolentes,
> Ie uos donroi cent mars d'argent
> Le matin au comencement.'

In FO, however, the lines occur earlier, at the beginning of the mother-in-law's interview with the *garcon*, before they come to the lady's chamber, and L, like C and H, has already reported this bribe in indirect speech at the appropriate spot (124-5). L thus seems to preserve authentic source material twice here, but the passage which corresponds rather more closely to FO occurs in the wrong position, and is not integrated into the verse structure. Is this in fact authentic source material, and if so, from where has L derived it, or is the agreement with FO more apparent than real? Both treatments in L employ the same rhyme on *knaue* : *hafe*, and it is possible that the closer agreement in 133-5 is coincidental, and results from reworking 124-5 in order to make it clear at this point that the mother-in-law is speaking to the youth.

There are several other curious features about the episode in which these lines occur. The *knaue* : *hafe* rhyme is also used in direct speech in the correctly placed corresponding passage in SO 157-8, and is one of a number of striking structural and verbal parallels between SO and NO in this episode. These include the description of the boy as a *kokes knaue*, NO 116, SO 122, 157, the decapitation of the boy, NO 175-8, SO 206-10, and several verbal and rhyme parallels. NO and SO here share some details, missing in FO, which in combination with the links in wording, show that either one of the extant English versions must have drawn on a representative of the other, or that both have derived material from another ME version of the story. Most of the parallels between NO and SO, which occur sporadically throughout, suggest that SO borrowed from NO, and there is no clear evidence for the existence of a third version; if such a version did exist, it could have been the source from which L derived 133-5 in the course of transmission, but I think it more likely that the lines are the handiwork of a zealous transmitter of L, anxious to clear up possible ambiguity. It is noteworthy that within these 'extra' lines, L uses in 135 the alien form *schall*, which otherwise occurs only once in L, beside regular *sall(e)*. This suggests that the lines are not integral, and have been added in the course of transmission.

138 vnclede: The use of this pp. and of the verb *vnclead* is rare in ME. *OED* records it in only four texts (all northern) for the period.

142 Compare *Cursor Mundi* 2293: 'Quat for luue and quat for doute'. C and H127 have an inferior reading and repeat a rhyme word used earlier in the stanza. The authenticity of L is confirmed by the stylistically parallel linking of two nouns in FO's account (218-19):

> Gran duel et sorsie demenant,
> Il se desueste et si se couche.

160 slepee: This could be an error for *sleepe*, but the forms *blyee* 50, *moree* 1221, *waree* 1318, *tydee* 1460, and [*p*]*esee* 1544 show that such forms are an occasional feature of Thornton's spelling practice. Since they occur always in line-final position, they should perhaps be associated with the occasional doubling of final *-o* in monosyllables in the same position (see p. 19) though C does not share any of the forms cited here. *Sir Gawain and the Green Knight* has similar forms occasionally: *madee* 1565 (within the line), and *eldee* 844, *trwee* 1274 (line-final position).

160-71 Prophetic dreams as omens of evil occur in various romances; the empress's dream here anticipates her exile into the forest and the animal theft of both children. In FO 251–4 and SO 196–200 it takes a slightly different form; an eagle carries off the children, and the theft is accompanied by the savaging of her body. In *The Earl of Tolous* 808 ff., before the virtuous wife is accused of adultery, the emperor dreams that she is attacked by two wild bears, and hastens home.

164 thyknes: For the rare sense of 'dense growth' cf. *OED thicknesse* 5, especially the Lydgate and *Promptorium Parvulorum* quotations.

175–83 L, C, and H agree with SO in their account of the emperor cutting off the boy's head, and tossing it at the empress (L, SO) or into the bed (C, H). This does not occur in FO, where the emperor, at the beginning of the scene, refuses to kill the apparently guilty pair as they sleep (FO 245–6), and, at the end of it, first has his wife taken off to prison, then beheads the boy, and has the body removed (FO 274–81). The agreements between NO and SO include some details of wording and rhyme, and are evidence of a special link between the English versions. On this see SO pp. 33–38.

The introduction of this detail has caused confusion and inconsistencies in the LCH texts, as they made efforts to accommodate material not fully integrated in their archetype. It would be hard to say which offers the most plausible version of the bizarre and improbable scene in which the empress sleeps while her husband kills the pretended lover he has found in her bed.

L and C agree against H142 ff. in having the emperor kill the boy as soon as he sees him (157 ff.). Meanwhile the lady, fast asleep, has a fearful dream from which she awakens in distress (C169) or, in the L and H version, begins to awaken. The emperor decapitates the youth he has already killed (C174), or, as H162 has it, kills him by beheading, and finally throws the head (LCH). In L, the head was presumably cut off in the initial act of violence, since the emperor merely picks it up at this point (175–7). C concludes with a three-line unit which is senseless in its immediate context; H has tried to improve on this, but L has a better reading.

H offers what is probably the least incredible version. It is possible that it has preserved best the sequence of *LCH, but I suspect that it shows later rationalizations of the inconsistencies introduced into *LCH when the scene was 'improved' by adding these details. The episode is interesting because it demonstrates a taste for sensational detail, and shows the perseverance with which the scribes hung on to the detail, despite their inability to assimilate it successfully.

184–6 It is remarkable that in NO, unlike other versions of the Octavian story, no action is taken against the empress until some time after the dramatic episode with the pretended lover. In FO 276, SO 218 the empress is thrown into prison at once, but NO abandons verisimilitude in order to introduce an episode, absent in the other versions, in which the emperor traps the King of Calabre (a new character) into condemning his own daughter to be burned.

The odd delay here probably results from the transfer of an earlier and reasonable delay in the source. When the wicked mother-in-law first accuses the empress to her son (FO 147-54), the emperor says he will hear no more about it until the empress recovers; if at this time his mother shows him the guilty pair in the act, he will take vengeance. From this the NO version has probably derived 184 (cf. FO 155: '*Dame,*' *dist il, 'n'en parles plus*') and the reference to church-going in 185, since in FO 167-72 the emperor helps set the trap by telling his wife that he is going to church to thank God for her recovery.

In the NO reworking the emperor decides to expose his wife's guilt at a feast celebrating the churching of the new mother. The practice of churching, or blessing, women after childbirth was common in the middle ages. It probably originated as a purification rite, derived from Mosaic law (Lev. 12: 6), but became simply a rite of blessing the new mother; the prayer-book of the Church of England preserves an ancient form of the ceremony, and the practice is still observed by the Catholic Church in some places.

196 duellyn: This is an untypical pr. pl. form for L and probably reflects the occasional occurrence of such forms in *LCH (see p. 35). C and H181 have pa.t. forms; C uses the historical present less frequently than L, and H uses it not at all.

214-19 The direct speech in L is probably archetypal, despite C. H199 ff. shifts from direct to indirect speech after the first three lines, and the rhyme-couplet 217-18, H202-3 differs in all three texts. The change probably reflects the elimination of *ouertaken* in *CH, since its use in the sense required here is rare and northern (see *OED, s.v. over-take* 3).

217 treson: Adultery involving the wife of the feudal lord or of the king was regarded as treasonable from the reign of Edward I at the latest, though it was first formally defined in law in the treason statute of Edward III (1352). The woman's consent to the adultery made her equally guilty. See O. Kratins, 'Treason in the Middle English Romances', *PQ*, xlv (1966), 668-87.

223-79 The judgement and execution scene here shows several parallels to the same scene in *Le Bone Florence of Rome*, and suggests that in his expanded and edifying account of the lady's conduct, the NO author may have been influenced by it, or some similar treatment of a Crescentia heroine. Compare first the call for the fire in NO 223-4 with *Bone Florence* 1663-4:

> He seyde, 'Syr, Y schall set a stake
> Wythowte þe towne a fyre to make'.

Compare also the pious prayer of both women (though Florence has no children), NO 256-67, *Bone Florence* 1675-80, and compare the wording with which mercy is granted in NO 275-6 with *Bone Florence* 1688-9:

> He seyde, 'Florence, also mote Y the,
> I may not on thy dethe see,
> For all the worlde to wynne.'

223-8 On burning as a punishment for treason (in this case adultery) see Kratins, op. cit., 686.

244–55 L, C, and H229–40 exhibit a typical network of partial correspondences here (cf. pp. 14 ff.). The sequence of three-line units in
C and H agree against L, but the verbal correspondences cut across this
division. I believe that C and H preserve the archetypal stanza better
than L, which occasionally alters the sequence of lines and three-line
units (cf. p. 16).

257 L and H242 preserve the original rhyme on *sette : grette*, replaced in C. See also the note on 313–17.

C269 The verb *tryllyd* 'rolled' is rare in ME. *OED* records the sense
required here only in *Erkenwald* and Chaucer.

281 L and H266 preserve here an alliterative phrase: *riche (rede)
and rownde*; C omits the first adjective, and has a short line.

288 L preserves the original reading *thede*, which was apparently
avoided in *CH. The word occurs three times in rhyme in L; at 1431
C has probably replaced it by *lede* (C1459), but lets it stand at 618
(where H602, however, replaces it with *londe*, and interrupts the rhyme
sequence). Here both C and H272 have introduced lines different from
each other and from L. H265 ff. has further serious troubles in this
stanza, having lost one tail-line, and expanded one couplet into a triplet.

293 bysett: Thornton has added *bestes* above the line, and *bysett*
may be an instance of miscopying, which he failed to delete when he
corrected the line. However, since the word occurs elsewhere (313,
871), and since L has many long lines, I preserve the MS reading here.

C291 In his note Sarrazin suggests that *streyght* represents OF
estreit, and that it replaces an earlier *tyght*. This is theoretically possible, since, though there is no evidence for the loss of the fricative in
the language of the archetype, C resolves a textual problem at C1525–6
by introducing the rhyme *fyȝt : smyght* 'smite'. See further the note on
1305. However, neither L nor H279 offers any support for the *tyght*
suggestion, and *streyght* 'straight' < *streccan*, in the sense 'extended,
broad' makes satisfactory sense as it is. C's reading may be a compro-
mise of some sort, for the different readings in L, C, and H suggest
some difficulty in the archetype.

307 ferly: In late use this word is chiefly northern. C here reads
veryly, and H292 *full*, but at 1337 L and C share the form.

C307–8 hylle : welle: H295–6 has the same rhyme. Here, as at
C373–4, C439–40, C508–9, C has an *i : e* rhyme which does not occur
in L, but which may be archetypal. On *i : e* rhymes see p. 34. For *welle*
L reads *schille*, which *MED* treats as its only example of *chele* adj. in
the sense 'cold'. This must be wrong; the word is ME *shill* 'resonant,
shrill, loud', generally used of voices or wind, but used here in a rather
strained sense of 'purling, gurgling' to give a correct rhyme. Thornton
uses the adverb *schill* in *Sir Eglamour* 300, and adjective and adverb
occur elsewhere in rhyme (cf. *Lybeaus Desconus* 781, SO 535, 563).

313–30 The repetitions here—three references to the lady sitting,
two references to her weeping, two references to the spring—are a
consequence of the introduction into *LCH of the lady's second prayer
(319–27), on which see pp. 62–4. Invention flagging, the redactor has

thriftily reused the local material that came to hand, and has, moreover, drawn on the lady's first prayer, 256-67.

313-17 The archetype probably repeated the *sette : grette* rhyme here. C and H both show reluctance to use *grette* 'wept', but they do not always remove it at the same point. Thus, in this passage C retains it at C314 but removes it and uses an inexact rhyme at C310-11, as it has earlier at C253-4. H removes it on both occasions here, but retains it earlier in H241-2.

318 L avoids here the infinitive in *-n*, though such infinitives are occasionally confirmed by rhyme in both texts. See p. 35.

319-20 C and H304-5 here repeat a rhyme which they and L already used in the first prayer at 259-60.

333 L has expanded this line excessively, but in view of its agreement with H318 the verbs *synge* and *ȝelle* are probably original.

334 Compare SO 447: *A gryyp com fle to take hys pray.*

342 L and C here present a corrupted form of the phrase *wede(n) of wit*; cf. *Cursor Mundi* 13975: *of witt to wede*, and the same idiom at L1511: *Of witt als he wolde wede*, beside C 1539: *As wyght as he wolde wede*. It seems that by anticipation of the rest of the line *witt* was replaced by *wode* in a common antecedent of C and L (and hence also of H, which has a quite different reading here). L has otherwise preserved the construction, apparently understanding *wode* as 'wood'; the MS shows that Thornton first wrote *wende* for *wede*. C, probably misreading the *f* of *of* as long *s*, has taken *wode* as an adjective 'mad'. Compare the *As wyght as* in C1539 for the same kind of reshaping, and for C's *os* 'as' see C41. On *f : s* confusion in C, see note to 1305.

344-5 Compare SO 313-14:

> And þoȝte hym bere as fast as hy may
> To þe stede þer hyr whelpys lay.

Both parallel FO 560-1:

> Lors pense qu'il l'en portera
> A ses lioneaus por mengier.

But while SO is closer in wording to FO, it has misapplied the material to the kidnapping by the ape, while NO correctly uses it with reference to the lioness. See SO, note to 310-15.

349-51 Compare SO 481-2:

> A chylde þat ys of kynges blood
> A lyoun ne struyd hyt for no good (etc.)

FO does not contain this motif, so the English versions have derived it from some other source. The tradition that lions will not injure those of royal blood occurs also in *Bevis*, where Josian is spared by two lions because she is a king's daughter, a queen, and a virgin. The wording and rhyme in L link it with the *Bevis* treatment; cf. *Bevis* (Auch.) 2391-4:

> For þe kind of Lyouns, y-wys
> A kynges douȝter, þat maide is . . .
> þe lyouns myȝt do hur no wroth.

SO's treatment is more diffuse and does not share the rhyme parallel.

This suggests that the motif was borrowed from *Bevis* into NO and made its way from there into SO.

In NO the motif occurs only in L, but I think it is likely that it did occur in *LCH, and that the crucial couplet was lost in *CH. C has instead a couplet which makes poor sense in the context, and which occurs again at C382-3, where it fits better, and is paralleled by L; H has only a weak one-line equivalent to the couplet.

The appearance of the motif illustrates well how motifs can drift from one romance into another. Two factors encouraged the drift here. *Bevis* has various links with the Octavian story (**Constance** and **Eustace** elements, twins, Saracen princess, wonderful horse, etc.), and details from it are likely to enter the mind of a redactor or free-spirited scribe dealing with similar material. Secondly, the lioness nursing the royal child is a striking feature of the Octavian story, and is likely to attract other motifs involving lions, such as the lion as protector of the virtuous royal lady, or the grateful lion fighting by the side of its master.

355-7 Compare FO 589-90:

> Qu'il porteroit un cheualier
> Trestuit arme sor son destrier.

358-60 Compare FO 596-601:

> Le lion en porte et l'enfant . . .
> En un ille que fu sor mer . . .
> A terre descent li grifons.

376-7 Compare FO 629-31:

> Vne fosse fist li lions
> As ongles qu'il ot grans et lons,
> L'enfant bonement i a trait.

C373-4 denne : *theryn*: H360-1 has the same rhyme; for *theryn* L has *þen*. Compare C439-40 for the same rhyme and variant in L, and see the note on C307-8.

379-80 Compare SO 467-8:

> And whanne he was anhungred sore,
> Of hym he eet.

411 L's reading makes better sense and is confirmed by H395. The line is misplaced in the manuscript, where it follows 405. The shift to the end of the stanza restores the tail-rhyme stanza pattern and is confirmed by C and H. Cf. 627 and see the note on 1560-5.

C426 strykyng: L and H agree here in using forms of 'run' against C's reading. The sense required here, 'running, flowing', is uncommon in ME, and may have been used most often in the west; of the few examples recorded in *OED*, s.v. *strike* 1. (c), three are from texts belonging to the *Katherine* group.

436-56 There are some striking parallels in wording and rhyme between NO and SO in this account of the empress's recovery of one of her children. These are discussed in SO, p. 31.

C439-40 denne : *therynne*: H426-7 has the same rhyme. Compare C373-4, and see the note on C307-8.

446 clappe: See *MED* s.v. *clappen* 5. for other examples of *clappen*

< OE *clæppan* used for *clippen*, though *MED* does not record for *clappen* the sense 'embrace each other' which is required here. For this sense, see *clippen* v. (1), 1. (a). Trounce (*MÆ*, ii (1933), 56) for some reason regards the *clappe* form in L as evidence of the Philistinism of its scribe, and apparently prefers the *pappe* : *cleppe* sequence of C. H429-30 has *pap* : *clap*.

455-6 Compare FO 713-14:

'He,' fait ele, 'por dieu merci
C'est mes enfes, ie soi de fi.'

474, 475 chippe: See p. 24.

484-5 Compare SO 613-14:

Good wynd & whedyr God hem sente,
Hy drogh vp seylle & forþ þey wente.

496-529 In NO the exiled lady is recognized by the King of Jerusalem and becomes an honoured member of his household. In SO 619-54 she becomes a seamstress in Jerusalem, and later works in the King's household. Both accounts differ from FO, and show similarities to F&O. See pp. 46-7.

C501, H488 The rhyme sequence here requires a form of *nerehonde* with *e* which I have not found elsewhere, though *hende* as a pl. of *hond* occurs, chiefly in northern and East Midland texts.

C508-9 dwelle : wille: For *dwelle* L reads *stille*. See the note on C307-8. H agrees with C on the other *e* : *i* rhymes, but here agrees with L against C and rhymes on *styll* : *wyll* (H495-6).

517-19 The corresponding stanza dealing with the knighting of young Octouian in SO (655-60) uses a similar rhyme-scheme: *ydwelled* : *eld* : *scheld* : *fyȝt* : *beheld* : *knyȝt*.

529 Compare SO 619: 'In Ierusalem sche gan dwelle'.

576 Clement þe Velayne: Clement is introduced by this name in all the English texts at this point (cf. H560, SO 402), though *Climens li uilein* does not occur in FO until 960, when the romance picks up again the story of Florent.

581-2 L and H565-6 agree on the second person pl. pronoun here, where C has wrongly employed the first person, suggesting that Clement plans to sell the child later.

607 fraynede: L's agreement with H591 shows that this word is archetypal.

610-21 In both English versions Clement claims the child as his own, begotten in the Holy Land (NO) or in *Marsyle* (SO 410-18). In FO he makes no admission of parentage, but F&O (P. Paris, p. 305) parallels the English versions, since Clement claims there to have begotten the child on a Saracen woman in the *terre Alexandrine*.

C613-14 The *was : flesche* sequence of C is shared by H, agrees with Clement's statement above (610-11), and is probably archetypal. The rhyme may depend on the dialectal and vulgar development of final [s] to [š].

627 This line is misplaced in the manuscript, where it follows 625 and is the last line of the column. The shift to the end of the stanza restores the tail-rhyme stanza pattern, and is confirmed by C and H. Cf. 411.

636 redis right: This collocation is apparently northern and Scottish; see *OED s.v. read* 16 (d), which records it from Scottish texts and *Awntyrs off Arthure*. The line is a filler, with little meaning; it is a parenthetical guarantee of careful reporting by the narrator. Compare the similar use of *ho so right redes* in *Awntyrs off Arthure* 16, 113, etc.

643-5 In FO 985 ff. Clement's wife suggests that their own son be made a moneychanger, and Florent a butcher. In distinguishing two children, L agrees with FO, while C and H agree in error by ignoring the natural son, and assigning both occupations to Florent. On the other hand, C preserves the *chaungere* paralleled in FO, while L has *chawndelere* 645, and H628 has *chauncelere*. The partial agreement between L and H is puzzling; without it, it would seem that C preserves the archetypal reading, and that the L form originated as a misreading of *chaungere* as *chaundere*, which, by analogy with *chaunderie* forms for *chaundlerie*, was taken as a form of *chaundeler*. MED does not record *chaunder* forms for *chaundeler*, but *chaunderie* is more common than *chaundlerie*, and *chaundere* as a back-formation is possible. The similarity between L and H, however, suggests an already corrupted *LCH reading (? *chaundelere*) which has been corrected in C. But it is hard to see why only one of the two errors in close proximity should have been corrected.

646-57 C's version of these lines is weak, and L's reliability is confirmed by FO, H, and external evidence. L and H agree in Clement's dispatching Florent over the bridge to a *bouchere* (648) to learn the trade, while in C he is sent to the bridge (C644, 649) to be a butcher. C thus presents the bridge as destination rather than route. FO 1015 ff. makes it clear that Clement sends Florent to the *boucherie*, and that on the way there, on Grant Pont (FO 1040), he meets the squire. This agrees with the layout of mediaeval Paris, where Grand Pont connected the Ile de la Cité with the Right Bank, and ended at the Chastelet, near *la boucherie*, the main trading centre and slaughter-house of the butchers of Paris, one of the oldest and best-known of the trade-guilds. L and H's prepositions are therefore correct, while C, perhaps through anticipation of Florent's second venture into trade (see the note on C710-14) is in error. *Bouchere* in all the English texts may reflect a misunderstanding of FO's *boucherie* (1015).

At 651, however, C and H634 agree on a weaker line against L's *To vse swylke mystere*. L's line probably perpetuates a misunderstanding of the French source; cf. FO 1016 *le mestre* 'the master (butcher)'.

664 On the lacuna in L following this line see p. 11.

C696 soche anodur: 'another of the same sort'. *OED s.v. another* 1. c records this for ME only in *Cursor Mundi* 1942, and *s.v. such* 26. in the *Satire on the People of Kildare* st. 4.

C704 sonys: H690 has the singular form which is correct, so this corruption must have been introduced in *C or C.

C710-14 In this case the bridge, i.e. Grand Pont, is the right destination, since Clement's other son is to become a money-changer, and Grand Pont, a fortified bridge, was occupied chiefly by money-changers. It was in fact officially renamed Pont au Change in the mid-twelfth century.

C720 molettys: A rare word; see the *MED* treatment, *s.v. molet(te.* L is defective here, but H706 uses another rare word, *molens*, on which see *MED, s.v. molaine*, and *Sir Gawain and the Green Knight*, 2nd edn., rev. Davis, note on 169. The use of the word *molet* in heraldry of a rowel-shaped figure, coupled with the plural form, and the adjective *gylte*, all suggest that the word here (and *molens* in H) refer to ornamental studs or bosses connecting the bit to the rest of the bridle, rather than to the bit itself, as some of the Scottish evidence suggests. Cf. *DOST, s.v. mol(l)et(t).*

C754-6 These words (paralleled in FO 1233-8 and SO 843-52) served to remind the audience or reader that Florent's apparently irresponsible conduct is the natural outcome of his noble birth.

C778 Compare SO 919-20: *þe sowdan . . . Wyth hym he broȝt a fowll geaunt.*

C787-92 In FO the sultan's daughter, having set up camp at Montmartre, sends an emissary to request safe conduct and protection from the king of France during her stay. Montmartre, at that time some three or four miles from the northern boundary of Paris, was a natural vantage point for viewing the city. The problem with the English poet's account is that *Borogh Larayn*, modern Bourg-la-Reine, is 9 kilometers south of the present southern city limits of Paris, and is hence a considerable distance from Montmartre and separated from it by the city itself and by the Seine running east-west through the centre of Paris.

665-83 C lacks L's incomplete stanza, 665-71, where the giant agrees to win Paris in return for the sultan's daughter. The differences between L and C in the next stanza, 672 ff., hinge on this. The English versions have condensed and modified the account of the giant's wooing in FO; the giant has become monstrous, the lady reluctant, and the authenticity of L or C cannot be confirmed from FO. The question is whether the discrepancy between L and C arises from condensation of the archetype in *C, or expansion of the archetype in *L.

I think that 665-71 are the remains of extra material which has been introduced in *L. The primary motive may have been to rationalize inconsistency arising from drastic condensation of the French source in the initial English redaction. The request and promise of a kiss in return for the King of France makes sense in FO, where the lady has accepted the giant as a suitor, but not in the English versions, where he is repellent to her. In L she understands that she has become part of a business deal, and submits, while in C her agreement is unexplained.

In both English versions the giant promises the King of France's head rather than his person (as in FO). This must therefore have been in the archetype; it was probably suggested by other versions of the motif of the Saracen giant who loved a Saracen princess where the same detail occurs (cf., for example, two separate instances of the motif in *Guy of*

Warwick (Auch. 3045-52, and stanzas 122, 126)), and prepares the way for the broad stroke of irony later, whereby Florent instead (at 915-21) presents the giant's head to the lady, in words which echo the giant's promise.

L's version of the promise, 678-83, differs from C, and, like 665-71, reflects further modification of the archetype. The wording here, and in the paraphrase which occurs at 723-31 (missing from C) resembles that in the Ff. 2. 38 version of *Guy* 2936-42, and suggests that a non-Auchinleck version of *Guy* may have been its source. If this view is correct, the differences between L and C in the stanza beginning 672 reflect reworking in *L to accommodate interpolated material, and C should be closer to the archetype. Two textual details confirm this: the request for a kiss in C corresponds more closely than L does to FO 2046-7:

Se de uos auoi' un besier
Le roi de France uos rendroie.

Secondly, C811-12 has a rhyme *day* : *may* 'maiden'. The noun *may(e)* is used freely in L; C uses it much less frequently, and only in rhymes. Except for this instance these are always paralleled in L and are presumably archetypal. It is most unlikely that a reviser of *C would introduce a rhyme on a word that he otherwise avoids.

720-43 These two stanzas, wanting in C, must have been in the archetype, and have been removed by editing in *C. See further the note on 744-55. The giant's direct challenge to Dagaberde, and his onslaught on the walls, though based on FO's account (especially FO 2059-62, 2147-9), are not closely paralleled there. The English version is therefore a blend of crude but colourful new material and material from the OF source. Despite various shifts, additions, and conflations, L preserves from the OF source the sequence of challenge, combat, challenge, followed by the crucial meeting with Florent, while C has eliminated the second challenge. 735-6 reflects FO 2065 ff. where kings and knights declare their intentions to fight the giant, but are all afraid to set out against him.

The tail-line sequence in the second stanza, which requires the form ʒynge at 734, offers some additional, though not conclusive, evidence that this stanza was in the archetype. See the note on the first line of the poem.

740 This line is echoed in the same context in *Eglamour* 556.

744-55 The differences between L and C here are a consequence of the omission in C of 720-43, discussed above, and they provide additional confirmation that the lines in L are archetypal. Since the stanzas containing the giant's challenge have been eliminated in *C, Clement can know nothing of the sultan's daughter, or of the promised kiss, and *C has been revised to remove the references to these which are preserved in L. Instead C859-64 paraphrases its earlier report of the giant's threats (C835-40). In the corresponding passage in FO 2123-52, Clement tells Florent that the giant is fighting to win his lady's favour; L preserves this, with the additional details present in the archetype, discussed above (note on 665-83).

Further confirmation of the presence of 720–43 in the archetype is afforded by the events following Florent's victory. His presentation of the giant's head to the sultan's daughter (915–20) does not occur in FO nor in SO, but has been transmitted to L and C from the archetype. It was presumably introduced into NO as a kind of rough and comic justice. The giant gets his deserts by being killed; the lady receives the giant's head, rather than the head he promised her, and Florent claims the kiss which was to be the giant's reward (915 ff.). C preserves these details (C1003–8), though, since it omits 720–43, and has edited 744–55, neither the French nor Florent should know anything about the giant's love for the lady nor his promise of the head.

It is possible that this 'head for a head' substitution in NO was suggested by *Bevis of Hampton*, which shares some details and motifs with NO. In a rather similar pattern of events, Bevis's evil mother sends her aged husband off to the forest to procure a boar (or in some versions, a boar's head); cf. *Bevis* 184 ff. There he is killed and beheaded by her lover, who, as she had requested (97 ff.), sends her the head as a love token (276–9).

746 The pa.t. pl. *ren*, in rhyme with *men*, is hard to explain. *OED* cites some other instances of pa.t. *ren(ne)*, pp. *renne*, in other texts, so it is apparently a genuine variant. In ME, *renne* < ON *renna* occurs widely (while *rynne* is chiefly northern), but its pa.t. forms coincide with those of *rynne*. Weak forms also occur, and the vowel of the weak form *renned* may occasionally have been transferred to the strong past.

759–60 L and C differ here substantially, and there is little to choose between them. C869 echoes C836 closely, while 759 in L is metrically awkward, and possibly corrupt. The sense in L apparently is: 'Ah, lord, for whatever reason so many men are afraid of him, it seems to me, etc.'

768–91 Revision in *C has removed these stanzas and patched up the gap by condensing and reassigning some of the debate between Clement and Florent. In C, the elimination of Clement's agreement to lend his armour makes for an awkward transition to the account of the arming which follows. L preserves from the OF source Florent's threat to go unarmed, and Clement's admission that he possesses some old-fashioned and dirty pieces of armour (cf. FO 2169 ff.). Clement's attempts to dissuade Florent are paralleled in FO and are there in keeping with his anti-heroic attitude. In SO, on the other hand, Florent is urged to action by a dream-vision, Clement welcomes the idea, and persuades the King of France to knight Florent before the fight.

792 ff. The account of the arming of Florent parallels FO quite closely; cf. 2197–200:

Le hauberc uesti uerement,
Qui fu plus noirs que arrement,
Molt estoit lais et enfumes,
Et de tote parz roilez.

What the English version fails to convey is the full mock-heroic tone of the OF account, where Florent is formally seated and armed as if in the ceremony of knighting. There are, in fact, close parallels between this account and that of the ceremony where Florent is dubbed a knight in FO 3010 ff.

805 Gladwyn: In FO, this is the name of Clement's son, who is nameless in L and C, and called Bonefey in SO 679. C and L agree in the transfer of this name to Clement's wife. The tug-of-war with the sword which follows parallels FO 2225 ff. closely.

822-3 These lines are apparently an inaccurate rendition of FO 2215-16, and follow on the transfer of the name Gladwyn from the son in FO to the wife in NO:

> Climens Gl[a]douain apela,
> Son fiuz estoit et molt l'ama.

C913 so bryght: Sarrazin, in his edition, suggests that this is ironical, anticipating the ironical comments which are to follow at 847 ff., C932 ff.; I think it is an error, probably arising from a misreading of the initial syllable of *vnbryght* in the exemplar.

C934 bre[ny]e: C does not use minim *i* within the word, though *i* occasionally begins *in, into* (beside *yn, ynto*, or forms with long *i*). This presumably prompted C's occasional misreading of *ni* in its exemplar as *m*. Cf. 1600, and see the note on 45.

847 ff. L and C preserve the mockery which greets Florent in FO 2275 ff.:

> Laissies aler
> Auant le hardi bachelier, etc.

C932 repeats the actual wording of FO with its *hardy bachelere*.

867-72 L and C preserve, and in fact expand, Clement's cry of encouragement to Florent in FO 2367-8:

> Biax fieuz, ore t'ai bien ueu
> A grant cop que tu as feru.

C958-60, however, continues with three lines omitted in L, but paralleled in FO 2369-70:

> Ben[e]ois soit qui t'engendra,
> Et la mere que t'aporta.

These lines probably were omitted because their echo of the words of the woman to Jesus (Luke 11: 27: *Beatus venter, qui te portavit, et ubera, quae suxisti*) struck Thornton, or the scribe of *L, as irreverent. As a result L has a 9-line stanza.

C961 Here, as at C913, Florent's armour is inaptly described. In this case, I think the scribe has slipped mechanically and momentarily into the idiom of the conventional account of a knight cutting a fine figure.

C995 C corresponds here more closely than L to FO 2562: *Droit a Monmartre s'en monta*. L's equivalent to *Monmartre* in FO and *Mountmertrons* in C is *Mont(e) Martyn(e)*. Cf. the single occurrence of *Mount Martyn* in SO 938.

915-29 On the presentation of the head to the sultan's daughter see the note on 744-55. This entire episode, which is quite carefully integrated into L (less successfully in C because of revision, see the note on 723-43) has been introduced into the source of L and C, and is not paralleled in FO or SO, where Florent carries the head back with him to

Paris. Here, as in other romances, the Saracen princess is presented as a lady of spirit, worthy of such peers as Josian, who in *Bevis* strangles Earl Miles after a forced marriage (3219-24), and Floripas, who in *Sir Ferumbras* connives with her chamberlain to throw her troublesome governess out the window (1360-73).

939 surkotte sleue: C reads *skarlet*, and FO 2694 has simply *manche*. The L reading coincides with SO 1180.

C1034 C here repeats a line it has already used at C962, where it is paralleled in L. The repetition has obviously been triggered by the preceding line of the couplet, which both L and C have already employed at 873, C961.

955 L and C agree on *Cleremont*, while FO 2764 has the sultan lodged at Dan Martin. The reference is probably to Clermont-en-Beauvasis, an important town and military post in the Middle Ages, but an unlikely base for the sultan's attack on Paris, since it is 63 kilometers north of the present-day city limits of Paris. On the significance of the French place-name evidence, see pp. 45-6.

958-62 This agrees with FO 2783-90. SO has transferred some of the details of wording and rhyme used here to describe Florent's visit to the princess (SO 1171-6). See further pp. 52-3.

C1071 hodyus: 'odious, loathsome, fearsome'. The scribe has either added an unetymological *h*, as in *hacton* C878, or the form has been influenced by the semantically similar *hidous*.

1008 Olyuayne: L uses elsewhere the form *Olyue* (3 examples) while C always uses *Olyuan, Olyvan* (5 examples). These forms in *-n* correspond to the *-ain(e)* oblique case ending in OF, which is used only with personal names. The name, however, does not occur in FO, where the lady is attended by twenty nameless maidens.

1029-31 These lines are repeated in both L and C at 1257-9.

1032-91 Sixty lines of authentic material in L are omitted in C. The passage contains the welcome of Florent in Paris after he has killed the giant (cf. FO 2895 ff.), the knighting of Florent (cf. FO 2925, 2994 ff.), Clement's beating of the minstrels (cf. FO 3079 ff.), and his confiscation and return of the mantles (cf. FO 3173 ff.). This is probably, but not certainly, another case of deliberate editing and compression in *C; it eliminates a tedious and not very comical exposé of Clement as a buffoon. Two factors, however, prevent us from being quite certain that the omission was intentional. First, the omission is masked by two stanzas being grafted together to produce one tail-rhyme stanza, but the combination produces a faulty tail-rhyme sequence (C1117-28). Secondly, C preserves a later stanza (1101-12), in which Clement concludes the omitted episode by throwing out money to pay his share of the expenses of the feast. But even in L's version, this detail has little connection with what has gone before, and besides, C has elsewhere retained unexplained details, after removing the earlier material which made them intelligible (see the note on 744-55).

1101-12 C and L share this detail in which Clement further demonstrates his bourgeois perspective and uneasiness in the face of conspicuous consumption. He discharges what he considers his own liability for the expenses of the feast, and disclaims any further responsibility. This gesture does not occur in FO or SO, and indeed, Clement's suspicions about high society scarcely needed further demonstration. In NO it makes Clement an object of mirth, embarrasses Florent, and moves the emperor to ask Florent if this man is his father. The result is the early recognition of Florent by his real father, which does not occur in other versions of the story. See further the note on 1125–60.

1110–12 These lines repeat material already used at 1077–9, where it is paralleled by FO 3195–6, and by SO 1297: *þe knyʒtys logh yn þe halle.*

1116–24 The question and answer here parallel FO 3136 ff., though they lead to a different conclusion. Cf. especially 3138–40:

> 'Sire,' dist Florens, 'ie ne soi,
> Mais unques autant ne l'amoi
> Come s'il m'eust engendre.'

and 3147–49:

> 'Mes sachies, sire, de mes eus
> Ne regardoi(e) si uolentiers
> Home come uos, ce sachies.'

1125–60 NO departs from other versions of the Octavian story, including FO, in having Florent identified by the emperor at this point (1137 ff.) instead of at the end of the poem, as part of the reconciliation and reunion that marks Eustace, Constance, and Crescentia stories. FO itself contains a line which may have initiated this remodelling in NO, for, following the interview between the emperor and Florent (NO 1116–24, FO 3136–53), the emperor surveys the young man and almost says: *'Mes fieus estes uerraiement'*. Nothing more comes of this, but NO, which shows other signs of dislocation in this section, proceeds to develop further inquiries, and the identification of Florent. Thus the corroborative testimony of Clement, which comes at the end of FO (5299 ff.), and which parallels this account, has been transferred to 1131 ff.

This modification is the source of later inconsistencies at 1470–2, 1482–5, where Florent's parentage is apparently still in doubt, and it weakens the dénouement, where the empress's recognition of Florent (1575 ff.) becomes redundant. The sequence of events has been reworked, and not very successfully; I think this is more likely to be the result of tampering in the course of transmission of NO than to have originated in the original English redaction of the French source.

C1175 The omission of the subject pronoun of the third person occurs quite often in ME when the subject is understood from the context. See Mustanoja pp. 138–44.

C1201–2 lawe : haue: This rhyme does not occur in L, but similar rhymes on ʒ : *v* occur elsewhere. Cf. *Guy* (Auch.) 3173–4 *haue : plawe*, *Havelok* 949–50 *knaue : plawe*, 2676–7 *of-slawen : Rauen*. They may be inexact rhymes, depending on the partial similarity of voiced fricatives, or may show the occasional development of ʒ > *v*. See *Havelok*, ed. K. Sisam, note on 949–50, Dobson, vol. 1, p. 182.

C1208-9 C omits the reference to the sultan in 1180; as a result C1208 is short, and *hym* in the next line makes no sense, as its proper antecedent, the sultan, is missing, and Florent is, of course, alone.

1182 reyngened: This is a reverse spelling from *reign*, for which *OED* records *reyngne, reingne* spellings in the fourteenth and fifteenth centuries.

1221 moree: See the note on 160.

1227-32 L and C have the two three-line units in different sequences. C probably has the original order, since in FO 3410 ff. the recognition (by the sultan's daughter rather than by the Saracens) comes first; then, because he provokes the sultan, Florent is attacked. On L displacing lines and three-line units, see pp. 15–16.

C1298 [to] fare: Compare *yare : to fare* C1585-6.

1293-328 In FO Marsabele's move nearer to Paris is differently motivated. She proposes to her father using herself as a bait to trap Florent, 3668 ff., secretly hoping for another meeting with him.

No formal battle takes place in FO at this point, but there is a sortie against the Saracens, 3565 ff., in which Florent does not play an important role. NO is here repeating Marsabele's earlier move to Mountmertrons to watch the encounters between the giant and the French opposition, C787 ff. The sortie is inflated into a major battle in which Florent distinguishes himself, but the inconclusive issue of the battle shows its functional irrelevance to the action.

The ineffectuality of the action is matched by the ineffectuality of the verse and language. The introductory stanza, 1293-304, is particularly weak. The first and final three-line units are repetitive, 1296-8 is a reworking of 1224-6, and 1299-301 repeat 1230-2. The battle itself is described in the most banal and conventional terms, and the first six lines are a reworking of the account of the authentic battle (1497 ff.) in which the Saracens defeat the French.

1305 The word *syte* 'grief, distress' is rare in ME, and chiefly northern; see *OED s.v. site* and Kaiser, p. 242. The alliterative collocation used here is first recorded in the *Ormulum*, and is paralleled by Old West Norse *sorg ok sút* (on which see E. S. Olszewska, 'Alliterative Phrases in the *Ormulum*: some Norse parallels', p. 127, in *English and Medieval Studies presented to J. R. R. Tolkien*, ed. N. Davis and C. L. Wrenn (London, 1962)). *OED* records one or other variant of the phrase also in *Wars of Alexander*, *Layfolks' Catechism*, Robert of Brunne, and *Legends of the Holy Rood*, to which may be added *York Plays* 480/2, *Towneley Plays* 5/147, *Northern Passion* 148/33.

The phrase has been obscured in L, and eliminated in C both here and again at C1525 (where L is defective). C and L agree on *sorow in . . .*, so the archetype was probably already corrupt. C has compounded this by further corruption resulting presumably from (i) unfamiliarity with the northern word, and (ii) a misreading of 'long' *s* as *f*, and a 'correction' of the supposed phonetic spelling to the etymologically appropriate one. Compare C's treatment of the phrase at C1525-6, and the hypercorrect spelling *smyght* introduced there. There is otherwise no evidence for the loss of the palatal fricative in this phonetic context in either text or in the archetype. For other instances of C's confusion of archetypal *f* and 'long' *s*, see the note on 342.

C1334 smyte: In view of the singular noun, the verb here must be intransitive, with the sense 'to be fought, to rage'. The same holds for C1526, where this, and the preceding line, are repeated.

1308-9 E. G. Stanley (*EGS*, vi (1957), 62–63) cites a long list of romances in which battles conventionally last for the period of daylight.

1318 waree: See the note on 160.

1389 Compare Marsabile's words to Florent at the same point in FO 3892: *Mes peres a un tel destrier*, and FO 3915: *S'a une corne enmi le front*. In SO the theft of the horse occurs after the sultan's daughter has been carried off by Florent to Paris, unlike the other versions, and the lady gives this information to Clement rather than Florent, but she uses similar wording: *My father haþ an horned stede* (SO 1335).

1421 brymly 'boldly, loudly': The etymology of ME *brim* 'grim, fierce' is uncertain. *MED* suggests it may be a blend of *breme* and *grim*. The senses and collocations in which it occurs overlap to some degree with those for *breme*, though its range of meaning is more restricted. *Brim* and the adverb *brimli* occur infrequently in ME, generally in northern or northerly texts. C's reading may be taken either as *breuely* or *brenely*. Both would represent a misreading or a misunderstanding of an earlier *bremely* 'boldly, loudly'. However, *breuely* 'briefly' makes adequate, though less colourful sense here, and seems to me typical of the kind of improvisation and dilution of meaning introduced by C or an antecedent when faced with a difficult or corrupt exemplar; compare the note on 1305.

1423 Compare FO 4094: *Sarrazinois sot bien parlier*.

C1459 lede: See the note on 288.

1460 tydee: See the note on 160.

1470-84 L and C agree on Florent's speculation about his kinship with the emperor, and on the general belief that Florent must be of gentle birth. The first of these is in accord with Florent's earlier expression of natural affection for the emperor, 1119–24, which is paralleled in FO 3147–50, but it is made nonsense of by the recognition scene earlier, at 1137 ff. See the note on 1125–60.

1479 ff. On the damage in L see p. 12.

C1525 See the note on 1305.

C1526 See the note on C1334.

C1539 On C's corrupt reading here, see the note on 342.

C1553 NO agrees with SO 1520 in reporting the capture of the king of France by the Saracens, while both FO and F&O develop with some nationalistic zeal the miraculous intervention of St. George (and, in F&O, also St. Denis) on behalf of the king of France. English versions of the story might well have eliminated this legendary material independently, but it is possible that their agreement in omission was inherited from a common source. SO may retain a vestige of it in its reference to *Seynt Georgys armys* (1612).

C1557 swelle: This use of *swelle* 'proud, arrogant' antedates by roughly three centuries the earliest use of the adjective in any sense in *OED*, though the corresponding senses for the verb are recorded from the thirteenth century onward.

C1567 ȝyng: See the note on line 1.

C1577 wele: This rare verb is otherwise recorded only in Robert of Brunne and in *Ywain and Gawain*, and is thus northern or North Midland in distribution.

C1590-6 The tail-line sequence of rhymes is broken here halfway through, and we are given no account of the journey of young Octovian and his men to meet the Saracen host. In FO they sail to Brindisi and then proceed towards Lombardy (FO 4917-22); in SO 1597 ff. they wait for the Saracens at Acre. It is likely that a limited amount of material has been lost here, perhaps two half-stanzas, and that the omission was accidental and connected with the scribe of C beginning a new column of text (f. 101vb) at exactly the point where material seems to be lost (1591).

1536 L and C always use *Florent* (L also has *Florente* once), except here and at C1552 (L defective), where forms corresponding to the OF nominative in *-s* are used, and confirmed by rhyme.

1560-5 C offers a better reading with the two groups of three lines in the reverse order. Young Octovian's defence of his mother is then continuous, occupies the first six lines of the stanza, and is followed by the emperor's reactions to the simultaneous restoration of son and wife.

1571 Following 1571 C has three lines, missing in L, which produce a 15-line stanza. Both C and L have dealt, though in different ways, with a problem presented by the archetype, where the injured wife's speech must have begun without any identification of the speaker. C has covered this by a three-line addition, while L inserts *scho said* into an already long and unwieldy line.

1609-10 The treason statute of Edward III (1352) included in its category of high treason compassing or planning the death of the king, his wife, or his child, and death by burning was the usual punishment for women convicted of it. See O. Kratins, *PQ*, xlv (1966), 686.

1610 a belle of brasse: 'A cauldron full of molten copper'; C reads: *a tonne of brasse*. The sense 'cauldron' required here is extremely rare; *MED* records it otherwise only in *Awntyrs of Arthure* and the *Life of St. Robert of Knaresborough*. All three examples involve burning; cf. *Awntyrs off Arthure* 188: *In bras and in brymston I bren as a belle*. In his edition of this poem R. Hanna rejects the sense 'cauldron' for *belle*, and instead derives the word from OE *bǣl* 'fire', with shortened vowel. He would therefore translate the *Awntyrs* phrase as 'I burn as a blazing fire', and would translate the similar *St. Robert* line in the same way. I do not find the derivation from *bǣl* convincing, and I think the word certainly means 'cauldron' in NO. Burning in a cauldron recurs frequently elsewhere as a typical punishment; cf. *Bevis* (Chetham MS) 3179-84:

Syr Beues, wythout any let,
Made a caudron on the fyre be set

> Ful of pytche and of brymstone:
> A wors deth was neuer none.
> Whan the caudron boyled harde,
> Murdour was cast in the myd-warde.

Pitch and brimstone are typically mentioned as the contents of the cauldron, as they are in descriptions of the punishments of the damned, but molten copper occurs also, both in earthly and hellish torture. Juliana is faced with *a chetel wol of iwelled bras* (Ashmole MS, 54), and boiling *in bras & brimston* in hell is promised in the *Castle of Perseverance* 3594.

In both NO and FO punishment is forestalled, since the wicked mother dies before it can be carried out, and in FO we do not learn what the projected punishment was. It is possible that the form planned in NO originated as a misunderstanding of *enbrasee* in Dagobert's recommendation much earlier (FO 1673-6):

> 'Sire, bien eust deserui
> Vostre mere, que ce basti,
> Qu'ele fust maintenant getee
> Dedans le feu et enbrasee.'

1626 ff. L and C differ in their conclusion. L has a concluding six-line stanza, which has probably been worked up as a finishing touch. It incorporates C1729-30, and has replaced the last three lines of the preceding stanza with three three-stress lines of minimal content.

GLOSSARY

The glossary is primarily a guide to words in L which may be unfamiliar. Words which occur commonly today are not usually treated here, unless they occur in L in some unusual form or sense, or in a phrasal construction whose meaning may not be transparent. Words which occur in C but not in L, and variant forms from C, are recorded only when they seem likely to cause difficulty; line references for such forms are preceded by C.

References are selective, chosen to give generous illustration of the forms of the words treated and of both typical and interesting uses. In the illustration of forms, however, I do not attempt to record all variation between *i, j* and *y* (as vowel), *u* and *w* (as vowel), *ʒ* and *y* (as consonant) and *þ* and *th*.

The arrangement of the glossary is alphabetical, but the following features should be noted: initial *ʒ* and *y* (as consonant) are treated together after *g*; initial *i, j* and *y* (as vowel) are treated together before initial *j* (as consonant); *þ* and *th* are treated together after *t*; initial *v* as vowel is treated before *v* as consonant; within the word *u* and *w* as vowel precede *u* [v] and *w* [w].

The sign ~ stands for the headword in one or other of its forms. The line reference for any emended form is preceded by *, and n. appended to a citation refers the reader to discussion in the notes.

abyde see habyde.
abowne *adv.* on top 795.
abowte *prep.* around, near 212, 268, 843.
aboue *adv.* on top C880.
actone *n.* jacket worn under the hauberk 793, hacton C878.
adowne *adv.* down C1025.
adrede *pp.* afraid 954.
afore *adv.* before C378.
aftir *adv.* in pursuit 476; afterwards 1053.
agayne *adv.* away, homeward 301, 718; back again 721, 1081.
agayne *prep.* towards, to meet 602, 1033; in front of 52; against 539, 1190.
agenste *prep.* against C780, C1219.
ay(e) *adv.* always, all the time 160, 423, 1160; continually 738; ~ when whenever 379.
ayerde *pp.* inherited 107n., heyred C107.
ayere *n.* heir 80, heyre C80.
aythire *pron.* each 96, aythere 1292.
aythir(e) *adj.* each 857, 1058. Cf. owthir.

al see all(e).
alkyn *adj.* of every kind 203.
all(e) *pron.* all, everything 159, 168; everyone 2, 129.
all(e) *adv.* all, entirely, quite 47, 169, al 811, 1226.
alle þoghe *conj.* although 1218.
almyghte *adj.* almighty 1139.
als *conj.* as, just as 10, 15, *righte ~* 1100; as, like 123, 303; when, while 37, 330, *righte ~* 1005, *so ~* 46; as if 342, 1184; (~) ... ~ as ... as 490, 711, os C41, ~ ... *so* when ... then 535.
also *adv.* also, moreover 261, 595, als 1286; ~ *(als) swythe* very quickly 609, 1140, *alsso swythe* 1084.
alþirmoste *adj.* most of all 1417.
amange *prep.* among, in among 11, 1236, amonge 1045, emange 199, amonges 1079.
am(e) see be(e).
amende *v.* change, alter 866.
amonge see amange.
amonges *adv.* here and there 1311.
and *conj.* and 1, 6; if 9, 761, 762.
anelase *n.* dagger 1616, analasse C1719.

any *adj.* 1277, **ony** C1258.
ankir *n.* anchor: *ryde one* ~ lie at anchor 436.
anone *adv.* right away, at once 432, ~ *ryghte* 1113.
appon(e) *prep.* upon, on 336, 408, 418, **oppon** 209, 1127; ~ *a daye* one day 37, 193.
are *adv.* before, previously 287, 381, **ore** 1313, 1600.
are see **be(e)**.
arewyd *pa.t.* regretted C1350.
aryght *adv.* properly, correctly C74, C633.
armede *pa.t. refl.* armed 690, 1171. **armed(e)** *pp.* 24, 357.
armoures *n.pl.* arms, weapons and armour 775.
arste *adv.* previously, earlier C1557.
art(e) see **be(e)**.
aske *pr. 1 sg.* call for 218. **askede** *pa.t.* asked 744, ~ *aftir* asked for, asked about 1072.
askynge *n.* request 688.
aspye *v.* notice, observe 49.
assent *n.* opinion 231.
atyre *n.* equipment, apparel 797, 828.
ato *adv.* in two C1718.
auentayle *n.* chain mail protecting neck 819, **ventayle** C904.
auenture *n.* event, outcome 13, 1023, **nawntir** 215; mishap 972. **auenturs** *pl.* exploits 1334, **awntirs** 1406.
auenture *v.* hazard 715.
awaywarde *adv.* away, in another direction 712, 766.
awen see **owen**.

bacenete *n.* helmet worn under the fighting helmet 819, **basenett** C904.
bachelere *n.* young knight 847.
badd(e), bad(e) see **byddis**.
bane *n.* bone: *blode and* ~ body, form 1009.
bare *adj.* empty 1317.
bare see **bere** *v.*[1]
barne *n.* child 384.
baselarde *n.* dagger 157.
basenett see **bacenete**.
batelle *n.* fighting, battle 934, 1226; single combat 835. **batells** *pl.* battalions, armies 1306.
be(e) *v.* be 60, 107, **bene** 971. **am(e)**

pr. 1 sg. 58, 71. **art(e)** *pr. 2 sg.* 869, 1461, **ert** 1367. **es** *pr. 3 sg.* 10, 141, **ys** C10. **are** *pr. pl.* 69, 113, **er(e)** 398, 1329, **es** 326, 491, **bene** 1203, **be** C395. **be(e)** *pr. subj.* 228, 671. **be** *imp. sg.* 883, 1410. **was** *pa.t. sg.* 14. **wer(e)** *pa.t. pl.* 31, 601, **weren** 90, **weryn** 546, **ware(e)** 268, 1318n., **wore** 1327. **were** *pa. subj. sg.* 55, **ware** 132, **wore** 1003. **bene** *pp.* 28, 64, **ben** C28, **byn** C64, **be** C572
be see **by**.
be- see **by-**.
bede *v.* offer 587, 659; summon 192. **bedd** *pa.t.* offered 415; **bede** prayed 825. **bede** *pp.* C189.
bedeene see **bydene**.
begyfte *pa.t.* entrusted, gave C675.
bey *n.* ornament, ring 921.
belyue *adv.* quickly, readily 678.
belle *n.* cauldron 1610n.
bement *pa.t.* signified 222.
bere *v.*[1] bear, carry 356, **bare** C353. **bare** *pa.t. sg.* 360, **bere** 818. **bare** *pa.t. pl.* 236, 286. **borne** *pp.* 347, 398; **born** 265, 1040.
bere *v.*[2] cry out, shout 1421.
besemyth *pr. 3 sg.* befits: *hym* ~ it becomes him C933.
besyde *adv.* nearby 1545; *here* ~ nearby 562.
bete *imp. sg.* beat C689, C702. **bete** *pa.t.* C677, C686. **beton** *pp.* C682.
betoke *pa.t.* handed over C280.
by *prep.* by, by means of 176; beside 46; along 424; concerning 216; (in oaths) by 1074, **be** 583.
byblede *pp.* stained, bloodstained 159, 179, **bebledd** C155.
bycome *pa.t.* became 1320. **bycomen** *pp.* in *where þay* ~ *were* what became of them 1073.
byddis *pr. 3 sg.* bids, commands 1189, **byddyþ** C1217. **bad(e)** *pa.t.* 284, 662, 841, **badd(e)** 144, 421, 702.
byde *v.* stop, halt, 425; remain, endure 770, 860, wait 1274, 1358.
bydene *adv.* together: *alle* ~ all together, completely 797; **bedeene** all together C882; forthwith 977.
bye *v.* buy C696. **boghte** *pa.t.* bought 1134.

byforne *adv.* in front 1034; *þer* ~ before that time, previously 304.

byforne *prep.* before, in front of 801.

byhete *pa.t.* promised 917.

byholde *v.* watch, look at 1095. **byhelde** *pa.t.* 40, 829.

byleues *pr. 3 sg.* remains, stays 383. **beleue** *imp. sg.* C1484. **belefte** *pa.t.* 521, **byleued** 523; **belafte** left, let be C380.

bynke *n.* bench 810.

birdis *n. pl.* ladies 995.

byrnand(e) see **bryne**.

bysett(e) *pp.* occupied, inhabited 293; filled 313; laid out, expended 871.

bystadde *pp.* pressed, beset: *seke* ~ gravely ill 141.

byta(u)ghte *pa.t.* handed over 283, 295, 646.

bytwene *adv.* in the midst 1262.

bytwene *prep.* between 29; in among 557.

bytwyx(e) *prep.* between 694, 835.

ble *n.* appearance: *blythe in* ~ joyful in appearance 663; **blyee** in *bryghte* ~ bright face, fair countenance 50.

blyee see **ble**.

blyn *v.* desist, stop 666, 1404. **blanne** *pa.t.* C1432, C1624.

blyschede *pa.t.* in ~ *vp* (?) looked up, (?) started up 178.

blysse *n.* joy, happiness 259, 397.

blyssynge *n.* blessing 5, 1633.

blythe *adj.* happy 6, 103; ~ *of* happy about, contented with 434, 490; ~ *in ble* see **ble**.

blode *n.* blood 159, 863; stock, lineage 1471; *of gentill* ~ of gentle birth 565, 1099.

bloo *adj.* grey, ash-coloured C166.

body *n.* trunk 1243.

bodworde *n.* message 94.

bofete *n.* blow 739. **bofettys** *pl.* C1270.

boghte see **bye**.

bolde *v.* grow bold 887.

bondys *n. pl.* fetters C1634.

borde *n.* table 1228, 1278. **burdes** *pl.* 910, **boordys** C998.

borne see **bere** *v.*[1]

borowe *n.* city 1288.

bot *adv.* only: ~ *littill* only a little, very little 72, 478.

bot *conj.* but, yet, however 32, 49; only, except that 782, 932, 1234; unless 771, 1381; but rather 351, 404.

bot *prep.* except 68, 757.

bote *n.* remedy 1233.

bote *pa.t.* bit *982.

bownden *pp.* fettered 1520.

bowne *adj.* ready, prepared 938; *all redy* ~ all prepared, quite ready 413; ~ *to* ready to go to, ready for 911, 934.

bowrde *n.* joke, jest C898.

boxe *n.* blow 1242.

brayde *n.* exchange of blows, armed encounter 724.

brasse *n.* molten copper 1610n.

braste *pa.t.* burst 792.

brede *n.* food 1046.

breke *v.* crush, crack 763; demolish 755. **brake** *pa.t.* broke 540, 856.

breme *adj.* bold, fierce *C1065.

brene *n.* corselet 849, **brenye** *C934. **brenyes** *pl.* *C1600.

brennand, brenne, brente see **bryne**.

brere *n.* briar, bush 41.

bretage *n.* wall, barricade 710, 722.

brethir see **broþir**.

breuely *adv.* quickly, without delay C1449.

brydale *n.* wedding feast 1599.

bryghte *adj.* fair 39, 50, 73; shining 440, 579, 849.

bryghte *adv.* brightly 167, 234.

brymly *adv.* loudly, boldly 1421n.

bryne *v.* burn, destroy by fire 707, 755, **brenne** C840. **birnande** *pr. p.* blazing 167, **byrnand** 169, **brennand** C164, **brennyng** C166: **brente** *pa.t.* C765. **brynt(t)e** *pp.* 228, 1609, **brente** C225.

brynge *v.* bring, lead 503, 1191. **broght(e)** *pa.t.* brought, escorted 605; ~ *to þe grounde* laid low C1037. **broght(e)** *pp.* brought 619; ~ *to bedde* put to bed 71; ~ *to grownde* buried 69; ~ *to a bettur man* raised to a higher station C707.

brode *adj.* large 579; broad 1289, 1290.

brondes *n.pl.* coals 234.

broþir *n.* brother 1536. **brethir** *pl.* 1585, **brethurn** C1688.

broune *adj.* shining 936.

buke *n.* book, source 353. **bukes** *pl.* 10, 896.

burdes see **borde**.

burdone *n.* club 853.

burgesse *n.* citizen 574, 640. **burgeys** *gen.* C697, **burges** C751. **burgesche** *pl.* 601, **burgeys** C598.

buskyd *pa.t. refl.* prepared C1549.

came see **com(e)**.

can *auxil.* (forming with inf. periphrastic tense) did C8, C49, C288.

care, kare *n.* distress, sorrow 54, 123; trouble 68; anxiety 180; *made full grete* ~ lamented greatly, expressed great distress 1151.

carefull(e) *adj.* sorrowful 324, 389.

cas *n.* chance: *par* ~ by chance 1236.

caste *v.* throw 227. **caste** *pa.t.* threw 177, **keste** 1104; ~ *on* put on 793.

certis, –es *adv.* certainly, indeed 112, 1411, **sertes** 1380.

chambir *n.* bedroom 38, 153; counsel chamber, reception room 98, 211.

charyte *n.* charity: *par* ~ for the sake of charity 1634.

chawnce *n.* event C1561.

chawndelere *n.* chandler 645.

chaungere *n.* money changer C642.

chere *n.* behaviour, bearing 213; appearance 999; mood, state of mind 866, 1149; *made euyll* ~ was sad 241; *make glade* ~ be in good spirits 991.

chese *pa.t.* chose 1598; ~ *for* acknowledged as 1562, **chees** C1665.

chide *n.* reproach, complaint: *gyffe a* ~ make an objection, complain 779.

child(e) *n.* offspring, child, infant 32, 65, 358; *with* ~ ȝode became pregnant 85; boy, youth 517, 634, 638; (as a title) ~ *Florent* 816, 873. **childes** *gen.* in *no* ~ *playe* no child's play, no game 878, 950. **childir** *pl.* 44, 115, 170, **chyldren** C83.

childbed *n.* labour, confinement: *in* ~ *laye* lay recovering from labour 128.

chippe see **schipp(e)**.

cytoles *n. pl.* citoles, stringed instruments 201.

clappe *v.* embrace each other 446n., **cleppe** C443.

clerkes *n. pl.* scholars, writers 27.

cleues *n. pl.* hills 308.

clyppyng *n.* embracing C1391, C1685.

colde *v.* grow cold 890.

coloure *n.* colouring, complexion 1000.

com(e) *v.* come 470, 1016, **comyn** C1514; ~ *to* come by 608, 1129; ~ *tylle (to)* reach, get to 1016, 1165; ~ *of helde* come of age 626; *comen (comyn) of* come from, descended from 565, 1099, 1471. **comes** *pr. 3 sg.* 532, **comyþ** C529. **com(e)** *pa.t.* 91, 341, **came** 407. **comen** *pp.* 31, **comyn** 565.

comforthe *n.* solace, peace of mind 60, 522; courage 883.

concelle *n.* private thought 56, 1012; **consaile** advice 1378.

contenance *n.* looks, expression 984, **countynawns** C1072.

cosse *n.* kiss C816, **kysse** C821.

costes *n. pl.* expenses 1066.

courses *n. pl.* runs, charges 1443.

couthe see **kan**.

couyre *v. refl.* recover 525.

crafte *n.* trade 649.

crafty *adj.* skilful C1412.

crye *n.* uproar, outcry 933.

crye *v.* wail, lament 181; cry out, pray 741. **cryede** *pa.t.* 317, 882, 1322.

crysten *v.* christen, baptize 629. **crystened** *pp.* 266, 515, **cristenede** 1369, 1596.

Crysten, Cristyn *adj.* Christian 971, 1156, 1257; **Crysten** as *n.* Christians C1059.

Crystendome *n.* Christendom C785.

Cristyante *n.* Christendom 986.

crown *n.* crown of the head 694.

curtayse *adj.* courteous 1050, 1096, 1107, **curtes** C1124.

curtasye *n.* good will, kindness: *for thi* ~ of your courtesy, if you please 725.

day(e) *n.* day 209, 332; daytime 438; appointed time, appointed day 1207, 1330; *this* ~ today 260, 972, 1025; *that* ~ (on) that day 255, 1065; *appon a* ~ one day, on a certain day 37, 193, 1605; ~ *and nyghte* day and night, constantly 378, 513, *by nyghte and by* ~ 1021; *hafe gud* ~ good day! 1399. **dayes** *gen.* 492, 1204. **dayes** *pl.* 326.

daylyght, -lyȝt n. daybreak C488, C1309, C1441.

dales n. pl. valleys 308.

dame n. lady, mistress (as term of address) 620.

damesele n. maiden, girl (as term of address) 915, 927, damysell C1003.

dare pr. 1 sg. dare 770. dare pr. 3 sg. 753. durste pa.t. 470, 477, 736.

dawnyng n. dawn C329.

dauwnsede pa.t. danced 1068.

debonorly adv. submissively, meekly 465.

dede n.[1] death 251, 275; to þe ~ to death 228, 791; to þe ~ goo (ȝode) die (died) 267, 1314; take ~ undergo death, die 239.

dede n.[2] deed, feat 1542; conduct 1052; battle 1386; doghety of ~ valiant in war, bold of action 18, 1410, 1586.

defawte n. insufficiency, want C1458.

deyse see dese.

dele see dole.

delyuered pp. delivered (of a child) 132.

dere n. injury C1206.

dere v. impede, hinder 1178, 1253; ~ to do harm to 483. deryth pr. 3. sg. afflicts C106.

dere adj. dear 747; ~ with dear to 642, 869; precious, excellent 5, 1633.

derke see dirke.

derkeness n. darkness C161.

dese n. dais 963, deyse C1051; heghe ~ high dais, dais for the high table 1127, 1568.

dewkys n. pl. dukes C1556.

dewre see dowre.

did see do.

dyghte v. refl. prepare, equip 439, 1414. dyghte pa.t. 1282. dyghte pp. prepared, made ready 240, 758; tended 328; treated 555; were ~ were gone 137; ~ to the dede destined to die 791.

dylfull see dolefull.

dynge v. batter 740.

dynt n. blow, stroke 868, 976.

dirke adj. dark 1309, derke C326.

dyskeuyr v. reveal C59.

dyuirse adj. different, various 189.

do(o) v. do, carry out, perform 649, 760, 827; ~ it no mys (woghe) do it no injury 350, 564; proceed, act 1344; cause 106; put, place 1296, 1447; (with inf.) cause, have 76, 101, 515; (representing another verb) 1111, 1120; auxil. (forming with inf. periphrastic tense) 932, 1125, 1170. dose pr. 3 sg. 106, 874, dothe C1385. did pa.t. 101, 144, dud C50. done pp. 230, 1447.

doghety adj. valiant 18, 847, doghty C18.

doghtynes n. feat of arms C1582.

dole n. sorrowful event 208; distress, grief, pity 232, 732, 1425, dele C229.

dolefull adj. sorrowful 161, 173, dylfull C158.

dome n. explanation 607, 1128; with ~ rightly, duly 1146.

done see do.

dose, dothe see do.

downe n. open tract of ground C1318.

dowre v. endure 399, dewre C396.

dowte n. fear 23.

drade see drede.

drawen see drewe.

drede n. fear: for ~ for fear 142, 348.

drede pr. pl. are afraid of 759. drede imp. 1019. drade pp. 147.

dreghe v. endure, have strength 461.

drewe, droghe pa.t. pulled, drew 157, 804, 806; refl. ~ awaye drew back 145; ~ vp saile hoisted sail 484; ~ till elde reached old age 35; drowe in ~ downe tore down C1615. drawen pp. drawn, unsheathed 803; as adj. 1229; ydrawe in ~ away withdrawn C1357.

dryve v. hasten 721. dryvand pr. p. driving 653.

dubbede pa.t. dubbed: ~ to knyghte conferred knighthood on 519.

dulefully adv. shamefully 555, delefully C552.

duelle v. stay, live 511, 529. duellyn pr. pl. spend time 196n. duellid pp. delayed, postponed 630.

ebbe n. ebb-tide 493.

eche adj. each, every C287, C705; ~ oon everyone C523, C1724. Cf. ilke.

eghe *n. pl.* eyes 572, **eghene** 989, **eye** C569, **eyen** C1077.

egre *adj.* eager 976, **egur** C964.

elde *n.* old age 35; age 517, **helde** 626.

eldyrs *n. pl.* forebears 11.

emange see amange.

emprice *n.* empress 25, 128, **empryse** 104, **emperes** C25, **emperyce** C503.

enoghe see ynoghe.

er(e) see be(e).

erly *adv.* early 100, **yerly** C100.

errande *n.* message C94; mission, business C1583, C1653.

ert see be(e).

erthe *n.* ground 808, 814.

es see be(e).

esyly *adv.* without difficulty 356.

ete *v.* eat 979. **ete** *pa.t.* 327, 368. **eten** *pp.* 1101, **eton** C1129.

euen *n.* evening 1309, 1501.

euen *adv.* completely 329.

euyll *adv.* poorly, badly C973.

euyll(e) *adj.* bad 241; hard, difficult 920.

euir *adv.* always, continually 145, 640; ever, at any time 1122, 1156; *alle* *þat* ~ whosoever, all who 1482.

euirylke *adj.* every 23, 1135.

euirmore *adv.* in *for* ~ forever more 1160.

fadir *n.* father 191; (as term of address) 756, 768; (of Christ) 4. **fadir** *gen.* 1215.

fay *n.* faith: *be hys* ~ on his word C795.

fay *adj.* fated to die 66n.

fayle *v.* fail: *withowtten* ~ truly 1377.

fayne *adj.* happy, pleased 601, 1080; eager 1203.

faire *adj.* beautiful, fair, pleasing 40, 79, 200; ~ *of* fair in, fair of 352, 1009; ~ *and fre(e)* fair and noble 87, 514. **fayreste** *sup.* 26.

faire *adv.* well 624, 1448; courteously 1042.

falle *v.* fall 795, 1238. **felle** *pa.t.* 52, 245, 269; happened, came to pass 88, 894, **fell** 215.

false *adj.* false, treacherous 1614.

fand(e) see fynd(e).

fare *n.* state, condition 57, 508.

fare *v.* go, set off 414, 543; get along 67.

farre *adj.* distant C185.

faste *adv.* quickly 134, 712; vigorously, eagerly, steadily 226, 558, 825; confined 160.

fawcon *n.* falcon 656.

fawte *n.* lack, want 1430.

fauoure *n.* benevolence 16.

fe(e)de *v.* feed 345; nurse, suckle 597; rear 624.

fedurs *n. pl.* wing feathers, wings C654, C671.

fee *n.* money 415.

felde *n.* plain, open ground, field (of battle) 255, 1289, 1338, **fylde** C243; *wyn the* ~ see wyn.

fele *adj.* many 12, 1141, 1158. See sythe.

felide *pa.t.* felt 372.

felle *n.* skin: *of flesche and* ~ of flesh and skin C723.

fell(e) see falle.

fellede *pa.t.* struck down 977.

fende *v.* defend 932.

ferde *n.* fear: *for* ~ for fear 713.

ferde *pa.t.* got on, fared 885, **farde** C973.

ferde *ppl. adj.* afraid: ~ *of* frightened of 480.

fe(e)re *n.* fear C444, C468.

fere *n.* spouse 58; fellow, companion 846, 1415.

ferly *adv.* very 307n., 1337.

ferre *adv.* far away 145; *als* ~ *als* as soon as, once 711; ~ *and nere* far and near 1588. **ferrere** *comp.* 315.

fethils *n. pl.* violins 200.

fewle see fowle.

fyghte *n.* armed encounter, battle 19, 785, 1328; fighting 703.

fynde *v.* provide 703. **fond(e)** *pa.t.* found 413, 442, **fand(e)** 102, 411, **found(e)** 311, 432, 910.

flemed *pa.t.* banished 279. **flemyd** *pp.* 289, **flemede** 1564.

flyande *pr. p.* flying 166, **fleyng** C163. **flowe** *pa.t.* flew 862, **flye** C947.

flyghte *n.* flight 352, 1357; *tuke his* ~ flew 171.

flode *n.* sea 418, 457; river, stream 1351, 1360; high tide 493.

florence *n. pl.* florins 281, 579.

flowe see flyande.

folde *v.* embrace 61; collapse, fall 893. **folden** *pp.* folded C654.

folke *n.* people 700, 708; retainers 1282, 1386. **folkys** *pl.* C833.

fond(e) see **fynde.**

for *conj.* for, because 7, 115; ~ *þat* in order that 1299; because 1503.

for *prep.* for, because of 47, 142; for, in exchange for, in return for 566, 578; for, as 506, 560, 1562; despite 1572, (with *to* + inf.) 56, 182.

fordredd *pp.* badly frightened C1042.

forfare *v. refl.* destroy 183.

forgete *v.* forget 1001. **forgetyn** *pp.* 1102, **forgeton** C1130.

forlorne *pp.* lost 305, 397.

forme *n.* bench: *mete* ~ bench to sit on at table 1246.

forsothe *adv.* truly 208; ~ *to saye* to tell the truth 553.

forthe *adv.* forward, out, away 121, 152, 302.

forthi *adv.* therefore 36, 754.

forthi þat *conj.* because 44.

forwhy *adv.* for what reason 207.

forwhi þat *conj.* provided that 1369.

foteknaue *n.* foot servant 1195.

fowle *n.* bird 660, 1204; ~ *of flyghte* bird of the air 1357; **fewle** winged creature 352, 355, 368. **fowlles** *pl.* birds 333, 491.

foulle *adj.* hideous, ugly 737, **fowle** 767, **fulle** 677.

found(e) see **fynde.**

fownde *v.* leave, depart 951, 1310, 1455; depart in death 66.

fourtenyghte *n.* fortnight 1591, **fowrtene nyghte** 1025.

frayne *v.* ask 53, 1212, 1223. **frayned(e)** *pa.t.* 508, 607.

fre(e) *adj.* gracious, noble, excellent 262, 622, 660. See **faire.**

fro *prep.* away from, from 338, 363, 398, **fra** 1216.

ful(l) *adv.* very, quite 7, 584.

fulle see **foulle.**

gaf(f)e see **gyffe.**

gamen *n.* pleasure, revelry 197, 809; *joye and* ~ joy and revelry 29, 1078; sport, joke 813; **games** *pl.* skills C648.

gamyd *pa.t.* rejoiced C1173.

gamnes *pr. pl.* rejoice 1145.

gan(e) *auxil.* (forming with inf. periphrastic tense) did 53, 61, 741.

gare *n.* sword C1527.

garte *pa.t.* (with inf.) made, caused 124, 511, 629, **gerte** 82.

gatt see **gete.**

geaunt(e) *n.* giant 685, 690. **geaunt** *gen.* 901, 922.

gedirynge *n.* assembly 205, **getherynge** C202.

gent *adj.* noble 289.

gentill *adj.* excellent 656, **jentyll** C653; *of* ~ *blode* of noble ancestry 565, 1099.

gerte see **garte.**

geste see **jeste.**

gete *v.* get, procure 595, 920, 925; beget, produce (a child) 33, 80, 83, **gatt** *pa.t.* 83, 595, ~ *fote* set foot 364. **getyn** *pp.* 33, 617.

gyff see **if.**

gyffe *v.* give, grant 78, **geue** C78; *refl.* surrender, devote oneself 403. **gyff(e)** *imp.* 5, 75, **yf** C75. **gyffe** *pr. 1 sg.* 779. **yeuyth** *pr. 3 sg.* inclines, is attracted C1151. **gafe** *pa.t.* gave 277, **gaffe** 686; *þerof gafe he noghte* he cared nothing for that 833. See **chide, ill(e).**

gylte *pp.* gilded, gilt C720.

glede *n.*[1] live coal 874, 1438.

glede *n.*[2] kite, bird of prey (used contemptuously) C680.

glee *n.* joy 478.

gleme *n.* light: *dayes* ~ daylight 492.

glente *pa.t.* shot, sprang 807.

go(o) *v.* go 118, 185; go away, depart 277, 296; walk 1348, **gone** C315. **go** *imp.* 990. **gon(e)** *pp.* gone, passed 31, 202, 326, **goon** C31. See **dede.**

Grekkes *adj.* ~ *se* the Mediterranean 407, 569, **Grekeysch** C404.

grene *n.* grassy place 556.

gret(e) *adj.* great, much 16, 274; large, huge 86, 1133; mighty, powerful 739; valuable 125; noble 1045. **gretteste** *sup.* largest 1237.

grett(e) *pa.t.* wept, lamented 314, 943, **gret** 317; prayed 257.

greue *n.* grove 310.

greues *pr. 3 sg.* distresses, agitates 1013. **greue** *pr. subj. refl.* be concerned, be anxious 620.

greuys *adj.* grievous C1335.
gryffone *n.* griffin 353, 360, 367.
grymly *adj.* horrible, dreadful 983, 1307.
grome *n.* servant, a fellow C172.
gronyng *n.* groaning 173.
gude *n.* money 566, 871. See kan.

ȝare *adj.* ready 568, 1269.
ȝates *n. pl.* gates 840, 842, 843.
ȝe *pron. 2 pl.* you 9, 210. ȝow *acc.* and *dat.* 3, 7, 207, yow C7, C75. ȝoure *poss.* 1075. (addressed to one person) ȝe 58, 76, 109. ȝow *acc.* and *dat.* 74, 780, 1020, ȝowe 1123. ȝow *refl.* 1019. ȝour(e) *poss.* 55, 56.
ye *adv.* yes C575.
ȝede see ȝode.
ȝelde *v. refl.* yield, submit 252; give, pay 1466. ȝolde *pa. t.* gave 589.
ȝelle *v.* cry 333.
ȝeme *v.* care for 625, yeme *C45n. ȝemede *pp.* kept 1574.
ȝere *n.* year: *to* ~ this year 216. ȝere *pl.* 31, 64, 575, ȝeres 28.
yerly see erly.
ȝif see if.
ȝyng(e) see ȝong(e).
ȝitt *adv.* yet, still 276, 1023; up to this time 547.
ȝod(e) *pa. t.* went 120, 121, 148, ȝede 95, 143. ȝode *refl.* 98. See child(e), dede.
ȝolde see ȝelde.
ȝone *adj.* that 1117, 1580.
ȝong(e) *adj.* young 597, 1116; ȝyng C1567; as *n.* in *olde and ~ (ȝynge)* old and young, everyone 1n., 734.

habyde *v.* wait for 437, abyde C422; linger, stay 765, 1055; face in combat 851. habode *pa. t.* waited 1291.
hacton see actone.
haf(e) *v.* have 104, 125, haue 115, han C44; get, receive 96, 125; give birth to 89; beget 115; ~ *no syghte* see nothing 165. haf(f)e *pr. 1 sg.* 70, 110, hase 392. hase *pr. 2 sg.* 871. has(e) *pr. 3 sg.* 116, 1389, haues 1352. hafe *pr. pl.* 64, hase 65. hafe *imp.* ~ *here* take this! 1105, ~ *gud daye* good day! 1399. had(e) *pa. t.*

28, 44, hadd(e) 96, 206, haued 1301; ~ *joye* rejoiced 1441; ~ *dowte* feared 23; ~ *lufe* loved 1119.
haghten *adj.* eighth 209.
haylsed *pa. t.* greeted *604.
halde see holde.
hale see hole.
halle see haulle.
halse *n.* neck 1615.
halsynge *n.* embracing 1582, haulsynge 1363.
hande *n.* hand 507, honde 976; *jn vncouthe* ~ in the power of strangers 108; *with herte nor with* ~ by wish nor by deed 276.
hardy *adj.* bold, brave 560, 935.
hare *n.* hair 176, 1613, herre C173.
hare *adj.* grey 354, 534.
has(e) see haf(e).
hawberke *n.* hauberk, coat of mail 440, 795.
haulle *n.* hall 909, halle 1068; dwelling 605, 1085.
haulsynge see halsynge.
haue(d) see haf(e).
hauen *n.* harbour 409, 485.
hede see heued(e).
hedir *adv.* here 1188.
hedouse *adj.* dreadful 984.
heghe *adj.* high, tall 410, 488; ~ *waye* highway 1179, 1458, *hye strete* 298; *on* ~ on high, high 449, 460, *on hye* 427. See dese.
heyre see ayere.
heyred see ayerde.
heythen *adj.* heathen 1196, 1250, hethen 618, hethyn 948.
helde see elde.
helme *n.* helmet 440, 692.
hende *adj.* courteous 48.
hent(e) *pa. t.* caught 176, 472; pulled 475; received, got 831.
herbere *n.* shelter 312, 331, erber C328.
here *n.* army 1181, 1256; crowd of men 1224.
herkyn *v.* hear, listen 323. herkyns *imp. pl.* 2, 210. harkenyd *pa. t.* C858.
hert(e) *n.* heart 36, 43; courage, spirit 887, 1323; will, desire 276, 1121; secret thoughts, mind 59. hertis *gen.* 63. hertes *pl.* 291. *in* ~ *es noghte to hide* it is not to be hidden, it is quite true *1277, 1364. See hande.

hete *n.* promise 924.

hete *pr. 1 sg.* promise 681. highte *pa.t.* promised 125, 928, was called 353, 489. highte *pp.* promised 680, 727.

hethen, hethyn see heythen.

hethynnes *n.* the heathen world C785.

heued(e) *n.* head 682, 820, hede 176, 750. heuedis *pl.* 1318.

hewe *n.* colour 484; complexion 1367.

hewe *pa.t.* cut C1603.

hye *imp. sg. refl.* hurry, make haste 134. hyed *pa.t.* C663.

hye see heghe.

hyght *n.* height: *on* ~ high up C457.

highte see hete.

hythen *adv.* hence, away 66.

hode *n.* hood: *be my* ~ by my hood 583.

hodyus *adj.* fearsome, loathsome C1071n.

holde *v.* follow 298; hold, keep 805, halde 581. *holde to pr. 1 sg.* agree with, consent to 231, *halde þertill* 670. holde *imp. sg.* be faithful to 1400.

hole *adj.* undamaged 1135; hale healthy 1313.

holtes *n. pl.* woods 354, holttis 534.

honde *n.* dog 1456.

honde see hande.

honeste *adj.* noble 188.

hope *pr. 1 sg.* hope, expect C869.

horsede *pa.t.* mounted 1437.

hungirde *pa.t. impers.* grew hungry 379.

if *conj.* if 55, 319, ȝif 337; ~ *þat* if 417, 1371, *gyff þat* 1412; ~ *all* even if, although 550; *bot* ~ unless 1381.

yf see gyffe.

ilke *adj.*[1] in ~ *a* each, every 1194, 1408, ~ *(a) man* everyone 254, 526.

ilke *adj.*[2] in *þat* ~ the same, the very 697, 1231.

ill(e) *n.* annoyance, resentment: *with* ~ resentfully, angrily 1218, *to* ~ C1246; *takes (it) to none* ~ do not be offended 768, 1124; distress: *gyffe ȝow nothynge* ~ do not be upset 75.

ill(e) *adv.* ill, badly 885, 1013. See lykes.

ynoghe *n.* enough, a lot 368.

ynoghe *adj.* great, much 809, 1078, ynowghe 1618, enoghe 567, ynowe C894.

inowe *adv.* completely, comfortably C1188.

intill *prep.* into, onto 288, 359.

into *prep.* into 143; in 239, 405.

yrons *n. pl.* fetters C1640.

jwhil(l)s *adv.* meanwhile, in the meantime 124, 738.

ywhil(l)s *conj.* whilst 1386; ~ *þat* for as long as 461.

jwysse *adv.* truly, certainly 349, 1346.

jentyll see gentill.

jeste *n.* story, tale, poem C628, C1695; yeste C279, geste C984.

juggement *n.* judgement, verdict 218, 225, 1608.

kan *pr. 1 sg.* know how to, can 74. kane *pr. 3 sg.* 1432. kan *pr. pl.* in ~ *littill gude* have little sense 584. couthe *pa.t.* could, knew how to 518, 1423; knew 570; *kouthe of* knew about 362.

kare see care.

kembe *v.* groom C742.

ken(e) *v.* recognize 711, 940. kende *pa.t.* 506, 923.

kene *adj.* bold, brave 550, 701; deadly, powerful 868.

kepe *v.* look after 1432. kepe *pr. 1 sg.* wish 1207. kepid *pa.t.* preserved 363; kepede looked after 378, kepte C375.

keste see caste.

kyn *n.* family, kindred 1372; kynn race 1396.

kynd *n.* nature: *of* ~ natural 650.

kirke *n.* church 185, 195.

kirnelle *n.* embrasure 1336.

kirtyll *n.* gown 238.

kysse see cosse.

kyssynge *n.* kissing 1363. kyssyngez *pl.* kisses 1582.

kythe *v.* make known, tell 3, 612.

knaue *n.* boy, servant 124, 133; *kokes* ~ cook's boy, scullion 116.

knauechilde *n.* male child 443, 451. knauechildir(e) *pl.* 83, 89.

knawe *v.* recognize, know 1224. knowe *pr. 1 sg.* 1579. knewe *pa.t.* 1340, 1373.

knyghte *pp.* knighted 1054.
kouthe *see* **kan.**

laghte *pa.t.* drew, caught 888.
laide *pa.t.* laid 557; *refl.* 369.
lay(e) see **lye.**
laye *n.* faith: *by my* ~ by my faith 1206.
layne *v.* be silent, withhold information 966.
land(e) *n.* land, kingdom 34, 81, **londe** 704, 975; dry land, shore 430, 441; *Holy* ~ Palestine 405, 610; *on(e)* ~ ashore, on land 364, 456; *in (one)* ~ in the country 105, 498. **londes** *gen.* 1589. **landis** *pl.* 45, 78.
lange, langere see **longe.**
lasse *adj.* less C171.
late see **lett.**
lawe *n.* practice, custom 186, 1173. **lawes** *pl.* skills, ways 872.
lawe *adv.* low 1319.
lede *n.* people, nation 186, 1589.
lede *v.* journey 285; convey, bring 594; lead, escort 1387. **led(d)e** *pa.t.* escorted 235, 1061. **led(d)e** *pp.* conducted, led 994, 1266.
lefe *adj.* pleasing 689; **leue** dear 969. **leuir** *comp.* more pleasing: *hir hade* ~ she would rather 675; *me ware* ~ I would rather 1155.
lefte see **leue.**
lely *n.* lily 1335, **lylly** C1363.
leman(e) *n.* loved one 727, 916; sweetheart (as term of address) 678.
leme *n.* brightness: *sonne* ~ sunlight C489.
lende *pa.t.* leaned 929, **leynyd** C832; **lenede** *refl.* 699.
lene *v.* lend 776; grant 826. **lende** *imp.* lend C866. **lent** *pa.t.* gave 1242.
lengare, lengere, lengir see **longe.**
lente *pp.* landed, arrived 498, **lende** C495, **ylente** C759.
leppe *pa.t.* jumped 903, **lepped** 479, **lepe** C476.
lere *v.* learn 649, 872.
lese *n.* falsehood 1565; *withowtten* ~ truly, indeed 1094, 1143.
lessynge *n.* false story, falsehood 1563. **lessynges** *pl.* 394.
lett *v.*[1] leave 611. **late** *imp.* let, allow 320, 456. **lete** *pa.t.* let, allowed 265, 795, **lette** 1088. **lette** *pp.* allowed to remain 1436.
lett *v.*[2] delay 502, 772. **lettes** *pr. 3 sg.* 1351.
lewte *n.* lute C198.
leue *v.* leave 705, 987. **leued** *pa.t.* 541. **lefte** *pp.* 318, **leued** 385.
leue see **lefe.**
leuede see **lyf(f)e** *v.*
leuir see **lefe.**
ly(e) *v.* lie 182, **lygge** 949; stay, lodge 970; ~ *ouer* lean over 722. **lay(e)** *pa.t.* stayed, lodged 92, 673; led 297, 1255; lay 128; ~ *doun* lay down 331; ~ *faste* lay helpless, lay in bed 160; ~ *one knes* fell to (its) knees 881.
lyf(f)e *n.* life 104, 399; *on(e)* ~ alive 26, 705, 1030, *one lyue* 987, 1157. **lyffes** *gen.* 57.
lyf(f)e *v.* live 68, 105, 404, **lyue** 1375. **leuede** *pa.t.* 17.
lygge see **ly(e).**
lyght(t)ede *pa.t.* ~ *down* alighted, dismounted 958, 1446, **lyght** C1474. **lyght** *pp.* fallen C1347.
lykes *pr. 3 sg.* in ~ *ill* displeases 114.
lyones *n.* lioness 341, **lyenas** C338. **lyones** *gen.* 361, **lyenas** C358.
lyre *n.* face 40, 1000, **lere** C40; cheek 272, 1150.
lystyn *v.* listen C9. **lystenyth** *imp. pl.* C2, C207.
lythe *v.* hear, listen to 9, 1556, ~ *of* 1138, 1570.
lyue see **lyf(f)e.**
loffed see **lufe.**
loghe *pa.t.* laughed 812, 1077, **loughe** 844, 900, **laghed** C929; ~ *on* smiled at 558.
lokyn *pp.* picked up C1274.
lond(e) see **land(e).**
longe *adj.* long 936. **langere** *comp.* later, more distant 1207, **lenger** C1235.
longe *adv.* for a long time, long 130, 538, **lange** 436, 581; *wyde and* ~ far and wide, all over 496, 637. **lengere** *comp.* 1274, **lengare** 1454, **lengir** 1055.
lordynges *n. pl.* (as term of address) sirs, masters 1269.
lore *n.* instruction: *sett to þe* ~ placed under instruction, sent for training 644.

lorne *pp.* lost 1031, 1259, **loste** 1457.
loughe see loghe.
lousede *pa.t.* released 1534.
louede see lufe.
louely *adv.* beautifully C693.
louyd *pa.t.* valued: ~ *for* valued at, put a price of C727.
lufe *n.* love, affection 142, 942.
lufe *v.* love 374. lufes *pr. 3 sg.* 1123. loffed *pa.t.* 641, louede 1051, luf-fede 823, louyd C638.
luke *v.* see, try 770. luke *imp. sg.* see to it, make sure 991. lukes *imp. pl.* 1269.

mad(e) see make.
may(e) *n.* maiden, girl 930, 955.
may(e) *pr. 1 sg.* may, can 399, 1016. mayste *pr. 2 sg.* C149. may *pr. 3 sg.* 60. may(e) *pr. pl.* 80, 1380. maye *pr. subj.* 884. myght(e) *pa.t.* 115, 461. moghte 34. (with inf. of motion understood) 315.
mayles *n. pl.* links, rings (of mail armour) 796.
mayn *n.* strength C1540.
maystir *n.* master (of a ship) 425; victor 838; ~ *owtlawe* chief outlaw 559.
maystres *n. pl.* feats 787.
make *v.* make, build 76, 224; do, carry out 787; cause to 946, 949; cause to be 6, 527; utter, express 248, 263; ~ *gronyng* groan, lament 173; ~ *a feste* hold a feast 187, 1587; *refl.* ~ *bowne (ʒare)* make (oneself) ready 568, 938. make *pr. 1 sg.* 263. mad(e) *pa.t.* 187, 233, 1587. See care, chere, mone.
mantil(l)s *n. pl.* cloaks 1069, 1081.
marchandyse *n.* goods for sale 1108.
mawngery *n.* feast, festivities 198.
mede *n.* reward 621, 1466.
mekill *adj.* great, much 194, 306; ~ *of myghte* of great strength, of great power 300, 355; as *n.* ~ *and littill* great and lowly, everyone 1.
mekill *adv.* much, greatly 1163.
mend *imp. s.* bring comfort to 324.
ment *pa.t.* meant, signified 745.
merueylle *n.* wonder, marvel 665.
messangere *n.* messenger 1184, **messen-**

gir 1212; ~ *lawe* the custom of messengers 1173. messangers *pl.* 1177.
messe *n.* mass 101, 122, **masse** C101.
mete *n.* food 327, 1049; meal, dinner 911, 1075; *at þe* ~ at table 1045. See forme.
mete *v.*[1] meet each other 1362; fight with 473; ~ *with* meet, encounter 299, 536. mett *pa.t.* met 545.
mete *v.*[2] dream 161.
metyng *n.* meeting 1585.
mynge *v.* relate C7.
mynstralsye *n.* musical entertainment 204.
myrk *adj.* dark 329.
myrthe *n.* joy, pleasure 197. myrthis *pl.* pleasures, entertainments 30, 199, 204.
mys *n.* harm, injury 350.
mysdo *v.* harm, injure C797.
myse *v.* notice the absence of 1071.
mystere *n.* trade, occupation 651.
mo(o) *adj. comp.* more (in number) 30, 326; *no* ~ no more, no further 119, 184; as *n.* no more 698.
mode *n.* heart, spirit, mind 301, 912; *with mylde* ~ with gentle heart, graciously 97, 684.
mody *adj.* brave C771.
moghte see may.
molde *n.* earth 1156.
molettys *n. pl.* star-shaped ornaments at each end of a horse's bit C720n.
mone *n.* lamentation 324; *made hir* ~ uttered her lament 386.
monyd *pa.t.* mentioned, spoke of C1246.
more *adj. comp.* more, further 643, 1227, mare 126; greater 522, mare 60; moree higher (in rank) 1221n.; *no* ~ no more, no further 781. as *n.* more 380, 860; *no* ~ 827, 1106. *sup.* as *n.* moste most 1010. Cf. mo(o).
more *adv. comp.* in *no* ~ no more, no longer, never again 905, 970, 1076, *no mare* 1154. moste *sup.* most 1123.
morow(e) *n.* morrow, next day 1281, morne 1413; morning 1308, 1500.
mote *pr. 1 sg.* may 772. moste *pa.t.* must 1075, 1272.

nay *adv.* no 112, 786.

name see nome.

nane *adj.* no, not any 44, 426.

nawntir see auenture.

ne *adv.* not 20, 67.

ne *conj.* nor 362, 706.

nede *n.* need, crisis 1408; *at* ~ in (time of) need 1390; *do alle his* ~ do what is necessary for him, take care of him (ironically) 760.

nede *adj.* scanty, scarce 586.

nede *adv.* needs 1272.

nedely *adv.* of necessity 1234.

neghe *prep.* near 470, nye C467.

nere *adv.* nearly, almost 471, 713; *wele* ~ very nearly 273; near 271, 574. See ferre.

nere *prep.* nearer to, near 242, 971.

nerhande *adv.* almost 156.

nese *n.* nose 811.

neuenede *pa.t.* mentioned, referred to 1218.

neuir *adv.* never 205, 287; not at all, in no way 650, 790; ~ *so . . . als* never so . . . as 858, 1560; ~ *one* not one 718.

newe *adj.* new, renewed 1376.

nye *adv.* almost C468, C846.

no *conj.* nor 988, 1391.

noghte *n.* nothing 833. See gyffe.

noghte *adv.* not 95, 113, nott 320, 966, not 630, 925.

noye *n.* trouble 1572.

noyes *n.* noise, uproar 745, noyse 933.

nolde *pa.t.* would not *765, 804.

nome *pa.t.* caught 1239, name took 406. nomen *pp.* taken 1401, 1540, ynomyn C1535.

none *n.* noon 438.

noresche *n.* wet nurse 595.

nothyng(e) *adv.* not at all, by no means 75, 549, 1351.

noþir *conj.* neither: ~ . . . *ne* neither . . . nor 705, 735, *nodur . . . nor* C1067.

not(t) see noghte.

odur see oþir.

of *prep.* of 4, 16; in, with regard to 18, 42; of, from, belonging to 574, 601; about, concerning 3, 10, off 8; from, out of 140, 265; consisting of, (made) of 281, 854.

ofdroghe *pa.t.* struck off 901.

oftesythe(s) *adv.* often 615, 930.

oftynsythe *adv.* often C12.

oght *pa.t.* ought, was entitled to C1643.

olyue *n.* olive 1172, 1174, olefe *C1200.

on(e) *pron.* one 26, 718, 1201, oon C523. See eche.

on(e) *adj.*[1] one 335, 1573, own C1676; the same 627.

one *adj.*[2] alone 1347.

on(e) *prep.* on, upon 24, 41, 52; about 999, 1000, 1162; to 460. See ankir, heghe, lyf(f)e, etc.

ony see any.

onsownde *adj.* unsound, unfit: *made* ~ injured C1614.

oppon see appon(e).

or *conj.* before 132, 683, are 100, 582, ~ *þat* 267.

or *prep.* before 1025.

ordeynede *pp.* destined, assigned 251.

ordynance *n.* practice 1176.

ore *n.*[1] oar 472.

ore *n.*[2] mercy: *thyn* ~ of your mercy C699, 969; *for Crystys* ~ for the grace of Christ C688, C752.

ore see are.

orysoune *n.* prayer 248.

os see als.

oste *n.* host, army 1416, 1429.

oþir *pron.* other (one) 1292, odur C1319; *none* ~ none other 726. oþer *pl.* 1530.

oþir *adj.* other 30, 344, wodur C341, odur C527; next 1054, toþir 332; different, otherwise 1484.

oþir *conj.* in ~ . . . *or* either . . . or 952.

ouirgo(o) *v.* overpower, overcome 704, 730, ouyrgone C862.

ouirtaken *pp.* ~ *with* caught in the act of 217.

owen *adj.* own 926, 1085, owun 644, 1621, awen 230, 605, own C227.

owthir *adj.* each (of two) 1310. Cf. aythir(e).

paye *n.* payment 588.

payneȝere *n.* pannier, basket 593, panyer C590.

payn(n)es *n. pl.* pains, suffering 86, 131.

palays(e) *n.* palace 1035, 1086, palese 1266, palesse 1469.

palmere *n.* palmer, pilgrim 575.

palmes *n. pl.* claws 169.

pappe *n.* nipple 445, 892. pappes *pl.* 372.

par *prep.* by 1246, 1634. See cas, charyte.

paramour *adv.* passionately C806.

parlement *n.* assembly, gathering C286.

partynge *n.* leavetaking 206, pertynge C203.

pawtenere *n.* purse, wallet C711.

paveleone *n.* tent 957, 1419.

pepille *n.* people 741.

perelle *n.* peril, danger 790.

pese *n.* peace 1559.

peté *n.* compassion, pity 232, 274.

petous *adj.* pitiful 745.

pyn *n.* suffering, pain 325.

playe *n.* amusement, sport 194, 1597; *childes* ~ see child(e).

playe *v.* play 444, 482; *refl.* take (one's) pleasure, amuse (oneself) 38, 452.

playne *n.* plain 1298.

playne *adj.* clear, visible 1226.

plesyde *pa.t.* pleased, indulged 526.

pownd(e) *n. pl.* pounds (of money) 126, 580.

pouerly *adv.* humbly, meanly C1500.

pray *n.* prey 334.

present *pp.* presented 1468.

presse *n.* crowd, throng 1091, 1417, prees C1445; prese thick of battle, fray 1541, 1604. See prowde.

pressede *pa.t.* hastened, pushed forward 1263.

preuaté *n.* inmost thoughts 1343, preuyté C1371; *in* ~ in confidence 1011.

preuely *adv.* secretly, stealthily 137, preualy 1007.

pryde *n.* pomp, splendour 1061, 1109; pride 563; source of pride, something valued 1457.

pryste *n.* priest 101, preest C101.

prodly *adv.* nobly, splendidly 1472.

prowde *adj.* proud: ~ *in prese* valiant in battle 1604. prowdeste *sup.* as *n.* proudest 1241.

proue *v.* prove, establish 117; test, try 1206. proue *pr. 1 sg.* assert, demonstrate 1565. proued *pp.* proved 1614.

qwene *n.* queen 261, 322, qwne 523. qwenys *pl.* C265.

qwykke *adj.* alive 718.

quyte *v.* pay C1494.

ran(e) see ryn(n).

rase *v.* tear: ~ *of* tear out 1613, race C1716.

raughte *pa.t.* dealt, struck 889, raght C977.

rauesched *pp.* carried off 1216.

rebawde *n.* rascal 973, rybawde C1061.

reches(e) *n.* splendour 146, ryches C143; wealth, riches 1159.

redd *n.* course of action, plan C241, rede C597.

rede *v.* counsel, advise 74. rede *pr. 1 sg.* 562. redis *pr. 3 sg.* in ~ *ryght* is correct, has the right information 636. rede *pr. pl.* read 15, 282. rede *imp.* counsel 260.

rede *adj.* red 238.

redy *adj.* ready, prepared 914, 1271, 1455; near, convenient 411; willing 512; immediate 588; *all* ~ *bowne (dyghte)* quite ready, all prepared 240, 413.

reyngened *pa.t.* tied up 1182n., reynyd C1210.

ren see ryn(n).

resceyuede *pa.t.* greeted, welcomed 1477.

reson *n.* reason: *with* ~ reasonable, fair 218.

rewle *v.* rule 45.

rewme *n.* kingdom 495, 637, realme C492.

rewarde *pp.* rewarded, recompensed 135.

rewyd *pa.t.* grieved C698.

ryaller *adj. comp.* more splendid C1703.

riche *adj.* fine, splendid, lavish 76, 187; of great value, valuable 281, 621; mighty, strong 92, 393; brilliant, rich 484.

ryght *v.* rule C45; set in order C684.

ryghte *n.* right, justice 1190; *one* ~ rightfully 45; *gude* ~ sound judgement, the proper thing to do 1148.

ryghte *adv.* properly, correctly 636, 761; just, right, exactly 877, 1005, right 419; *ful(l)* ~ directly, at once

ryghte *adv.* (*cont.*)
598, 674; very well 74, 570; straight ahead 297; ~ *so* thus, accordingly 253; just then 341. See anone.

rightwyse *adj.* rightful 225.

ryn(n) *v.* run, go quickly 456, 712, renne C453. rynnande *pr.p.* running 341, rennyng C338; flowing 429. ran(e) *pa.t.* 43, 461, 709, ren 746n.

riste *n.* rest: ~ *ne ro* rest nor peace 1164, reste C1192.

ro *n.* peace, rest 1164.

roche *n.* rock 427, 431.

rofe *pa.t.* tore 939.

roght *pa.t.* cared C918.

ros(s)e *pa.t.* arose 97, 933.

ruysty *adj.* rusty 796, rowsty C881.

sadill *v.* saddle 1170. sadull *imp. sg.* C865. sadulde *pa.t.* C1198.

saye *v.* say, tell 553, 585; speak 1606. saye *pr. 1 sg.* 1053. sais *pr. 3 sg.* 55, 388, sayse 109, 353. saye *pr. pl.* 109, sayne 27. said(e) *pa.t.* 103, 151.

sayland *pr. p.* sailing 424.

sayne, sayse see saye.

sake *n.* offence, crime 223; *for* . . . ~ for (someone's) sake 77, 247.

sall(e) *pr. sg.* shall, will 67, 152, 773, schall 135. sall(e) *pr. pl.* 66, 1027, schall 76. sold(e) *pa.t.* should, would 284, 425, 502, sulde 985; was to, was supposed to 805, 1054; had to 1066.

samen *adv.* together 28, 64, 80, same C1685.

sampnede *pp.* assembled 193.

sande *n.* decree, will 99, 402, sonde C99.

Sarazene *n.* Saracen, Moslem 1418, 1428, Sarezene 946. Sarazen(e)s *pl.* 1235, 1268.

sare see sore.

sary see sory.

sawtrye *n.* psaltery 201, sawtre C198.

sauely *adv.* safely 1177.

saw(e) see se(e).

sawis *n. pl.* tales 7.

schall see sall.

schamede *pa.t.* was ashamed 1112.

schapen *pp.* made, shaped 1393, schapon C1421.

schare *pa.t.* cut C1027, C1718.

schawebereke *n.* scabbard 805, scabard C890.

schene *adj.* bright 1037, 1205.

schewe *v.* show, display 1174, 1205; ~ *till (to)* reveal to 56, 1012.

schille *adj.* gurgling, purling 311n.

schipmen *n. pl.* sailors 415, schippmen 469.

schipp(e) *n.* ship 416, 424, schipe 413, 1493, chippe 474, 475.

scho *pron. 3 sg.* she 51, 52. hir *acc. and dat.* 61, 62; *refl.* 256, 314. hir *poss.* 40, 50, hyre 104, 939.

schoke *pa.t.* shook 982.

schone *pa.t.* shone 168.

schrede *v.* cut up 1049.

sckarlett *n.* rich cloth 238.

se(e) *n.* sea 359, 407. See Grekkes.

se(e) *v.* see, look at 90, 711, sene C809; agree to, countenance 275; know, recognize 849, 1299. se *pr. pl.* 941. saw(e) *pa.t. sg.* 154, 179, seghe 409, 571, sey 922. sawe *pa.t. pl.* 777, 1030, seghe 448, 469, see 428. sene *pp.* 676, 1208. See semly.

seges *n. pl.* seats 996, 1044.

seghe see se(e).

sey see se(e).

seke *v.* seek, look for 334. soghte *pa.t.* 1036. soghte *pp.* 1557.

seke *adj.* ill 141. See bystadde.

sekirly *adv.* certainly, surely 1123.

selcouthe *adj.* strange, marvellous 1394.

selden *adv.* seldom C72.

semblyd *pa.t.* gathered C190.

semes *pr. 3 sg. impers.* suits 848. semed *pa.t.* seemed 294.

semly *adj.* fair, beautiful, pleasant: ~ *of syghte* beautiful in appearance 42, 237, ~ *to see* beautiful to behold 90, 657. semelyest *sup.* C786.

sen *conj.* since, seeing that 617, 774.

send *v.* send, dispatch 702, 1383. sende *pr. subj.* grant 789. sende *pa.t.* sent 1188, sent(e) 418, 430; *sente aftir* sent for 501. sende *pp.* 926, sent 1594.

sene *adj.* clear, apparent 803.

sene see se(e).

sertes see certis.

set(t)e *n.* seat, place at table 914, 996.

sett(e) *pa.t.* placed, put 963; launched 457; *refl.* seated (oneself), sat down 314, 556; ~ *one knes* went on (her) knees, knelt 256. sett *pp.* put, set, placed 820, 1044. See lore.

seuenyghte *n.* week 202.

syde *n.* side (of the body) 1312, 1625; bank, shore, in *by an ile* ~ 424, *by the reuere* ~ 1355; *on ilk a* ~ all around 1440; *one aythir(e)* ~ on each side 857, 1280.

syghede *pa.t.* sighed 51, 174.

syghte *n.* sight 154, 490; *a* ~ *of* a view of, a look at 764, 1220; *of* ~ in appearance, to behold 573, 677, *to* ~ 294, 639; *se by* ~ set eyes on, see 941. See hafe, semly.

syte *n.* grief, distress 1305n.

sythe(n) *conj.* since 1223, 1374, sethyn C1106.

sythen *adv.* afterwards, then 182, 1370, sethyn C742, syth C1398.

sythes *n. pl.* times 962, 1567; *fele sythe* repeatedly, many times 12, 1141. Cf. oftesythe(s).

skapede *pa.t.* escaped 718.

skyll *n.* cleverness, reason 117; *with* ~ ably, well 81.

sklauyn see slavyne.

skorne *n.* taunt, insult C916.

skornede *pa.t.* mocked 845.

skryke *v.* shriek 181.

slayne see sloo.

slavyne *n.* pilgrim's mantle 603, sklauyn C600.

slepe *pr. 1 sg.* sleep 72. slepee *pa.t.* 160n., slepid 361, slepede 129.

sloo *v.* kill 707. slewe *pa.t. sg.* 895, 1217. sloghe *pa.t. sg.* and *pl.* 158, 1516. slayne *pp.* 435, 717, slon C432, yslayne C1622.

smertly *adv.* quickly 1360.

smytte *v.* strike, deliver blows 1306, smyght C1526. smote *pa.t.* 1323, 1509, ~ *to* struck at 855, 861, 879. smetyn *pp.* 902.

socoure *n.* help 390.

sighte see seke *v.*

soyty *adj.* dirty 800, 821, sutty C885.

solace *n.* pleasure 194.

sold(e) see salle(e).

solempnyte *n.* ceremony 965.

somdele *adv.* somewhat, rather 1249.

somedele *n.* some part, some C866.

somewhate *n.* a certain amount, something 1027.

somtym *adv.* once 13; sumtyme at times 999.

sone *n.* sunlight 777.

sone *adv.* quickly, at once 229, 840, son 542; soon 83, 305; *als* ~ *als* as soon as 1611.

sonondaye *n.* Sunday 1596.

sore *adj.* grievous, severe 86; sore, sad 1002.

sore *adv.* bitterly, with great distress 51, 257, sare 174, 423; greatly, exceedingly 147, 379; violently 861.

sory *adj.* sad, sorrowful 122, 301, sary 206, sorye 968; distressed 837, sorye 1065; sore, painful 1312.

sothe *n.* true facts, truth 152, 612; *þe* ~ *to telle (saye)* to tell the truth, truly 244, 1594.

sothe *adj.* true 7.

sothe *adv.* truly 1094, 1130.

sowdan(e) *n.* sultan 670, 1180. sowdan *gen.* 751, sowdans 1442.

sowkand *pr. p.* sucking, feeding from 443. sowkyde *pa.t.* 370, sowkede 445, soke C367.

sown *n.* sound 317.

sownde *adj.* sound, uninjured 1313.

sownde *adv.* soundly C72.

spake see speke.

sparkyll *n.* spark C962, C1034, sperkull C1466.

speche *n.* words 886; language 1423.

spede *n.* haste, speed: *gud(e)* ~ speedily, quickly 904, 1453.

spede *v.* succeed, fare 826, 1472. spede *pp.* 1267.

speke *v.* speak, say 119, 155. spekes *pr. 3 sg.* 905, 1113. speke *pr. subj.* 762. spake *pa.t.* 274, 454, 1479. spoken *pp.* 184.

spylle *v.* perish 320.

spoken see speke.

sprede *pp.* laid out, decked 993, spradd C1081; spread 1278.

sprent(e) *pa.t.* leapt 476, 1357.

sprete *n.* pole 472, sprytt C469.

sprynge *v.* spread 8; (of day) break 100. spronge *pa.t.* spread 497, 638; sprang, leapt 874, 1438, sprange C962.

stande *v.* stand 242, 273; **stonde** withstand, endure 976, ~ **agayne** 1397, 1513. **stode** *pa.t.* 122, 212, **stodyn** C1468.

stede *n.*[1] steed, horse 756, 881; *on(e) (his)* ~ on (his) horse 24, 817. **stedis** *pl.* 1315.

stede *n.*[2] place 287. **stede** *pl.* 189.

stele *n.* armour 691; steel 854.

steuen *n.* voice 323.

stye *n.* path, way 297.

styffe *adj.* strong, stalwart 539, 1384.

styfly *adv.* bravely, boldly 365.

stille *adj.* soft, quiet, in a low voice 1115.

still(e) *adv.* quietly 120, 1002; undisturbed, without moving 383, 511; secretly 1007.

stynte *v.* stop, halt 1404. **stynt** *pa.t.* C1432.

stirte *pa.t.* leapt 1228. **start** *pa.t.* C1259.

stode, stonde see **stande.**

stownde *n.* short time 948; *a* ~ for a short time 9; *bot littill* ~ for only a short time 72.

strande *n.* place, region 166, **stronde** C163; **strand** 408.

streyght *adj.* (?) broad, (?) dense, thick C291n.

streme *n.* water, sea 486. See **welle.**

stremyd(e) *pa.t.* streamed, flowed 863, 1316.

strenghe *n.* strength 1513, **strenkyth** C1541.

strete *n.* road, path 535; *hye* ~ highway 298.

strykyng *pr. p.* flowing C426n.

stroke *n.* blow 889, 1063.

stronge *adj.* powerful, mighty 366, 668; severe, intense 131; gross, outrageous 1563.

sufferd *pa.t.* permitted 467.

sulde see **sall(e).**

sumtyme see **somtym.**

surkott(e) *n.* surcoat 913, 939.

swayne *n.* man of low degree, servant 1213.

swelle *adj.* proud, bold C1557n.

swete *adj.* sweet, gracious, dear 77, 552; delightful, fond 1363.

sweuenynge *n.* dream 161.

sweuyn *n.* dream C158.

swylke *adj.* such 585, 651; ~ *a(n)* such

a(n) 215, 1599, *soche a* C214; ~ *als* such as 775.

swythe *adv.* quickly, at once 629, 841, *als(o)* ~ 609, 1140.

swoghe *n.* swoon: *lay(e) in* ~ fainted 348, 815.

swonede *pa.t.* fainted 1567. **swownyng** *pr. p.* C1715.

swonyng(e) *n.* swoon: *felle in* ~ fainted, swooned 269, 339; *ly in* ~ fall or lie in a swoon 182.

swore *pa.t.* swore 984, **swere** C795.

tak(e) *v.* take, bring 278, take (possession of) 662, 1087; take hold of 853; seize, capture 358, 1518; take, follow (a road) 598, 696; *refl.* 1458; ~ *daye* set an appointed day 1207, 1330; ~ *hir dede* die 239. **takes** *pr. 3 sg.* 1179, 1254. **takes** *imp.* 768, 1124. **tuke** *pa.t. sg.* 358, 662, **toke** 906; ~ *vp* snatched up 170. **tuk(e)** *pa.t. pl.* 127; ~ *þaire leue* took their leave 1619. **taken** *pp.* 1330, **tane** 1382; ~ *with* seized by 1131, 1576; **takyn** taken (as a lover) 116. See **flyghte, ill(e).**

talkynge *n.* words, discourse 2.

tane see **take.**

taryed *pp.* delayed, postponed C627.

teyʒt *pp.* trained, shown C672.

teynt *adj.* convicted C214.

telde *n.* tent, pavilion 1442.

tell(e) *v.* tell, narrate 207, 244; ~ *of* speak of, talk about 530, 1407; *herde* ~ *of* heard about 1611; count out money, pay 578, 590. **telles** *pr. 3. sg.* 1590. **telle** *imp. sg.* 1116. **tolde** *pa.t.* 62, 448. **tolde** *pp.* 10, 220; ~ *by thre* thrice told, three times over 1192. See **sothe.**

tene *n.* distress, vexation 980.

tydandes see **tythande.**

tyde *n.* time: *this* ~ at this time, now 776; *that (ilke)* ~ at that time, then 845, 1434; **tydee** 1460n.

tydes *pr. 3 sg.* in *hym* ~ it falls to him 1234.

tyghte *pp.* determined 754.

till *prep.* to 35, 98; (postponed) 56, 251, **tylle** 1016.

tyte *adv.* quickly 136, 149. **tittir** *comp.* more quickly 771.

tythande *n.* (piece of) news 91, 981. tydandes *pl.* 1570.

to *conj.* until 185, 1309, ~ *þat* 626, 838.

to *prep.* to 118, 133; (postponed) 1345, too 1119; as, for 25, 519; down to 810, 814; at, against 773, 889; for, to go to 911, 914; (with *inf.*) 56, 90. See com(e), dubbede, ill(e) *n.*, etc.

tobraste *pa.t.* broke open, were injured 811.

toke see tak(e).

tolde see tell(e).

tonne *n.* barrel, tun C1713.

too *n.* toe 694.

tornament *n.* tournament 19, 1391.

toþir see oþir.

towre *n.* castle 92, 393; tower 1336. towris *pl.* 410.

traylyd *pa.t.* flowed C1178.

trekelide see trykylde.

treson *n.* act of treason 217.

trewe *adj.* true, faithful 924, 1370.

trewly *adv.* in truth, indeed C1151.

trykylde *pa.t.* trickled 272, trekelide 1150.

tryllyd *pa.t.* flowed, ran C269.

trompes *n.pl.* trumpets 1287, 1488, trowmpes 1620.

trow(e) *pr. 1 sg.* believe, think 584, 763. trowest *pr. 2 sg.* C148. trowed(e) *pa.t.* 151, 1143.

tuk(e) see take.

þay *pron. 3 pl.* they 28, 35, they 298, 484, C32. þam *acc.* and *dat.* 29, 33, thaym 1520, þem 1373. þair(e) *poss.* 34, 45, ther C288, hur C1559.

þan *adv.* then 43, 50, thane 690, þen 250, 377.

than *conj.* than 676, 1155, then C21; than if 1222.

þare see þer(e).

þat *rel. pron.* that, which, who(m) 26, 42, 206; that which, what 1400, 1462; in which, in what 327, 1020; (of time) when, on which 88, 1331; (with postponed prep.) ~ . . . *in* in which 146, 340, ~ . . . *till* to which 251; (with pers. pron.) ~ *þay* who 572; ~ . . . *þam* whom 707, 977.

þat *conj.* that 80, 104; so that 119, 140; *so* . . . ~ so much . . . that 305; *swilke a* . . . ~ such a . . . that 1243; because 944, 1566; when 1308; (with subj., introd. command or wish) 137, 782; (forming compd. conjs.) see for, forthi, if, ywhil(l)s, or, to, whills, etc.

the *v.* prosper 772.

thede *n.* country 288; people, nation 618, 1431.

thedir *adv.* thither 192, 994, thethur C189.

they see þay.

theis see this.

þen see þan.

þer(e) *dem. adv.* there, in that place 129, 256, þore 85, 102, þare 177, 428; (antic. and indef.) 14, 20, þore 878, 975, thare 334.

þere *rel. adv.* where 92, 128, þore 1291, 1417, þare 710, 1180, 1210.

þerat *adv.* at that 1617, thereatt 1077.

þerby *adv.* nearby 312.

therefore *adv.* therefore, on that account 70, therforne C563.

þerin *adv.* in it 451, 705.

þer(e)of *adv.* of that, about that 628, 661, 1304, þoreof 1083.

þer(e)till *adv.* for that purpose, to that 78, 670.

þerto *adv.* to it, to that 252, 650.

þer(e)with *adv.* with it 351, 375, thereupon 172.

thi see with thi.

thies see this.

thyke *adv.* thickly, densely 293.

thykke *adj.* dense 307. thykest *sup.* C1265.

thyknes *n.* dense growth 164n.

thyn *adj.* few, sparse 1320.

thynge *n.* creature 737.

thynke *pr. 1 sg.* think 978. thoghte *pa.t.* thought 716, 951; intended 860; *grete dole* . . . *of hym* ~ felt great pity for him 1425; *grete joye* . . . *of hym* ~ took great pleasure in him 1449.

thynkes *pr. 3 sg.* in ~ *mee* it seems to me 665, *me thynke* 760, 870. thoghte *pa.t.* in *hym (hir, þam) thoghte* it seemed to him (her, them) 163, 830, 1100.

this *dem. adj.* this 67, 81. **thies** *pl.* 27, 437, **theis** 1353, **þis** 777.

þo *dem. adj. pl.* those 434, C431, C662.

tho *adv.* then 616, 1017.

þoghe *conj.* though, even though 1040, 1142, **þofe** 357; if 258, **þofe** 346.

thoghte *n.* distress, anxiety 70, 131; thought, preoccupation 998, 1014.

thoghte see **thynke.**

þore see **þer(e).**

thorow(e) see **thurgh(e).**

þou, þow *pron. 2 sg.* thou 113, 1369. **þe** *acc.* and *dat.* 323, 389; *refl.* 136, 620. **thy** *poss.* 5, 116; (usually before vowels and *h*) **thyn(e)** 113, 230, 688.

thrange *n.* throng, crowd 1237.

thritty *adj.* thirty 476, 1104.

thro(o) *adj.* bold, fierce 550, 701.

thrugheowte *adv.* everywhere 22.

thurgh(e) *prep.* because of, by means of 117, 367, **thorow(e)** 394, 894. through, among 533, 832, 1224; right through 1324.

thurgheowte *prep.* right through 1256, **thorowowt** C762.

thus *adv.* thus, so in this way 27, 382; **þus many** so many . . . as this 759.

vmwhile *adv.* at times 445, 446.

vnbryghte *adj.* dull, shabby 828.

vnclede *adj.* undressed 138n., **vncladd** C135.

vnclene *adj.* dirty 800.

vncomely *adj.* unsightly C884.

vncouthe *adj.* unfamiliar, alien 108, 288.

vndir *prep.* at the bottom of 310; under 1516. See **wede.**

vndirtake *v.* undertake, guarantee 667. **vndirtake** *pr. 1 sg.* 786. **vndirtuke** *pa. subj.* undertook, took on 785.

vndone *v.* unfasten, undo 841, **ondone** C926.

vnfaire *adj.* ugly, unsightly 816, 873.

vnfrely *adj.* wretched, unsightly 1415.

vnycorne *n.* unicorn 1393.

vnkynde *adj.* strange, unlawful C108.

vnnethes *adv.* only with difficulty 554, **vnnethe** C551.

vnryde *adj.* huge, of great strength 854.

vnryghte *n.* injustice, wrong 510.

vnsemly *adj.* unsightly, bad looking 799.

vnto *conj.* until 528.

vnto *prep.* to 59, 458.

vphelde *pa.t.* raised, lifted up 246.

vpstande *v.* stand up 365.

vse *v.* carry on, practise 651.

venge *imp. s. refl.* avenge 884. **vengede** *pp.* 992.

venquyscht *pa.t.* won C1533.

ventayle see **auentayle.**

veryly *adv.* really C304.

wafull see **wofull.**

way(e) *n.* way, road 305, 309; *heghe ~* highway 1179, 1458; *tuk(e) þe ~ to* went to, set off towards 127, 674. **weyes** *pl.* C284.

wake *v.* wake up 172; watch over 373. **wakyd** *pp.* in *had ~* had been sleepless 130.

wakyn *pr. subj.* wake up 140.

wan *adj.* dark 486.

wan see **wyn.**

wanttes *pr. 3 sg.* in *~ me* I lack, I need 757.

wapen *n. pl.* arms 1283, **wepyn** C1311.

ware(e) see **be(e).**

warne *v.* deny, refuse C821.

warre *v.* make war C1563.

was see **be(e).**

wate *adj.* wet 47.

watir *n.* water 426; stream, river 1402; *~ banke* river bank 1333.

wedde *v.* marry 1602, **weedde** 669; *~ . . . to wyfe* marry 1374.

wede *n.* garment, clothing 603, 627; armour 757, 816; (in tag) *vndir ~* in clothing 21.

wede *v.* become mad 342; *~ of witt* go out of one's mind 1511.

weyle see **will** *adj.*

weite see **wete.**

welde *v.* rule 34, 81, **wellde** 249; control, manage 1448; wield (weapons) 518, 1283.

wele *n.* prosperity 1159; *~ ne wo* joy or sorrow 362.

wele *v.* choose, select C1577n.

wele *adj.* lucky, fortunate: *~ is me* I am fortunate 1365; *~ were me* I would be contented 1346.

wele *adv.* well 690, 826; clearly, without doubt 113, 401; properly, fittingly 916, 992; wisely 871; very 273, 904.

welke *pa.t.* walked 408.

wellde see **welde**.

welle *n.* spring 311, 316; ~ *streme* stream flowing from a spring 428.

welthis *n. pl.* joys, pleasures 203, riches 1158.

weme *n.* injury, hurt 952.

wende *v.* go 1189, 1276. **went(e)** *pa.t.* went 175, 301; came away, parted 1243. **went** *pp.* gone 290, 504.

wend(e) see **wene**.

wene *n.* doubt: *withowtten* ~ without doubt 1202.

wene *pr. 1 sg.* believe, think 867. **wend(e)** *pa.t.* 1031, 1108.

went(e) see **wende**.

wepyn see **wapen**.

were *v.* bear, carry 799.

were see **werre** *v.*

wer(e), weren, –yn see **be(e)**.

werkys *n. pl.* deeds C756.

werre *n.* war 68.

werre *v.* defend 474; **were** *refl.* defend (oneself) 1247.

werreys *pr. 2 sg.* make war 1190, **werryst** C1218.

wete *v.* know, understand 422, **wytt** C419. **wote** *pr. 1 sg.* 67, 401. **wote** *pr. pl.* 58. **weite** *pr. subj.* 1202, **wiete** 1601. **wete** *imp. sg.* 113. **wyste** *pa.t.* 222, **wist(e)** 1230, 1496. **wyste** *pa.t. subj.* 1157.

wex(e) *pa.t.* grew, became 47, 865, **waxe** C85. **woxe** *pp.* C326.

whaym *pron.* whom 3, 8.

whan(e) see **when(e)**.

whatt(e) *adv.* somewhat, partly: ~ *for* . . . *and* ~ *for* partly for . . . and partly for 142.

whedir *adv.* whither, where 746, 1004, **whodur** C854.

whedur see **wheþir**.

when(e) *conj.* when 24, 1260, **whan(e)** 364, 412; since, because 925. *Ay* ~ see **ay(e)**.

wheþir *pron.* which (of two) 838.

wheþir *conj.* ~ . . . *or* whether . . . or 1028, 1213; **whedur** if C725.

why *adv.* why 109; ~ *euir* (?) for whatever reason 759.

whilde see **wilde**.

while *n.* time: *that* ~ at that time, then 1497, C1333, C1525.

whilke *pron.* which 1264.

whills *conj.* while, as long as 404, 1068; ~ *þat* 1514.

whyte *adj.* white, fair 41, **whitt** 1335.

whore *adv.* where 1461.

whoso *pron.* whoever 1590.

wyde *adv.* widely, far 8, 863; fully 842. See **longe**.

wyefe see **wyf(f)e**.

wiete see **wete**.

wyf(f)e *n.* wife 606, 640, **wyefe** 679, 1598; *to* ~ as (for) wife 25, 679, 1374; woman 706, 988.

wyght *adj.* bold C1539n.

wyghte *n.* creature, person 162, 303.

wyghte *adj.* strong 420.

wykke *adj.* dangerous 308.

wylde *adj.* wild, savage 293, 473, **whilde** 299, 366.

wilde see **will(e)**.

wyldirnes *n.* wilderness, wild uninhabited area 163, 292.

will(e) *pr. 1, 3 sg. auxil.* (forming with inf. periphrastic future) will, wish to 3, 79, 769. **willt** *pr. 2 sg.* 774. **will** *pr. pl.* 9, 577; (with omission of inf.) wish to do (so) 1018. **will** *pr. subj.* 729. **wold(e)** *pa.t. sg.* would, wished, would wish 183, 766, 783, **wilde** 966; ~ *awaye* wished to be off 931. **wolde** *pa.t. pl.* 580, 715.

will *adj.* lost, astray: ~ *of wone* wandering without shelter, at a loss for shelter 321, **weyle** C318.

will(e) *n.* wish, desire 55, 84; *to* ~ at her pleasure, at her disposal 512. **willes** *pl.* 417.

wylsom *adj.* lonely, wild 294.

wyn(n) *v.* win, get, obtain 667, 944; ~ *the felde* be victorious 1321; come, go 1405, 1419. **wan** *pa.t.* 149, 551; ~ *vp* lifted up, took up 542. **wone** *pp.* 748, **wonne** 778.

wirchipe *n.* glory: ~ *to wyn* win glory 789.

wyrke *v.* construct, build 82. **wroghte** *pp.* made, built 312, 593; contrived 394; done 1572.

wysse *pr. subj.* guide, direct 260.

wyst(e) see **wete**.

with *prep.* with 29, 81; surrounded by, amid 194, 197; by 1132, 1576; against 726, 753.

withdrawen *pp.* retired, departed 1329.

withowtten, -yn *prep.* without 95, 952; outside 224, 233.

with thi *adv.* in return for that 728; ~ *þat* provided that 671.

witt *n.* senses, mind 1511. See wede *v.*

wittirly *adv.* surely, certainly 681.

wo *n.* sorrow, grief, misery 325, 362; (with dat. of person) 258, 337, woo 36.

wo *adj.* sorrowful, sad 547, 858, woo 254.

wode *pa.t.* went through, penetrated 1324; waded 1315.

wode *adj.* mad, demented 156, 471.

wodur see oþir.

wofull *adj.* sorrowful, sad 162, 387, wafull 303.

woghe *n.* harm, injury 564.

wold(e) see will(e).

wombe *n.* belly C1559.

wonde *n.* wound, hurt, injury 63, 1307, wounde 952. wondes *pl.* 1502.

wondid *pp.* wounded 553.

wondir *n.* marvel, wonder 448, 830; *what* ~ *was ȝif, whate wonndir was þofe* it was no wonder if 337, 346, *no* ~ *þoghe* 258.

wondir *adv.* exceedingly, very 960, 1115.

wondirly *adv.* wonderfully, extremely 538.

wone *n.* dwelling place, abode 203; shelter, lodging 321. See will.

wonndir see wondir.

won(n)e see wyn(n).

worde *n.* word 155; fame, renown 8; news, report, word 497, 638; cry, comment 831; discussion 1227; *speke a* ~ *to (with)* have a word with, speak briefly to 1345, 1366. wordis *pl.* 119, 184, 274.

wore see be.

worthi *adj.* fitting, appropriate 223; ~ *of* fitting for, deserved by 219.

worthier *comp.* finer, more worthy 21.

wote see wete.

wounde see wonde.

wrange *adv.* wrongfully 107.

wroghte see wyrke.

NAMES OF PERSONS AND PLACES

Full references are given for forms in L, and for all variants in C. Forms in C identical with those in L are not cited. Discussion in the Notes of forms listed here is indicated by n. following the appropriate line references.

Arageous Arageous, the giant killed by Florent 672, 738, 967; **Aragonour** C805, **Araganour** C1055.

Borow Lerayne Bourg-la-Reine 1216, 1332; **Borogh Larayn** C790n., C1244, **Borough Larayn** C1360.

Calabire Calabria 221, 241, **Calabre** 190n.; **Calabur** C187, C218, C238.

Clement Clement, foster-father of Florent 589, 592, 602, 604, 616, 628, 744, 747, 762, 786, 798, 804, 810, 815, 822, 837, 864, 882, 886, 1041, 1062, 1065, 1069, 1074, 1081, 1083, 1102, 1107, 1110, 1125, 1158, 1405, 1414, 1437, 1441, 1446, 1451, 1452, 1458; ~ þe Velayne 576. Clement *gen.* 792; **Clementys** C668, C737, C877, C974, C1433.

Cleremont Clermont 995n., 1180; **Cleremount** C1043, C1208.

Crystys *gen.* Christ's C688, C752. See **Jhesu.**

Dagaberde Dagabert, king of France 723.

Florent Florent, son of Octavian 633, 646, 652, 658, 663, 744, 840, 915, 937, 951, 1030, 1114, 1161, 1210, 1233, 1251, 1258, 1296, 1311, 1323, 1326, 1332, 1338, 1356, 1398, 1401, 1464, 1479, 1491, 1506, 1509, 1515, 1518, 1569, 1598, 1602, **Florente** 812, **Florence** 1536n.; **Florawns** C1552, **Floraunce** C1636; **Child(e)** ~ 816, 873, 945, 1090, 1112; ~ of Paresche 1038, ~ of Rome 1147.

Fraunce France 596, 682, 723, 1059, 1080, 1188, 1200, 1537, **France** 919, **Frauncce** 985.

Gladwyn Gladwin, wife of Clement 805n.

Jerusalem Jerusalem 489, 529.

Jhesu Jesus 4, 388, 1632; ~ **Christe** 257, 386, 825; **Jhesu** *gen.* 247.

Lerayne see **Borow Lerayne.**

Mary Mary, the Virgin Mary 262, 322, 466, 1631, **Marye** 742.

Marsabele Marsabele, daughter of the sultan 1162, 1293, 1593, **Mersabele** 669; **Marsabelle** C782, C1321, C1696.

Mont(e) Martyn(e) Montmartre 970, 1026, **Mount Martyn** 673; **Mount-mertrous** C788, C790, C811, C995, C1058, C1114, C1522; ~ **appon Seyne** 1295; **Mountmertrous ouyr Seyn** C1323.

Octouyane Octavian, the emperor 22; **Octouean** title of romance 1629; **Octavyan** C22, **Octauyon** C769.

Octouyane Octavian, the son 516; **Octauyon** C513, C1606, **Octauyon þe yong** (ʒyng) C1567, C1651.

Olyue Olive, attendant to Marsabele 1011, 1017, 1342, **Olyuayne** 1008n.; **Olyuan** C1099, C1105, C1370, C1372, **Olyvan** C1096.

Paresche Paris 600, 601, 668, 680, 697, 953, 1015, 1038, 1403, 1459, 1595, **Pareche** 574, **Parische** 1255; **Parys** C571, C598, C715, C770, C775, C789, C830, C1041, C1103, C1283, C1431, C1487, C1523, C1698.

Rome Rome 10, 14, 107, 392, 506, 1147, 1467, 1603, 1624.

Seyne Seine 1295, **Sayne** 1333; **Seyn** C1323.

Sodam Sodom C1097.

APPENDIX

Huntington Library 14615 (STC 18779)

This text has been transcribed from photographs. The punctuation and capitalization are modern; capital *I* and *J*, which are not differentiated in the print, are here distributed according to function. In the three cases where *y* has been used in the function of *þ*, the form *þ* is printed; the distribution of *u* and *v* in the print is preserved. The few abbreviations which occur other than numerals, and the ampersand, have been expanded without notice, and on several occasions word-division has been regularized without notice.

A good number of printer's errors appear in the quarto; these have been emended, and are enclosed in square brackets in the text; in each case the quarto reading is given in a footnote. The errors are mostly obvious and mechanical slips in compositing: transposition of letters (96, 313, 401, 522, 630, 635), repetition of words (77, 577, 719) and of a line (461), the choice of the wrong type, based on the similarity of the characters (the use of *u* for *n* 268, 377, 522 (and probably 440), *h* for *b* 337, *c* for *t* 460, *n* for *m* 620, *n* for *a* 32), or the selection of a character which upside down resembles the one required (the uses of *u* for *n* mentioned above, *p* for *d* 34, and perhaps *g* for *h* 55)), and, finally, the misreading of minims (560).

Here begynneth þe hystory of Octauyan Emperour of Rome

A1ᵛ   Lysten, lordynges, both olde and yinge,   1
       And herken to my swete talkynge,
       Of whome I wyll you lythe;
       Jhesu that is our heuen kynge
       Gyue vs all his dere blessynge,   5
       And make vs gladde and blythe.

       1 *Large L filled with a flower, six lines deep*

Trewe tales I wyll you saye,
How it befell vpon a daye,
And ye wyll lysten and lythe;
In bokes of Rome as it is tolde 10
How it befell amonge our elders olde,
Ofte and fell sythe.

Somtyme there was an emperour
In Rome, of grete honoure,
In romayns as men can rede; 15
That man was of grete honour,
He lyued in joye and fauoure,
As a doughty man of dede.
In tournement and in fyght
In the worlde was none so wyght 20
As he was vnder wede.
Octauyan the emperour hyght,
Of all the worlde he was the noblest knyght
And a noble man of dede.

An empresse he hadde to his wyfe, 25
One of the fayrest that euer bare lyfe,
Thus say clerkes vs vnto.
Seuen yere they hadde togyder ben
With joye and myrthe them betwene,
As hyt befell tho. 30

A2ʳ

The emperour vpon a daye
In his ch[a]mbre gan sporte and playe
With his empresse bryght;
He behel[d]e her fayre chere,
That was as whyte as blossome on brere, 35
And semely was on syght.
A sorowe to his herte come
That he myght haue chyldren none,
Theyr londes to welde by ryght.
By his lady he hym sette, 40
For vpon her his mynde was knette,
He was so kynde a knyght.

32 chambre] chnmbre   34 behelde] behelpe

Whan the lady gan it se
She chaunged all her fayre ble,
And syghed wonder sore;   45
She fell on knees her lorde agayne,
And of his sorowe gan hym frayne,
And of his grete care.
'Good lorde, yf it were youre wyll,
Your counseyll that you wolde brynge me tyll,   50
And of your lyues fare,
Your counseyll to me that ye dyscouer,
And for me hit shall neuer forther,
I shall it kepe whyles I maye dure.'

And in his armes he gan [h]er folde,   55
And all his counseyll to her tolde,
How his hert was ybounde:
'We haue seuen yere togyder bene
And haue no chyldren vs betwene,
We shall lyue bothe but a stounde.   60

'I ne wote how my sone shall fare
And lyue in sorowe and in care.
Whan I am to bedde brought
I slepe full yll vnsunde on nyght.'
Thenne answered that lady bryght,   65
'Syr, I can tell you, I haue bethought,

A ryche abbaye we wyll make
For our dere ladyes sake,
And londes gyue theretyll;
We wyll praye her sonne so fayre   70
That we may gette a good ayre,
Our londe to welde at wyll.'

They lete make an abbaye tho,
The lady wexte with chyldren two,
As hyt was Goddes wyll fre.   75
At the last hit befell tho,
The lady was delyuered of chyldren two,

A2ᵛ

                    55 her] ger   77 of] of of

That semely was to se.
Tythynges came to the emperoure
There he laye in his toure,   80
A gladde man was he;
Two ladyes brought hym worde,
They had gyftes that were good,
The had bothe golde and fe.

The emperoure rose with mylde mode,   85
To his chapell there he youde,
He thanked God of his sonde;
Erly or ony daye dyde sprynge
He made a prest masse to synge,
His moder ther he founde.   90
'Sone,' she sayd, 'I am full blythe
That the empresse shall haue her lyue
And lyue with vs in londe;
A3r   But moche sorowe dredeth me
That Rome shall wronge arayed be   95
And in strau[ng]e mennes honde.'

'Moder,' he sayde, 'why saye ye so?
Nowe I haue men chyldren two,
I thanke God of his sonde.'
'Naye,' she sayd, 'sone myne,   100
Well I wote they are not thyne,
It lyketh me full yll in londe.

'For thou myghtest no chyldren haue,
Thy wyfe hath taken a cokes knaue,
I wyll hyt proue by skyll.'   105
A sorowe to the emperours herte came,
That worde myght he speke none,
She yede away full styll.

To her chambre forthe she yode;
The emperour styll at masse stode   110
As a man that was in care.
The emperours moder called a knaue

96 straunge] straugne

And hyght hym gyftes for to haue
A .c. pounde and more.
To thempe[r]ours cambre þe knaue take þe waye,   115
There the empres in chyldebed laye,
Aslepe was she there;
For why she had waked so longe
In payne and in care stronge,
Or she delyuered were.   120

'Hast the with all thy myght
Preuely that thou were vndyght,
And that thou be vncladde,
Softely by her thou in crepe,
That she wake not of her slepe,   125
Full seke she is bestadde.'
Hastely was the knaue vncladde,
And in he wente as she hym badde,
In to the ryche bede;
But euer the knaue drewe hym awaye,   130
Of the ryches that on hym laye
He was full sore adradde.

To the emperour sowne she wente,
And bad hym come in good entent,
At the masse there he stode.   135
'Sone, yf thou beleue not me,
The sothe mayste thou now se.'
To the chambre with her he yode,
Whan he sawe the syght than
A sorowe to his herte ranne,   140
That well nere he wexed wode.
The grome he sawe in the bedde,
The ryche clothes were ouer hym spredde,
Of that gylte he thought not good.

The lady laye fast on slepe,   145
A dolefull dreme gan she mete,
That was so lyght a wyght.
She thought that she was in a wyldernesse

115 themperours] thempeoours

In sorowe and in grete heuynesse,
That she myght haue no syght.   150
She thought there came fleynge
A dragon, with the fyre brennynge,
That all the worlde was lyght,
And in his paues brunnynge blowe
Up he toke her chyldren two,   155
And awaye toke his flyght.

Therwith the lady began to wake,
A4^r   A doulefull gronynge gan she make
And she syghed full sore;
The emperour sterte to the grome,   160
The here in honde he hent anone,
The heed he smete of there.
In he keste it to the bedde,
The ryche clothes were all to bledde,
Of ryche golde thoughe it were.   165
The grete treason that there was wrought,
The lady slepte and knewe it nought,
Her dyscomfort was the more.

Worde of this they spake no mo
Tyll the empresse to chyrche sholde go,   170
As the lawe was in that lede.
The emperoure made a feest, I vnderstande,
To kynges that were in dyuers londe,
Of many a londe of far stede.
The kynge of Calebre without las,   175
That the empresse father was,
Theder gan hym bede;
All they sembled vpon a daye,
With joye and game and moche playe,
To the chyrche the lady yode.   180

The kynges dwellyde there in same
There was bothe joye and game,
At that ryche dynere;
With good metes and drynkes amonge,
Of harpe, lute, and good songe,   185

Lute and good sautre;
Tyll the seuen dayes we[r]e all gone,
With all welthes in that wone,
And myrth of mynstrelsy.

A4ᵛ   There was neuer so ryche a gaderynge,   190
That had so sory a departynge,
I shall tell you why.

Grete dole it was to tell
Upon a daye howe it befell,
Herken, and ye maye here!   195
The emperour to his chambre yode
And his knyghtes aboute hym stode,
With a full gladde chere.
The emperour sayd, 'I vnderstonde
Suche auenture was in that londe,   200
By a lady, as ye shall here.'
All that treason he tolde them sone
And asked what jugement shoulde be done,
And what she worthy were.

Whan the emperour had his tale tolde,   205
The kynge of Calebre answered bolde.
He wyst not what it ment.
'Syr,' he sayde, 'for her sake,
A grete fyre I shall do make,
This is my jugement.   210
Whan the fyre is brounynge fast,
She and her chyldren to be cast,
To deth for to be brente.'
The emperoure answered full sone:
'Thy owne doughter hath this done,   215
I holde to myne assente.'

There was dole and grete pyte;
A fyre they made without the cyte,
With brondes brennynge bryght.
To the fyre they layde the lady there,   220
Two squyers her chyldren dyde bere,

187 were] weee

A5^r　That semely were to syght.
　　In a kyrtell of scarlet reed,
　　To the fyre they led her to be deed,
　　All redy she is dyght.　　　　　　　　　　　　225
　　The kynge of Calebre made euyll chere,
　　For sorowe myght not stande his doughter ne[r]e;
　　There wepte bothe kynge and knyght.

　　The lady sawe no better reed
　　But she must nedes be deed　　　　　　　　　230
　　That daye in the felde.
　　With sory herte, the sothe to tell,
　　Before the emperour on knees she fell,
　　And bothe her handes vp helde.
　　'Graunt me, lorde, for Jhesus sake,　　　　　235
　　That I myght a prayer make
　　To hym that all shall welde;
　　And than to do with me your wyll,
　　What deth that ye wyll put me tyll,
　　Therto I wyll me yelde.'　　　　　　　　　　240

　　The lady on her knees her sette,
　　And Jhesu Cryst ofte she grete,
　　No wonder thoughe she was wo.
　　She sayd, 'Lorde and kynge of blysse,
　　This daye thou wylte me rede and wysshe,　　245
　　And heuen quene also,
　　Mayde Mary, moder fre,
　　My prayer wyll I make to the
　　For my chyldren two.
　　As thou lete them be borne of me,　　　　　250
　　Graunt that they may crystened be,
　　Or they to deth sholde go.'

　　Kynges and quenes that aboute were,
A5^v　And ladyes, fell in sownynge there,
　　And knyghtes stode wepynge.　　　　　　　255
　　The emperoure stode her full nere
　　The teres fell downe on his lere,

Full sory he dyde there stonde.
The emperour spake a worde of pyte;
'Dame,' he sayd, 'thy deth I wyll not se,   260
With herte ne with hande.'
The emperour gaue her leue to go
And toke her her chyldren two,
And badde her go out of the londe.

The emperoure gaue her forty pounde   265
Of florences that were rede and rounde,
In geste as we nowe rede.
He comma[n]ded her knyghtes two
Out of the londe her for to lede tho.
The two knyghtes her chyldren bare   270
To what londe that she leuest were,
She was full sore aferde there.
The kynge frome the parlyament,
Euery lorde to his owne londe went,
And there dwelled with good entente,   275
For sorowe theyr hertes gan blede there.

That lady came in to a wyldernesse
That full of wylde beestes was,
The woode was stronge and thycke.
The knyghtes toke the lady her chyldren two,   280
And toke her golde, and bade her go,
As the waye laye full ryght.
They bade her holde the hye strete
For drede with wylde beestes for to mete,
That moche were of myght.   285
A6ʳ   Agayne the knyghtes wente with sory mode,
Alone the empresse forth yode,
As a wofull wyght.

She had so wepte here beforne
That her ryght waye she had forlorne—   290
So moche she was in thought—
In a woode that was full thycke,
What for hylles and leues eke,

268 commanded] commauded

Her waye founde she nought.
In a sloughe vnder an hyll   295
Sowne she founde a fayre well,
And an arbere redy wrought,
With olyue trees the arbere was sette;
The lady set her downe and wepte,
Ferther go she ne myght.   300

The lady by the well her sette,
With dolefull chere and heuy herte,
She myght no ferther gone.
'Lorde,' she sayd, 'of heuen blysse,
This daye thou me rede and wysshe,   305
God sende me some socoure sowne.
Mayde Mary, moder fre,
My prayer wyll I make to the,
To amende my sorefull mone.
I am full of sorowe and care,   310
And thre dayes I haue gone and more,
That mete had I none.'

By that she had her chyldren dy[gh]t,
Forsothe it was full nere the nyght,
As she satte by the well.   315
In the arbere downe she laye
Tyll it was lyght of the daye,
A6ᵛ   That foules gan synge and yell.
There came an ape to seke his praye,
One of her chyldren he bare awaye   320
Up into one hye hyll;
No wonder yf she were wo,
The ape bare her chylde her fro;
In swonynge downe she fell.

In all the sorowe that the lady in was,   325
There came rennynge a wylde lyonas,
That was in dede there.
In a sownynge as the lady laye,

313 dyght] dyhgt   319 *Large* T, *two lines deep*

Her other chylde she bare awaye,
Her dyscomforte was the more. 330

The lady was full heuy there
For the wylde beestes awaye her chyldren bere,
For sorowe her herte gan blede.
To Jhesu Cryste she made her mone
And syghynge forth she yode. 335

There came a foule fayre of flyght,
A gryffon he was called [b]y ryght,
Ouer the hylles hore.
The foule was so moche of myght
That he wolde well bere a knyght, 340
All armed yf he were.
The lyonesse and the chylde vp toke he
And flewe in to an yle of the se,
Bothe with hym he bare;
The chylde slepte in the lyonesse mouth, 345
Of wele or wo it ne cowth,
But God kepe it frome care!

Whan the lyonesse had fote on londe
Stowtely she can vp stonde,
As beest that was stronge and wylde. 350
Thoroughe Goddes grace the gryffon she slewe,
And of his flesshe ete ynoughe,
And layde her by the chylde.
The chylde souked the lyones,
As it Goddes wyll was, 355
And the pappes gan to welde.
The lyones gan of the chylde moche make,
And all for her whelpes sake,
She was therwith full mylde.

With her fote she scraped a den 360
And brought the yonge chylde therin,
And kepte it daye and nyght.
Whan the lyones hongred sore

337 by] hy

She ete of the gryffon euermore,
That was so stronge and wyght.   365
And as it was Goddes wyll
The lyones loued the chylde full well,
That was so fayre and bryght,
The lady set her on a stone,
To Jhesu Cryste she made her mone,   370
As a wofull wyght.

'Jhesu Cryste, kynge of blysse,
This daye thou me rede and wysshe,
Of all kynges thou arte floure;
As I was kynges doughter and quene,   375
And empresse of Rome hath bene,
And of ma[n]y a ryche toure;
Through this treason that on me is wrought
To moche sorowe I am brought,
And out of my honoure.   380
This wordes lyfe I haue forlorne
And my two chyldren frome me borne,
This lyfe I maye endure.

'A, lorde, the sorowe that I am in
Well I wote it is for my synne,   385
Welcome be all thy sonde;
To the worlde I wyll me neuer gyue
But serue the, lorde, whyles I lyue,
Receyue me with thy honde.'
Downe by a hyll the waye she founde,   390
And to the Greke see she came,
And wente by the stronde;
Before her an hauen she sawe
And a cyte with toures gaye,
The redy waye she founde,   395

Whiche brought her to the towne;
A shyppe she founde redy bowne
With pylgrymes for to fare.
She bad the shypmen golde and fe

A7ᵛ (margin marker beside line 381)

377 many] mauy

With that she myght therin be,   400
If that the[yr] wyll were.
A bote the set vpon the flode
And rowed to the londe there the lady stode,
A wyght man in he[r] bare.
By the mast they bade her sytte,   405
Of her wo no man myght wyte,
But euer she wepte full sore.

The shypmen sayled by an yle syde,
The mayster badde them they sholde abyde,
For fresshe water had they none.   410
Besyde them there was a roche on hye
And a well streme rennynge by
Come rennynge ouer a stone.
A8ʳ   Than two men to londe they sende
And sowne to the well streme they wende,   415
The well they founde, as I you sayne.
The lyonesse laye in her den
And was full gladde of these two men,
Full sowne she had them slayne.

So longe at an anker gan the ryde,   420
These two men for to abyde,
Tyll noune was of the daye.
Twelue men gan them dyght
With helme, and with halbarde bryght,
To the londe wente they.   425
They founde the lyonesse in her den,
And a man chylde they sawe therin,
With the lyonesse gan playe.
Somwhyle he souked the lyonesse pap,
And other whyle gan kysse and clap,   430
For drede they flede awaye.

They went agayne and tolde what they sawe,
And how they founde a roche on hye,
And in the yle a lyonesse den;
And there the lyonesse began to playe   435

     401 theyr] thery   404 her] he

With a chylde that therein laye,
And dyde slee bothe theyr men.
The lady sayd, that was so mylde:
'Mercy, lordes, that is my chylde,
And on londe lette me ryue.'   440
A bote they sette vpon the flode
Alone the lady forth youde,
Full sore wepte all they thenne.

Whan she came to the roche on hye,
A8ᵛ   She ranne as faste as she myght hye,   445
With full sory mode.
The lyonesse, thoroughe Goddes grace,
Whan she sawe the ladyes face,
Full fayre and styll she stode.
Thoroughe the myght of Mary mylde   450
She suffred the lady to take her chylde,
And to the see with the lady she yode.
Whan the shypmen the lyonesse se
They durst not come the londe nye,
For fere they were nere wode.   455

Some hente an ore, and some hente a spete,
This wylde lyonesse for to mete,
Out of the bote for to were.
The lady in to the shyp they hente,
Therty fote after [t]he lyonesse sprente,   460
There durst no man cum hym nere.
There myght men se game and gle,
Foure men lepe into the see,
So aferde they were of the lyonesse there.
By the lady the lyonesse laye,   465
And with the chylde gan playe,
And no man wolde she dere.

The shypmen drewe vp sayle of ryche hewe,
The wynde frome londe theym blewe
Ouer that wanne streme.   470

460 the] che   461 *This line appears twice*
463 into the] into to the

The fyrst londe that they myght se
Was a cyte with toures hye,
That hyght Jherusalem.
Full blythe they were of that syght
As is the foule, whan it is lyght,   475
Of that daye leme.
B1^r Whan hyt was ebbe and no flode,
The shypmen and the lady to londe yode,
In that ryche realme.

Ouer all the cyte wyde and longe   480
Of that lady the worde spronge,
That there to londe was lente;
And how she hadde a lyonesse
Brought with her out of wyldernesse,
The kynge after her sent.   485
The kynge bade lette for no thynge,
But the lyonesse with the lady to brynge,
To a castell there nere hande.
Whan she to the kynge come,
For the empresse of ryche Rome,   490
The kynge full well her knewe.

The kynge her frayned of her fare,
And she tolde hym of her care,
As a wofull wyght.
Thenne with the quene she dwelled styll   495
And had maydens at her wyll,
To serue her daye and nyght.
The chylde that was fayre and fre
The kynge made hym crystened be,
And sayd that Octauyan shall hyght.   500
Whan the chylde was of elde
That he coude ryde and armes welde,
The kynge dubbed hym a knyght.

The lyonesse that was so wylde
Dwelleth with the lady mylde,   505
Her comforte was the more.
The lady dwelled styll with the quene

With joye and game them betwene,
B1ᵛ   To couer her of her care.
Euery daye he serued that lady bryght,   510
To make her gladde with all his myght,
Tyll she better mended were.
In Jherusalem that lady dwelled styll;
Of that other chylde tell you I wyll,
That the ape frome her bare.   515

There came an ape that was so wylde
Thorough the forest with the chylde;
The holtes was bothe hye and hore.
As the ape came ouer the strete
With a knyght gan she mete,   520
The chylde as she bare.
Tho fa[u]ght the k[ny]ght full longe
Agaynest the ape that was so stronge,
His swerde he brake there.
The ape lefte the chylde and awaye wente,   525
The knyght frome her the chylde hente,
And with hym gan he fare.

Forthe with the chylde he rode then,
And in a forest he mette outlawes ten,
That moche were of myght.   530
The knyght was neuer so wo
That his swerde was broke in two,
That he myght not fyght.
If the knyght were neuer so wo
The outlawes wane the chylde hym fro,   535
That was so stoute and wyght.
The knyght was wounded that daye,
Unethys his horse bare hym awaye,
So dolefully he was dyght.

B2ʳ   The outlawes set them on the grene,   540
And layde the chylde them betwene:
The chylde was fayre and on them loughe.
The mayster outlawe sayd then:

516 *Large* T, *two lines deep*   522 faught] fanght;   knyght] kynght

'It were grete shame for hardy men
The chylde yf we it slewe.   545

'I rede we bere it with moche pryde
To Jherusalem, here besyde,
And do hyt no harme.
It is so fayre and gentyll bore
That we maye haue tresoure therfore,   550
Golde and syluer full yarne.'

The two outlawes made them yare
To Jherusalem for to fare;
It was so swete a wyght,
There was no man that the chylde se   555
For dole they wepte with theyr eye:
So fayre he was to syght.
A burgeys of Parys came full nere
That palmer had ben seuen yere,
Clement l[i vi]layne he hyght.   560
He sayd, 'Lordynges, wyll ye the chylde sell?'
'Ye, for monaye, yf ye wyll to vs it tell,
Florences brode and bryght.'

For fyfty pounde sell hym they wolde;
Clement sayd, 'Longe ye maye hym holde   565
Or ye hym so sell maye;
I swere by myne hode,
I wene can but lytell good,
Suche wordes for to saye.
Golde ond syluer is to me nede,   570
But .xx.li. I wyll you bede,
And make you redy paye.'
B2ᵛ
The chylde they hym solde,
And .xx.li. he them tolde,
And wente forthe his waye.   575

Whan Clement had the chylde bought,
He made a panyer to be wrought,
The chylde therin to lede.

560 li vilayne] lunlayne   577 be] be be

He toke hym the waye ryght
And asked hym with all his myght   580
What was his best reed.
A norse he gate hym also
Into Fraunce with hym to go,
The chylde for to fede.
The burgeys of Parys were full fayne,   585
Full many wente Clement agayne,
All rente was his wede.

They clepte hym and kyst hym all,
And brought hym home into the hall;
His wyfe was full blythe.   590
She frayned hym the ryght dome
How that he by the chylde come,
He tolde her full swythe:
'Dame, in Jherusalem I hyt gete,
And there I wolde hym not lete,   595
The sothe I wyll you lythe.'
His wyfe answered with herte mylde:
'Syr, it shall be my owne chylde.'
She kyste it many a sythe.

'Dame,' sayd Clement, 'whyle I palmer was,   600
I gate this chylde with my flesshe,
In the hethen londe;
B3ʳ   Into this londe I haue hym brought,
Wherfore, dame, greue the nought,
For ryche shall be thy wede.'   605
She answered hym with wordes fre:
'He is welcome to me, so mote I the,
For fayre I shall hym fede,
And kepe hym with our owne chylde,
Tyll he become of elde,   610
And clothe them in one wede.'

Clement was therof full blythe,
He dyd crysten the chylde swythe,
It dwelled but a nyght.

                588 *Large* T, *two lines deep*

Anone after they hym calde,   615
Florent the chylde hyght.
Whan the chylde was seuen yere olde,
He was fayre, wyse and bolde,
The man that redeth ryght.
In all the real[m]e wyde and longe   620
Of the chylde the worde spronge,
So fayre he was by syght.

Euer the burgeys and his wyfe
Loued the chylde as theyr lyfe:
With hym he was full dere.   625
Whan he was seuen yere and more,
Clement set the chylde to lore,
To be a chauncelere.
Than Clement betoke to Florent oxen two
And badde hym ouer the b[ry]dge to go   630
To a bocher, as ye shall here,
To lerne the crafte to do—
As his kynde was neuer to do so
B3ᵛ   Suche games for to lere.

Florent ouer the b[ry]dge gan go   635
Faste dryuynge his oxen two;
He sawe a semely syght.
A squyer ther was, as I you tell,
A gerfaucon he bare to sell,
With fethers folde full ryght.   640
Florent to the squyer youde,
And bothe his oxen to hym bode,
For that faucon bryght.
The squyer was wonder blythe
And gaue to hym the faucon swythe,   645
With herte good and lyght.

The squyer hasted hym full swythe
His oxen awaye for to dryue,
That he were out of syght.
And Florent to fle was full fayne—   650

620 realme] realne   630 brydge] byrdge   635 brydge] byrdge

He wende he wolde haue his faucon agayne—
He ranne with all his myght.
He wente hym home the nexte waye
To Clementes house as it laye,
And he in went full ryght.   655
He fede the faucon whyles he wolde,
And sythe his fayre fethers folde,
As the sqyer had hym taught by syght.

Clement the burgeys came en full sowne:
'Traytour, where hast thou the oxen downe,   660
That I toke the full ryght?'
Grete dole men myght se there:
Clement bete the chylde full sore,
That was so swete a wyght.
'With other mete thou shalt not lyue   665
B4ʳ   But that this kyte wyll the gyue,
Both by daye and by nyght.'
As sore beten as the chylde stode
Yet to his faucon he youde,
His fethers for to ryght.   670

Clementes wyfe thought wonder thore
That Clement bete hym so sore;
He asked his fader why:
'Father,' sayd the chylde, 'for Crystes ore,
Be in peas, and bete me no more,   675
But you wote why.
Wolde ye now a whyle beholde
How fayre he dothe his fethers folde,
And how louely they lye,
Ye wolde praye to God with mylde mode   680
That you hadde soulde halfe your good,
Suche one for to bye.'

The burgeys wyfe besyde stode,
Full sore she rued in her mode,
And sayd, 'For thyne ore!   685
For Marys loue, that mayde mylde,
Haue mercy on your fayre chylde

And bete hym no more!
Let hym be at home and serue vs two,
And lete our other sone out go, 690
Eche daye for to lere.
Suche grace for hym maye be wrought
To a better man he maye be brought
Than he a bocher were.'

After all this hyt befell 695
Clement began forty pounde to tell
In his chambre there;
Clement toke it to chylde Florent,
And to the brydge he hym sent,
The monaye his brother to bere. 700
As the chylde thorough the cyte yede,
He sawe where stode a fayre stede
That was stronge in euery stoure;
The stede was whyte as ony mylke,
The brydell raynes were of sylke, 705
The molens were all gylde.

Of wordes the chylde was wonder bolde,
He asked how the stede sholde be solde,
The monaye wolde he tell.
The man badde hym for thyrty pounde 710
Of florences rede and rounde,
No lesse he wolde hym sell.

Florent sayde: 'To lytell it wore,
Ten pounde I shall gyue the more.'
And ten pounde he than tolde in faye. 715
The squyer was wonder blythe
And toke the syluer to hym full swythe,
And hasted hym awaye.
Florent lepte vp for to ryde
To Clementes hous with moche pryde, 720
And toke the hye waye.
He thought to ryde in at the hall,

B4^v

719 lepte] lepte lepte

He sought none other stall,
He sette hym vp there in faye.

Florent was gladde, as I you saye,   725
And gaue his stede corne and haye,
He kneled downe and fayre hym dyght.